The Arabian Horse in America

THE GODOLPHIN ARABIAN

The
Arabian Horse
in America

New and Revised Edition

George H. Conn

South Brunswick and New York: A. S. BARNES AND COMPANY
London: THOMAS YOSELOFF LTD

© 1957 by The Countryman Press
© 1972 by A. S. Barnes and Co., Inc.
Library of Congress Catalogue Card Number: 74-37245

A. S. Barnes and Co., Inc.
Cranbury, New Jersey 08512

Thomas Yoseloff Ltd
108 New Bond Street
London W1Y OQX, England

By the Same Author

How to Get a Horse and Live With It
The Arabian Horse in Fact, Fantasy and Fiction

ISBN 0-498-01093-7

Printed in the United States of America

Table of Contents

Preface

The principal aim and purpose of this book is to put into permanent and historical form, material dealing with the introduction of the Arabian horse into America and his influence upon the light horse breeds. Available information is at present widely scattered and cannot be secured from any single source.

The importation of Arabian stud horses was begun in 1730 in the original thirteen colonies, long before most of the United States was settled, and written information on the subject can only be gained through extensive reading of early newspapers and sporting papers, privately printed sales catalogues, stud books and breeding records, and out-of-print documents. The material herewith presented has been so compiled and a great deal of it has been taken from my own library — a library collected over several years and containing the only known copies of many pertinent books and other printed works.

The publication of books dealing with horses and other sporting subjects in the United States dates back to about the beginning of 1800, one of the first being "Mason's Farrier," begun in 1811. During subsequent years a number of other books were published and, in general, writers of the period recognized the value and influence of the Arabian breed on American horses, and references and comments (many of them quite unreliable) are to be found in these publications. Two periodicals which I found to be the most satisfactory sources of early information were *The American Turf Register and Sporting Magazine* (founded in 1829 and continued for fourteen years) and the *Wallace Monthly* (founded in

1875 and continued for nineteen years). Among modern sources of information of value were: *The Arabian Horse News, The Western Horseman, The Bit and Spur,* and *The Horse Lover.* Special thanks are extended to Thornton Chard, custodian of Randolph Huntington's papers, and William R. Brown, author of "The Horse of the Desert," for their valuable assistance.

My reasons for extensive use of carefully selected quoted material is twofold. First, so that the reader may reach a clear understanding of it and may conduct further research if he so desires. Second, so that he may make independent judgments concerning blood lines, families and other matters about which there is still much controversy among breeders. I make no attempt to rewrite these early documents and thus inject my own personal opinions. My experiences over almost fifty years as a graduate veterinarian and in animal husbandry, as well as for some years in the breeding of Arabian horses, cause me to have naturally formed many ideas on the subject, but I prefer to avoid the expression of opinions or conclusions which may be unacceptable to various breeders.

No effort is made in this book to recount complete details of the breeding of Arabian horses in America and only brief mention is made of some of the better known Arabians, together with the names of their importers, owners or breeders. I have tried, rather, to trace, in a general way, the relationship of the Arabian breed to the development of several other breeds of light horses in this country. The Arabian breed supplied the foundation stock for all light horse breeds, including the Thoroughbred, Morgan and Saddlebred, about which considerable information is given.

During the very early days of the importation of blooded horses into the United States, frequently little heed was paid to their possible Arabian ancestry. This led to records that are incomplete and sometimes sketchy as far as the students of this particular type of horse are concerned. It was not until after the Godolphin Arabian, the Byerly Turk and the Darley Arabian became famous as sires in England and their offspring were imported to America to become the foundation stock for numerous studs, that considerable interest was taken in tracing their Arabian bloodlines.

Before 1730, horses in America consisted principally of imports from England, France and Holland and were commonly known as "stots," "rounceys," "hobbies," "bidets," etc. They were used principally for riding or for general transportation and were in no way similar to the horses that were imported from England in subsequent years. From 1730 to 1830, when the importation of horses of Arabian breeding was in full swing, the general designations were English, Spanish and Oriental. A few of the sires were listed on English records as Turks, Barbs, etc., but for all practical purposes it is generally agreed that most of the imports that arrived during this period were probably of Arabian breeding.

Until 1689, when the Byerly Turk, generally considered to be an Arabian-bred horse, was brought to England, the equine population of that country was of a mixed character. The Byerly Turk became famous in the stud in a very few years as a sire of improved race horses. From this time on, rapid progress was made in producing blood horses suitable for racing.

The Darley Arabian, imported in 1705 or 1706 into England, was the next great influence on the production of improved running horses. A great sire, the Darley Arabian helped materially, through his progeny, in building up the blood horse population of this country.

The greatest of these early Arabian horses was the Godolphin Arabian, introduced to England in 1730. He became the most famous of the three listed here, although all are generally considered to be the forefathers of all Thoroughbreds and practically all other light horse breeds to the present time.

Virginia, Maryland and South Carolina planters and breeders — most of them sons and grandsons of English horse breeders and owners — were the principal importers and improvers of the breed during the closing years of the 17th century. Racing at that time was almost entirely quarter racing, an ancient English sport consisting of short races on a straight track. (It is reported that the first race in America on a round, or circular track, occurred in 1737 in Hanover County, Virginia, on a track three miles in length.) The plantation owners' preference for races longer than the quarter races led to greater importation of blood horses, mainly sires, from England, to be bred to the native mares and thus better production of distance runners. While most of these importations were from England during 1740 to 1770, there is evidence that seven mares were imported from Old Spain. These mares were classified as Arabians and undoubtedly had much to do with the improvement of the racing stock of the period. It also appears that at least eight stallions were imported from Spain, or from the West Indies, in the early 1800's, probably well before 1830, and that these horses also played a very important part in producing better race horses in the United States.

Horse racing in the United States took on an organized form when a group of young planters from Virginia and Maryland took charge of the racing on the Rappahannock and the Potomac in 1745. Ralph Wormeley IV, Marmaduke Beckwith, Joseph Morton, Benjamin Tasker,

Jr., John Colvill, John Taloe II, John Spotswood, and William Byrd III, were all very prominent in the early foundation families of their locality and this group sent to England for mares suitable for mating with English blood horses already in America. Some of the mares so imported during 1733-1829, were Mary Grey, Muslin Face, Primrose, Selima, Miss Colvill, Jenny Cameron, Creeping Kate, and The Randolph-of-Chatsworth mare. The arrival of these animals marked the beginning of the breeding of race horses for the turf in America. From 1733 to 1829, a total of ninety-two mares were imported into Virginia, of which possibly as many as one out of five had sufficient Oriental or Spanish blood (now called Arabian), to be known as mares of Arabian breeding. They played an important part in the early racing history of Virginia and many of the prominent Thoroughbred horses of recent years can be traced to several of these dams and their offspring. From 1747 to 1804, a total of fourteen mares were imported to Maryland, several of them of Arabian breeding.

Eighteen mares were imported into South Carolina from 1760 to 1804. Though not pure-bred, they had sufficient Arabian blood to be classed as horses of Arabian breeding. Only five mares were imported into North Carolina from 1752 to 1809. New York imported twenty mares from 1765 to 1829, an indication that horse racing was spreading northward from Maryland and Virginia.

Pennsylvania imported seven mares from 1765 to 1798, New Hampshire one in 1770, Connecticut one in 1797, and Massachusetts three from 1799 to 1829. The listing of these small importations indicates that the aquisition of blooded mares for breeding purposes was somewhat general throughout the eastern part of the United States even though the principal importations were made into three or four states.

Records compiled by Fairfax Harrison, in his "Early American Turf Stock, 1730, to 1830, Volume I," (1934), show that a total of 265 individuals imported blood horses into the United States. During this period, some individuals who were not race horse breeders made a business of importing horses for breeding purposes, purely on a commercial basis.

In listing and discussing many of these early horse importations into the United States the term "English Thoroughbred" is not used. The English Thoroughbred was not known by that name in 1730, nor for several years after that. The English horse was known as the English blood horse or the English horse. When the General Stud Book began the term "English Thoroughbred" came into use. Later on the term "Thoroughbred" became the common designation of the racing horse of America.

Preface

The growth of the Arabian breed in America has been so rapid over the last ten years — much more so than with any other breed — that it is difficult to evaluate what, of the volume of available information, should be included. I have attempted to select that material which has some direct influence upon the Arabian breed as a whole, rather than to select information that has only a personal value to some breeder or owner. During the past several years many new Arabian studs have made their appearance and while time elapsed has been too short to evaluate their importance, it is my opinion that many of them will fail to be of historical significance, nor do I believe they will be of any great value in the further development of the Arabian breed in America. Too little attention has been paid to blood lines, families and types, and for that reason they have not produced, up to the present time, many impressive animals or ones that are likely to make history in the years to come.

At the close of 1939 registrations with the Arabian Horse Club of America showed approximately 1,800 Arabians. At that time there was only a small number of Arabian studs in the United States which had more than twelve or fifteen head of pure-bred Arabs. The Secretary's report reveals that as of January 1, 1951, a total of 6,192 Arabian horses have been registered during the Club's existence (founded in 1908) and that it was estimated that there were still living approximately 5,000 head of registered Arabs in America. There are probably four times as many owners of such pure-breds in America today as there were on January 1, 1940.

Because of this rapid expansion of breeding activities in the United States, it must be evident that we are, at the present, making a lot of Arabian history, but it cannot be recorded with any certainty until several more years have elapsed; therefore information on this aspect of the case is being overlooked and is not a matter of record in this volume.

GEORGE H. CONN

Chapter I

Arabian-Bred Horses First Introduced Into America Through The Spanish Conquest

IN the words of the early Spanish Conquistadors, "For, after God, we owed the victory to the horses." Hernando Cortez was the first of the Spanish conquerors to bring the horse to the mainland of the Western Hemisphere when, in 1518, he laid siege to Mexico with a cavalry force of eighteen.

In 1539, Fernando (or Hernando) de Soto landed in what is now Florida with 300 horses and in 1540, Francisco Vasquez de Coronado took 250 horses to the Rio Grande country and ranged over Arizona, Texas and Mexico and as far north as Kansas.

It is generally believed that some of these horses escaped and bred in the natural state throughout both North and South America. It is certain that after the Spanish conquest ended and Spanish colonists began to arrive in numbers, they brought with them many horses which thrived and multiplied to the point where, by 1570, enormous herds of wild horses ranged throughout northern Mexico, over the great prairies of Texas, Arizona and New Mexico right up to the Canadian border.

Almost certainly, the Spanish horses brought to this hemisphere traced back to Arabian bloodlines. It is said that all the horses bred and raised in Cuba during the thirty-five years after the discovery of the New World were directly descended from the famous breed of Cordoba. The breed was formed during the Arab Caliphate in Cordoba, Spain, from four sires brought from the Yeman or the Hejaz and crossed with native mares.

During the first few years after the discovery of America, horses were brought from Spain to Cuba, Jamaica, Santo Domingo and other Antilles Islands. There they were bred for the specific purpose of supplying cavalry horses to Spanish conquerors who set out for the mainland from one or the other of the islands. They did so well in these areas that by about 1522, it was no longer necessary for the Spaniards to transport animals from Spain.

By 1630, horses were plentiful although history records that the American Plains Indians seemingly had none and there are no records of mounted Indians for thirty years more. Some time during this period the Indians began to steal and otherwise procure horses from colonists and the use of the horse spread rapidly throughout Indian tribes all over the country. By 1719 mounted Indian tribes were common.

DU CARAM. Chestnut Arabian colt.

2

The following excellent speech on the subject of the Arabian horse and his history in America, made by the late John L. Hervey (pen name Salvator)* in 1942, tells the story as clearly and concisely as it can be told:

"All of you are familiar with the term 'Classic'. When you hear or see it used it at once arouses in your mind the idea of something singularly pure and perfect that for thousands of years — or at least centuries — has been by general consent accepted as a type or model by which everything else of the kind is tried or tested. The most frequent association of the word is with the culture of ancient Greece. Modern civilization is in effect founded upon that of ancient Greece. Almost everything that we have today reposes upon it — art, architecture, literature, science, philosophy and ethics. The Greeks by their achievements endowed us with that precious store of classics which remain the ideals and the standards of our entire scope of activity. The beauty of them is that they have never worn out. They are still going concerns.

"If you should wonder what all this has to do with my avowed subject, let it be said that there is only one classic type or breed of horse and that we owe our knowledge of him as well as our debt to him, not to the country from which originally he came, but to classic Greece. For it was Greece that introduced the Arab to Europe, whence he was disseminated all over the world.

"While Greece stamped its entire culture with its own sign-manual, it did not just reach up into the air and pull it down from there. On the contrary it was a very cosmopolitan culture, which it derived in large part from other, older countries of what is called the Mediterranean world. The Greeks were the great colonizers, travelers, explorers and traffickers of their age, as well as the great warriors and conquerors — and from wherever they went they brought back home and wove into the pattern of their life the things that they thought the best.

"Among many other lands that they penetrated were those of Asia Minor — and there they found the Arab horse. He was not, however, then an Arab. He belonged to the greater part of all that region — and had from time immemorial. The origin of the Arab (as we now call him) is the world's greatest zoological mystery. When we first encounter him he is already exactly the same fixed and eternal type of animal that he is today, with the sole exception that he is not quite so large. Otherwise he has remained through all the centuries, ages and cycles, to all intents and purposes unchanged. There he stands, just as he always has stood — the one and only equine immortal.

---

*Hervey was known for many years as the greatest living historian on the light horses of the United States.

"Modern zoology inclines to the belief that the historical equine race of today originated in Central Asia in prehistoric times. It might be thought, then, not much to wonder at, that in those dim and unimaginable ages it was easy for the species to find its way down into Asia Minor and there, in the course of time, to evolve into the Oriental type, of which the Arab is the ultimate flower and ideal. But the mystery lies in the fact that we are unable to link up the two kinds of horses. There are no intermediate types connecting them. Nowhere else that he went in all his world-wide roamings did the original Central Asiatic horse evolve into anything but what he might have been expected to — a coarse, rough, rugged, wild or semi-wild animal, without a trace of the characteristics that somehow he developed in Asia Minor. There he gained them to such an intense and irrevocable degree that he came to possess a power of stamping himself upon whatever he encountered. For ages now this power of his has been one of the wonders of natural history. In fact, there is nothing else to match it.

"When the ancient Greeks brought the Oriental horse across into Europe, with their unrivaled sense of the beautiful and their fanatical cult of physical perfection, they at once realized his ineffable character. In token thereof they made a god of him in the form of Pegasus. To the Greeks poetry which Homer and Sophocles and Sappho raised to heights never since attained, was the utmost flight of human achievement. So they made Pegasus its incarnation — a winged Arabian horse, that occasionally visited the earth but otherwise abode in heaven with the rest of the Olympians.

"Not satisfied with this, they carved his image all over their temples, especially the chief one of all, the Parthenon at Athens, which, now nothing but a ruin, remains the world's most famous and beautiful building.

"After the Greeks had acquired the Arab, they took him with them wherever they went in their travels, their voyages and their conquests. Above all, into Italy, where in time the Romans took him over. At the same time he was spreading through North Africa, where he developed into the sub-breed which we call the Barb.

"At one time there must have been immense hosts of Arabian (or Oriental) horses dispersed all over the then known world of the Greeks and Romans. It is difficult to conceive today, when they have become so scarce and so precious and so difficult to procure, in their best estate, that they are really 'articles-de-vertu'. In the prime of Ancient Asia Minor, they were bred on a gigantic scale. Whenever conquerors from other countries got into it and triumphed, among the first of their exactions in tribute were its horses. There was a strain of white ones that was especially coveted and we read of one conquerer carrying off with him no less than twenty thousand of them at one swoop.

"Wherever they went, the Arabs stamped their impress. When their blood was poured into that of the common horse stock of Europe, it was like pouring a rich dye into what before had been colorless; or, to change the figure, a drop of attar of roses into scentless compound. Their influence was so ‘profound that it broke down, remoulded and recreated whatever alien elements it was mixed with.

"What we call the Dark Ages following the downfall of the Roman Empire not only set back civilization for centuries, in human terms — it did the same thing for the equine race. The deluges of Huns, Goths and Vandals that overran Europe and passed down through Spain and Italy into North Africa brought with them hordes of their semi-wild and wholly uncultivated horses, the descendants of the original Central Asiatic breed that, all the while the Arab had been reaching his classical perfection, had remained the same coarse and common plebians that they are to this very day, as all who have studied the modern Tartar horse are well aware.

"This was a staggering blow to European horse culture which did not begin to recover from it to any great extent until, after centuries more, the age of the Crusades took the flower of European chivalry to Palestine and immediate contact was once more restored with the true Oriental horse. Once more he began to find his way to western Europe and take up his historic mission of refinement and enrichment.

"The discovery of America soon followed. By one of those providential circumstances which, as we look back upon them, seem to have been divinely appointed, the discoverer of America was an Italian and was in the service of Spain — and those were the two countries where, above all, the Arab stamp upon the horse stock had been the deepest, the Arab impress upon art had been the strongest and most wide-spread and the whole tradition remained most alive. This was particularly true of Spain, which had become the breeding ground of Europe's finest and most valuable types of horses — due wholly to its constant infusions of Oriental blood which reached all the way across North Africa and back to Arabia itself, where now all that was best and purest of the entire classical breed of Asia Minor had found its final home and refuge.

"Beginning with his first voyage of discovery, Columbus and all the subsequent Spanish explorers brought horses with them. Always and constantly horses, and, for the most part, horses of definitely Arabian type. For it was useless to bring ordinary ones. They would not stand up and live under the terrific hardships that they were called upon to endure. It required the utmost of strength, endurance, courage, constitution and soundness to withstand such ordeals.

"The testimony to this effect is unanimous. Itemized lists are still extant of the horses that Cortez brought to Mexico — the first landed upon the North American continent — that Pizarro took to Peru — the first used in the conquest of South America of which we have knowledge — and that de Soto brought to Florida, which were the first introduced into what is today the United States. Their praises were sung by all the chroniclers in the most enthusiastic terms. Not only were they beautiful and fleet — they were the saviors to which, in the last analysis, success was due. 'Before God we owed it to the horses' wrote Bernal Diaz, when he was penning the epic of the conquest of Mexico. Without them all would have been lost.

"It is one of the well-known basic facts of our horse history that the animals introduced by the Spanish Conquistadors were the progenitors of the vast herds of Plains and similar types that soon spread over the south and west of this country. Their characteristics were strongly Oriental. Hardship, privation, abuse, their constant lot, often caused degeneration, but the foundation remained and would reassert itself in remarkable ways. Three hundred years later, when the Plains were first being systematically explored and their vast herds of wild horses observed and examined, there were constantly turning up individuals whose beauty, speed and courage caused wonder and amazement. The horse lore of the Indians teemed with traditions of such steeds, which were often pursued for years before they could be captured — and sometimes never were. Tribal wars were caused by attempts to wrest from some band or chieftain some coveted animal, whose fame had spread far and wide and whose possession was held to be a token of supremacy.

"These legends and traditions have never been collected and collated as they deserve to be, for behind them was and is something perdurable — the indestructability of a type.

"One of the most remarkable demonstrations has been of but recent occurrence. It is now but two or three years ago that a band of dwarf horses, never before known to exist, was found in an isolated part of the Grand Canyon, from which they had been unable to escape for centuries. Lack of subsistence had reduced them to pygmies, but in their miniature forms lurked strength and vigor. Despite their stunted frames, they remained definitely Oriental in type.

"The Arab influence, through the horses of the Spanish explorers and colonists, was exerted upon our riding types in three ways; through the Plains stocks, in the west-central part of the continent, through the so-called Palominos, of California, and through the Chickasaw and allied sub-species that were developed in Florida, Alabama and the Mississippi Valley. The Palominos were undoubtedly produced by the introduction of Mexican ancestors deep in Oriental blood but bigger, bulkier and less refined through the crossing in of heavier strains, originally in Spain before they had crossed the Atlantic. Spain, it must be again remembered, was the purveyor to Europe at large of its finest horses for centuries. They were of two types — the Arab or Barb coursers and the larger, stouter, less active animals that were used for ceremonial purposes, and the like, both under saddle and in harness. Spain for a long while dominated what we call the Low Countries — Holland, Belgium, etc., — and there had been developed in the Middle Ages the so-called 'Great Horse' — the charger of giant size and strength that was necessary to carry the knight in full armor, with which the animal himself was also encased. It must have been ancestors of this type from which the Palomino was developed.

"The Plains and Floridian sub-species descended from the Arab and Saracenic ancestors brought in by the Spaniards were quite different in character. They declined in size somewhat from the parent stock because of the hot climate where they were propagated and the ignorance of the Indians and indifference of the white settlers toward their proper care and mating. To be correct, they for the most part mated themselves — and when that occurs a reversion toward the wild and uncultivated state always begins. Nevertheless there were many beautiful animals thus produced which were in wide request both among the colonists and the Indians for riding and racing purposes. For racing among the Indians, both of the Plains and the Gulf tribes, speedily became a passion once they were equipped with horses.

"The next great infusion of Arabian blood came with the settlement of Maryland, Virginia and the Carolinas. When Cromwell and his Roundheads overcame, deposed and executed King Charles I toward the middle of the eighteenth century, it caused a general exodus from England of the Cavaliers, the chief adherents of the Stuarts. Over 1,000 of them then came to Virginia, bringing with them many choice animals that must have been deep in Arab blood. For at that time racing in England was wholly in the hands of the aristocracy and their horses, whether for the course or for the saddle, were bred up from Oriental stock upon native strains.

"About that time Virginia became a hot-bed of racing, not over the long courses but the so-called 'race-paths' of the quarter-horses. These quarter horses became a distinct type. The blood of the earliest ones is known only through deduction, but everything points to its having been a combination of the best and fastest elements in the colony with the 'bred' sires and dams that were imported from England. The early course racers were known first as 'bred' horses, the later 'Thoroughbred' conception not taking shape until in the period preceding the Revolutionary War. The four-mile horses then were introduced in great numbers — all largely Oriental in blood and sometimes purely so. There was one of these early thoroughbred sires, imported Janus, that exercised a most remarkable influence upon the Virginia quarter-horse. The speed in his blood far surpassed anything hitherto known in Virginia and he begot a breed of quarter-horse that remains the most famous of all. It was the origin of the distinctive type that still exists in Texas and the Southwest — low and stocky, with tremendously developed hind quarters, but an utter inability to go farther — at best a half-mile being the limit.

"Somewhat later than his introduction into Maryland, Virginia and the Carolinas the Thoroughbred was imported into the North, especially New York. But the development of good roads in the North being much more forward than in the South, the riding horse there much sooner gave way to the coach, carriage and wagon horse. This became a standing condition which was to endure — and when the Civil War came, eighty years ago, the great superiority of the cavalry horses of the South to those of the North enabled them to stem the tide of northern victory for years, the Southern horses being in many cases pure thoroughbred and almost universally deep in Oriental blood, while those of the North were of a different type not nearly so well adapted to military use.

"To this however, one exception must be made. Shortly before the year 1800 there was foaled in New England the horse known today as Justin Morgan. He was one of the equine phenomenons of all time. Living his life in obscurity, used much of the time for the hardest menial labor, valued in his prime at not much more than a hundred dollars and covering only the common country mares, he begot one of the most valuable and popular families of horses that America has ever known — horses almost equally useful under either saddle or the collar, whose popularity became so immense that they were distributed over the entire U.S.A. and Canada. The ancestry of Justin Morgan is a matter of long-standing dispute. But one thing is certain — no horse of other than Arabian descent ever could have begotten him. He was small, fleet, active, fearless, docile, spirited, courageous and long-lived, and so unerringly did he transmit his peculiar and unmistakable individuality that horsemen can still pick out his descendants because of their inheritance of it, sometimes to an amazing degree.

"As this is merely an informal address and not an essay or a thesis, only one other race of American riding horses will be mentioned. That is — or was — the breed that flourished in America long ago but now for over a century extinct: the so-called Narragansett Pacer. As the name implies, he was originally a product of the region around Narragansett Bay. In Rhode Island and in pre-Revolutionary times, he was the favorite saddle horse of the Colonies, especially among the upper classes. His antecedents are unknown, the tales and legends regarding them being fantastic. As there was much trade back and forth between Narragansett and the West Indies at that time he may have possessed Oriental blood. But the fact that despite his great popularity and wide dissemination, as a type he was unable to endure but faded away into the past in no very long time after that of his hey-day, belies that idea.

"For the dominant quality of Arab blood is its eternal, its immortal persistence. Wherever, as the horseman of today looks about him and among these horses, observes beauty, speed, grace, fire, activity, docility and fineness yet toughness of fibre, he sees that eternity, that immortality, incarnated. It has triumphed over everything mundane — thousands of years, hap and circumstances, time and tide, incredible hardships and immemorial adversities, misuse, and abuse, the exigencies of mankind's daily life and the flame and blood of the battle-field — unconquerable, indestructible and victorious. Everything worth while in the shape of a horse in the world today partakes of it. The Greeks believed it godlike — and verily they made no mistake."

Chapter 2

The Introduction Of The First Arabian-Bred Horses To America From England

THE introduction of the blood horse, and particularly the Arabian-bred blood horse, into America dates from the year 1730. The wealthy Virginia planters of this era generally came from England and were closely related to the English gentlemen, most of whom were associated with the racing and hunting of blood horses.

At the time the importation of English stallions started to the American colonies the Byerly Turk (which reached England in 1689) and the Darley Arabian (1705 or 1706), were already making substantial names for themselves as sires of English racing horses. Through the use of these two Arabian stallions (then known as Orientals) the English breeders were making great improvements in their racing studs. The great Godolphin Arabian did not appear in England until 1730 and his first offspring to appear in America was the filly or mare, known as Clarke's mare, Post, in 1733. The records will show that the Godolphin Arabian rapidly came to the front as a sire of English racing stock, and after standing at stud for several years in England a large number of his offspring were imported to America.

From these three studs all English and American Thoroughbreds have sprung. All Thoroughbreds, therefore, can be said to be nothing more or less than specialized Arabians.

One important chronicler of much information on some of the very early importations of Arabian-bred horses — almost all of them progeny of the three sires mentioned above — is Fairfax Harrison of Richmond, Virginia, a former president of the Southern Railway. During researches into early Virginian history, Mr. Harrison became interested in the relationship between horse breeding, racing and the ownership of blood horses in the old dominion as it was related to the social life of the period. His enthusiasm grew to a point where he hired a full-time employee, a Mr. O'Conner of New York, and a staff of part-time workers to collect data on the subject. The project took a good deal of time and effort and resulted in the private publication and distribution to friends of a collection of eight books. The plates were then destroyed and, as far as is known, only fifteen sets existed at the time of Mr. Harrison's death, several years ago. The titles are as follows:

The Equine F.F.Vs. (which means the Equine First Families of Virginia) (1928).
The Belair Stud, 1747-1761 (1929).
The Roanoke Stud, 1795-1893 (1930).
The John's Island Stud (South Carolina) 1750-1788 (1931).
The Background of the American Stud Book (1933).
Early American Turf Stock, 1730-1830, Vol. 1, Mares (1934).
Early American Turf Stock, 1730-1830, Vol. 2, Horses.

Volumes 6 and 7 state in their sub-titles: "Being a critical study of extant evidence for the English, Spanish and Oriental horses and mares to which are traced the oldest American turf pedigrees."

Other common source books on early Arabian-bred horses in America are:

The American Race Turf Register, by Patrick Nisbett Edgar (1833).
The American Stud Book, by S. D. Bruce.
The Gentleman's New Pocket Farrier, by Mason, which contains some attempt at a listing of pedigrees in 1828.
Blooded Horses of Colonial Days, by Culver (1922).
Horses and Horsemanship of the United States, by Frank Forester (1857).
The General Stud Book — Weatherby's, published in England.
American Stud Book, by J. H. Wallace (1867).

Other papers that gave breeding information about the popular horses of the day were *The American Farmer* (1819-1829), and the *American Turf Register* (1829-1835), both published by J. S. Skinner, of Baltimore, Maryland.

Annals of the Turf by George W. Jeffreys, was published for several years after 1826 in the Petersburg *Intelligencer,* of Virginia.

Many other sources are available, such as racing registers, racing calendars and other newspapers published in Virginia, Maryland, South Carolina, and the other states where the blood horse was bred and owned in colonial days.

The first horses imported into Virginia in 1610 were, of course, not of Oriental blood lines but were common stock from England. This first importation was listed as six mares and one horse, but during the winter food was exceedingly scarce and these animals were eaten by the colonists. The next year, Sir Thomas Dale imported seventeen horses and mares, and in 1614 a Mr. Samuel Argall brought a further shipment of horses to Virginia. In 1620 twenty mares were brought in by the Virginia Company. The number of horses did not increase very rapidly for several years in Virginia, and by 1639 there were so few horses available that a Mr. Thomas Stegg was encouraged to import horses and mares, and by 1649 there were about 200 head of horses and mares in the colony. It appears that the growth of the horse population was very rapid from this period on and by 1668 it is reported that there was a very satisfactory number of horses in the Virginia colony. This information is given principally to show the foundation upon which the imported stallions were used for the development of racing stock in the Virginia colony, starting in 1730 with the importation of the first Arabian bred stallion into the colony.

Fairfax Harrison's study of the importation of the blood horse was centered chiefly in those importations made into Virginia. In his first book there were listed thirty-eight noted English horses and twenty-one mares imported into Virginia before the Revolution. Very complete and detailed information about them is supplied. The following is from "The Equine F.F.Vs.":

"By way of introduction to these records, several generalizations deduced from them are ventured. It will be noted that before the Seven Years War, and again after 1763, the importation of horses and mares to Virginia was almost exclusively to the Rappahannock valley; including in that geographical description the counties of the Middle neck, which were subject to the same social influences. But about 1768 the centre of horse breeding shifted to the James River valley and centered for a time on the mouth of the Appomattox. The indication of this change was not so much in the importations direct to that region, though there were several (including conspicuously those of the third William Byrd of Westover) as in the fact that, trailing clouds of glory, Jolly Roger, Janus and Fearnought then successively migrated, to end their careers in the Southside.

"Again, it may be noted that of the fifty-nine individuals here listed, only twenty-two, or say one in three, have been identified in GSB. Considering the history of GSB, inaugurated in 1791 after all this stock had left England, and never purported to be exhaustive, as Mr. Prior has shown, the failure to find official English records for the others is rather an inconvenience than an impeachment of their legitimacy: it means merely that no general census was contemporaneously kept of the matings of eighteenth century horses, such as is kept today in both England and America.

"The argument on this point of a recent correspondent of the Thoroughbred Record (1927, cvi, 263) is judicious:

" 'Mankato' and others maintain that quite a number of pedigrees in the first three volumes of the American Stud Book are wrong, specially so of imported stock, because links with the entries in the General Stud Book are missing; but what unbiased person will ever be able to prove that the entries in the General Stud Book are exhaustively correct and that the papers and pedigrees which accompanied the horses sent to America in the last half of the 18th century, were erroneously and falsely made out? Is it not more plausible, not to say logical, to assume that the records compiled in those times by British breeders from their own private stud books and handed over to the American buyers, deserve more credit for correctness than the official records which rested on what the keepers of the various English Stud Registers considered acceptable, or not, amidst the welter of contradictory evidence?'

"Taking, then, the traditional breeding as correct in every case for which we have contemporary evidence, it will be further noted that J. F. D. Smyth knew what he was talking about when he made his sympathetic observation on Virginia horses in 1772 and commented:

" 'The stock is from old Cade, old Crab, old Partner, Regulus, Babraham, Bosphorus, Devonshire Childers, the Cullen Arabian, the Cumberland Arabian, and a horse from Arabia named Bellsize which was imported into America (i.e., to Philadelphia) and is now (1772) in existence'.

"As these hallowed names are perhaps no longer familiar except to the antiquarian horseman, it will better carry home the significance of the horses here considered to interpret their breeding in terms of descent from the three accepted 'corner stones' of the thoroughbred horse, the Byerly Turk, the Darley Arabian and the Godolphin barb. On that test, it appears that all but three of the horses and all but five of the mares here in question brought to Virginia the blood of one or more of the 'corner stones;' the exceptions among the horses representing other Levantine stock, namely, the Cullen, Cumberland and Belsize Arabians mentioned by Smyth.

SARTEZ. No. 2500 as a foal.

"Of the 'corner stone' horses, fourteen were Byerlys; eleven Godolphins; two Darleys; four a combination of Darley and Byerly; two a combination of Darley and Godolphin; and one a combination of Godolphin, Darley and Byerly. Of the 'corner stone' mares seven were Godolphins; six Darleys; and two Byerlys. Stating this another way, the reputation of Flying Childers gave predominance to Darley blood in the earliest importations; then the success on the English turf of the get of Mr. Crofts' Partner and the arrival of his son, Morton's Traveller, gave the Byerly blood a predominance in Virginia which, measured in numbers, it maintained until after the Revolution; and, finally, when Fearnought came and achieved, locally, his justly great reputation, there was a strong swing to Godolphin blood, which, before 1770, had nearly balanced the number of Byerlys."

It appears justifiable to consider Bulle Rock the first Arabian horse in America, and Mr. Harrison is further quoted:

"On this testimony of a horseman's tradition, most of the discussions of the bred horse in America published since 1833, have, without criticism, hailed Bulle Rock as the first 'Arabian' horse in America. On this the Germans (See von Oettingen, *Horse Breeding in Theory and Practice,* English translation, 1909, p. 428) have recorded him among the sons of the Darley Arabian; but the Messrs. Weatherby have not yet given him the consecration of inclusion in GSB, for all that they have been accused (W. Allison, *The British Thoroughbred Horse,* 1907, p. 238) of undue hospitality to American horses."

The only reproductions of animal life in 1730 were paintings by artists. Photography was not yet available and therefore most of the illustrations in "The Equine F.F.Vs." consist of reproductions of well-known English paintings of many of these imported horses or their ancestors. A noticeable factor about these illustrations is that practically every one represents a well known Arabian or horse of principally Arabian breeding, such as Old Crab, the Byerly Turk, the Darley Arabian, Flying Childers, Crofts' Partner, the Godolphin Arabian, the Cullen Arabian, Old Babraham and Old Regulus.

THE BELAIR STUD, 1747-1761

The Belair Stud of Prince George's County, Maryland, one of the oldest and most prominent of the several studs formed from 1730 to 1830 in the colonial states, was established by Samuel Ogle (1694-1752) resident lieutenant governor of Maryland at intervals from 1731 to his death. During 1731 to 1742 he imported a Spanish or Barb horse and several Spanish mares. It is reported that Governor Ogle was persuaded to import what are referred to as Spanish horses by the inhabitants of Maryland who apparently preferred these horses to the English blood horse. It is said, however, that Governor Ogle himself preferred what we generally speak of as the English blood horse or Thoroughbred and that before 1735 he sent one of his mares to Virginia to be bred to Gist's Bulle Rock, the first imported Thoroughbred or blood horse.

When Governor Ogle returned to America from England for his last tour of official duty he brought with him an importation of Darley Arabian blood, a horse named Spark and a mare named Queen Mab, with her filly, Moll Brazen. This together with the earlier importation of Spanish horses was the foundation for the Belair Stud.

NURIDAB No. 4689. Arabian horse foal 2 days old.

Benjamin Tasker, Jr., Governor Ogle's brother-in-law, took over Belair Stud after the death of Governor Ogle in 1752. Tasker crossed the Spanish mares with the stallion, Spark, and also bred many native and quarter racing mares to this same stallion. The results were very satisfactory, and some very fine animals were realized from this cross-breeding. In 1751 one of the most famous mares ever imported into the colonies, the five-year-old Selima, arrived. She was of the new Godolphin Arabian blood, and after a short but satisfactory career on the turf she was put to breeding and produced some fine offspring. She ranks with Kitty Fisher as one of the two most famous early blood mares of Virginia.

The following comments are quoted from "The Belair Stud," by Fairfax Harrison:

"A few years later (1755) Governor Horatio Sharpe followed the example of his predecessor and also imported an English horse, Othello, which he sent to the Belair Stud as the one place then available in the province where he might have proper care; and to this stock Col. Tasker added about the same time (by acquisition from the estate of John Colvill of Fairfax County, Virginia) Spark's dam, a mature matron, bred by Colvill's kinsman, Lord Tankerville, and known, in honor of the breeder's wife, as 'Miss Colvill'.

"Col. Tasker died in 1760 and his Belair Stud was dispersed during the following year. Unfortunately for the history of the Thoroughbred horse in America, Col. Tasker's father (President of the Maryland Council and, on occasion, acting Governor), was a potentate of the eighteenth century school of public officers, with many of the characteristics attributed by the historians to the Virginia 'King Carter', and did not deem it necessary to do for his own son what men of less local importance were required to do for their families; that is to say, he did not file, as the law required, an inventory and administration accounts of the estate of Benjamin Tasker, Jr. For us today the consequence of this omission is that we lack that primary and specific evidence of the content and disposition of the Belair Stud which we have for other contemporary Maryland stud of less importance. But, despite that lack we are not altogether without information in the premises, for we have a precious shred of contemporary evidence directly in point, viz:

"(1761, May 14, MG) 'To be sold at public auction pursuant to the testament of the Hon. Colonel Benjamin Tasker, deceased, on Thursday the 21st of May, at Bellair in Prince George's County, near Queen Anne, the noted bay mare called Selima, four of her foals (probably Sharpe's Traveller mare, Stella, Selim & Ebony); the breeding mare (Moll Brazen) belonging to the late Governor Ogle, and their increase: in all 30. The subscriber will attend the sale.

" 'ROBERT CARTER, (*Executor.*

of Nomini in

Westmoreland County, Virginia)'.

"When the facts arrayed in this advertisement are read with the testimonies for the subsequent history of the Tasker horse stock it is possible to deduce, with conviction, that in 1756 the first stud of English blood in Maryland consisted of two imported horses, Spark and Othello, and four imported mares, viz: the two old ladies, Queen Mab and Miss Colvill, Queen Mab's English begotten daughter, Moll Brazen, the peerless Selima, the Bulle Rock mare, and the young stock they had then produced; but in 1760, when Col. Tasker died and the Belair Stud was dispersed, it is probable that Spark, Queen Mab and Miss Colvill were dead. The evidence for the others is that Othello was then removed to Whitehall by Governor Sharpe; that Selima and Moll Brazen (the last named being the sole survivor of the original Ogle importation) were sent to Virginia; and that the young stock was scattered among breeders in both Maryland and Virginia."

The Spanish mares and the Spanish stallion that made up a part of Belair Stud are not listed by name, but many references were found in the principal papers published at that time, such as the *Maryland Journal, Maryland Gazette, Pennsylvania Chronicle, New Jersey Gazette* and others. So many references are made to these horses and their Spanish origin that there can be no doubt about their authenticity.

Among the horses imported and used in furthering the Belair Stud was Ogle's Spark, a son of Darley's Arabian. The next stallion of prominence imported for use in this stud was Sharpe's Othello, who got his name from Horatio Sharpe, lieutenant governor of Maryland in 1753.

One of the most important and widely known mares bred in the Belair Stud was Gantt's Millie, sired by Ogle's Spark, and foaled in 1752. This mare was the dam of True Briton, the sire of Justin Morgan, founder of the Morgan breed. Students who have made an exhaustive study of the Morgan horse, have found that Justin Morgan was an inbred Arabian. His pedigree shows this to be an established fact.

THE ROANOKE STUD, 1795-1833

The most satisfactory and complete information on the Roanoke Stud of Virginia is contained in Fairfax Harrison's book of the same name.

Prior to the formation of this Stud, in 1795, there is considerable information on the activities of John Randolph, of Roanoke, the founder, who was also an enthusiast of quarter racing. Fairfax Harrison is once again quoted:

"John Randolph of Roanoke (1773-1833), a scion of the penultimate Randolph house, that of 'Curls', was, however, the freeman of the Virginia fraternity of horsemen, who loomed largest of any of his kin by the extent, if not the success, of his breeding operations. As a lad he may have felt the allure of the adventure while listening to the conversations of his maternal uncle, Dr. Theodorick Bland (1742-1790), who before the Revolution had maintained at Cawsons an important stud of English blood; but Randolph's immediate initiation to the mystery of horsemanship was effected by his cousin, David Meade III (eldest son of the David Meade II, 1744-1834, of Maycox, remembered in Virginia for the hanging gardens he constructed over the broad brown waters of James river) who was Randolph's habitual companion (Garland, i, 63) during the two years (1794 & 1795) after Randolph came of age and had entered into his inheritance.

"Randolph's statement (W. C. Bruce, i, 127) is that these years were spent riding 'about from one race field to another'; and in the last speech he ever made, that at the dinner following the Petersburg races in May, 1833, a few days before he died, his mind went back to these haunts of his youth and he named them. A correspondent of C. R. Colden who heard him testified to the charm of the discourse, saying:

" 'He spoke of his attachment to the sports of the turf, to the blood horse; told us of the origin of racing at Petersburg, of Pride's Old Field, of Gilles Field, of Ravenscroft; told us of the horses Ugly and Comet, of Brimmer and Flag of Truce; spoke of their owners, in language high and complimentary, as examples of the men of refinement and sentiment of the olden time, who followed the turf for amusement and achievement'.

"There have survived two testimonies that young Randolph was not merely a spectator at these long forgotten 'race fields' of the seventeen nineties. The first, of a Southside quarter race, was preserved by Edgar in his entry of an obscure horse known as Webster's Koulikhan:

" 'I rode Koulikhan once in a race, and beat, one quarter of a mile, against a horse in Nottoway County, whose name at this time I do not know. Koulikhan was as good a running horse as any, as far as he was tried. He was raised by a poor planter, and never was tried to run until he was aged. His breeder was a religious man, and Koulikhan was put into the hands of his kinsman, the late Mr. Wiltshire Binns, to run; and he ran several times with success, and then was kept as a covering horse. J.R., 30 October, 1830.'

"The second is the often quoted anecdote of a match at Charleston, S.C., in 1796, 'owners up', with the Scottish baronet Sir John Nesbit:

" 'On a bright sunny morning, early in February, 1796', said Thomas, (i, 56) 'might have been seen entering my book-store, in Charleston, South Carolina, a fine looking, florid complexioned old gentleman, with hair as white as snow; which, contrasted with his complexion, showed him to have been a free liver, or bon vivant, of the first order. Along with him was a tall, gawky-looking, flaxen-haired stripling, apparently of the age of from sixteen to eighteen, with a complexion of a good parchment color, beardless chin, and as much assumed self-consequence as any two-footed animal I ever saw: - this was John Randolph . . .

" 'He had come to Charleston to attend the races (cf. W. C. Bruce, i, 135 ff). There was then living in Charleston a Scotch baronet, by the name of Sir John Nesbit, with his younger brother, Alexander, of the ancient house of Nesbits of Dean Hall, some fifteen miles from Edinburgh. Sir John was a very handsome man, and as "gallant, gay Lothario" as could be found in the city. He and Randolph became intimate, which led to a banter between them for a race, in which each was to ride his own horse. The race came off during the race week, and Randolph won: some of the ladies exclaiming at the time, "though Mr. Randolph had won the race, Sir John had won their hearts." This was not so much to be wondered at, when you contrasted the elegant form and graceful style of riding of the baronet, with the uncouth and awkward manner of his competitor'.

"Randolph never forgot his quarter racing experience. Not only did it colour his breeding philosophy, but his later descriptions, of himself (ATR i, 462), as 'an old lover of the smack of the whip'; and (in a letter to W. R. Johnson, Bouldin, p. 225) of the need to 'plumb the track, as I have heard old racers say', conjure visions of that earliest form of Virginia horse sport which had its origin in the mists of Saxon England."

The principal sire used in founding the Roanoke Stud was Janus, imported some time before 1761 a son of the Godolphin Arabian. This horse lived to be 34 years old and died in 1780. The first reference to show that Janus was in Virginia was a letter dated May 13, 1757.

It is reported on good authority that John Randolph was not very successful in the development of his breeding stud, even though it existed for thirty-eight years, principally because he neglected to purchase some of the finest mares and fillies then being produced in Virginia and neighboring colonies, but instead decided to import some fillies direct from England as foundation stock.

Those animals bred by, or members of, the Roanoke Stud of Arabian breeding will be listed elsewhere in this book, and for that reason no further reference will be made to them here.

THE JOHN'S ISLAND STUD (S.C.), 1750-1788

Of the early importers of English blood stock to America the Fenwick family of South Carolina is of historical interest because of its traditional interest in racing in England. Edward Fenwick, who founded John's Island Stud, was born in 1720 and died in 1775.

John's Island is off the east coast of Carolina between Charleston and Port Royal. It is a flat lowland of very rich soil thirteen miles long and six miles wide, and on it the Fenwick breeding stud had a fine pasture of 200 acres for brood mares and their foals. At least 1,000 acres of the balance of the plantation was given over to the production of other crops. The original dwelling on this plantation, known as Fenwick Hall, was built in 1730. As late as 1931 several of the buildings of this famous stud were still standing and in a fair state of repair.

The early breeding operations of John's Island Stud were on a foundation of Narragansett pacers and Chickasaw or Indian horses. Upon this foundation Edward Fenwick, Sr., added imported English horses, particularly those of Godolphin Arabian blood. He is generally known as the founder of the turf in Carolina. The following is a list of his importations:

"1756 Brutus, son of Martindale's Regulus (GSB, i, 133; Bruce, i, 9).

"1758 Tarquin, son of D. of Ancaster's Tarquin (Bruce, i, 56).

"1759 Black-and-all-Black (probably) son of Ld. Portmore's Oroonoko (not in any stud book).

"1759 A Squirt mare.

"1759 A Tartar mare.

"1763 Pam, son of Martindale's Regulus (GSB, i, 382; Bruce, 1, 41).

"1766 Centinel, son of D. of Ancaster's Blank (GSB, i, 145; Bruce, i, 11).

"1766 Fallower, son of D. of Ancaster's Blank (GSB, i, 151; Bruce, i, 21).

"1766 A Brilliant mare.

"1766 A Bajazet mare.

"1767 Shadow, son of Rogers' Babraham (GSB, i, 202; Bruce, i, 48).

"1773 Matchless, 'the last surviving son of the Godolphin Arabian' (GSB, i, 196; Bruce, i, 36).

"1773 A Villager mare, with her colt (Matchem) by Stamford's Bosphorus.

"1773 A Merlin mare.

"Here, finally, during the Revolution Edward Fenwick, jun., brought another horse of the Godolphin blood, which had been imported into Carolina in 1772:

"1778 Flimnap, son of South (GSB, i, 73; Bruce, i, 22)."

Historical evidence shows that the first horses in use in Carolina were Narragansett pacers brought from Rhode Island in 1682, and it is therefore assumed that John Fenwick, an early ancestor of Edward Fenwick, Sr., used these horses for transportation, in the Indian wars and for other purposes, but that later on they were replaced by a breed known to Carolinians as Chickasaws.

In 1762 after Edward Fenwick had imported several English stallions to Carolina he started the importation of mares largely of the Godolphin Arabian breeding. In Fairfax Harrison's book on the John's Island Stud he comments:

"These mares came to America in three installments, each pair showing the importer's steadily increasing appetite for concentrated blood of the Godolphin Arabian, viz:

"1762 The two earliest mares (by Squirt and Tartar), representatives respectively of Bartlett's Childers and Croft's Partner, were apparently selected to nick with the Godolphin blood of Brutus, as they triumphantly did.

"1766 The next pair (by Brilliant and Bajazet) were representatives respectively of Panton's Crab and the Godolphin Arabian, while

"1773 the final pair (by Villager and Merlin), intended to be mated with Matchless, were, like him, both straight Godolphins.

"They were all duly mated with their contemporaries among the English horses in Carolina who were their peers in breeding, but no adequate or in any sense comprehensive record survives of their stud careers. We have testimonies for only some of their produce; notably that of the Squirt mare. It is curious and perhaps significant that later pedigrees did not play any of them up with such a chorus of historical retrospect as would certainly have been raised if they had gone to Virginia. The witty pen of John Davis, the English tutor who was in the Drayton family at the very time (1799) most of the Virginia historical pedigrees were put together, might, indeed, have used this illustration to point his remark that 'Cotton in Carolina and horse racing in Virginia are the prevailing topics of conversation: these reduce every understanding to a level'.

"On the other hand, it may be that the lack of detailed testimony for the John's Island mares is merely casual. Most of the surviving evidence for them is derived from certificates made by Edward Fenwick, jun., after the Revolution. By comparison of those certificates with the evidence for the maker's own racing activities it will be apparent that we have but a small part of all the certificates he may have given. In addition to those turf horses which are hereinafter noted because we know their breeding, the Racing Calendar shows that Edward Fenwick, jun., introduced the following colts and fillies on the turf: 1788 Adventurer, Cleopatra; 1789 Cincinnatus, Dungannon; 1790 Oronoko, Busiris; 1791 Angelina; 1792 Boxer; 1793 Pantaloon; 1794 Aeolus; 1798 Highflyer. Bruce has no record of any of these horses and we have been unable to supply the want. That they were all high bred is apparent both from the fact that Fenwick trained them and from their turf form. It is probable that he himself bred most of them so it seems to follow that if we had their breeding it might be possible to extend the list of the produce of the Fenwick imported mares.

"It seems expedient to note here that the advertisement of 1767 by Edward Fenwick of his intention to put down his stud during a prolonged absence in England did not result in any break in the continuity of his breeding operations in Carolina. At that date there seem to have been at John's Island, with 'bred up' representatives of the Chickasaw foundation stock, all of the first four imported mares (by Squirt, Tartar, Brilliant and Bajazet), as well as some brood mares of their produce. Detailed evidence is lacking as to what was sold in 1767; but there is evidence that the Stud was carried on until 1773 by Robert and John Gibbes, later Mr. Fenwick's executors, and the importations of 1773, made in contemplation of Mr. Fenwick's return from England, were thus not a foundation for a new Stud, but a refreshment of a stock on hand. So it was that when the importer died in 1775 and his son succeeded him, the breeding plant was as fully equipped with English blood as ever it had been. The inventory then recorded suggests, indeed, that it included at least two English mares, in addition to those here listed, which are not identified by later pedigrees."

There is considerable historical reference to the Chickasaw horse in Carolina. One of the first such was in the South Carolina *Gazette* of December 16, 1745, which advertised several Chickasaw and Choctaw horses for sale. Other references are to be found in 1763, 1764 and 1786. The following quotation is from Ramsey, the historian, and is in the nature of a comment on the Indian horse in Carolina. This comment was made in 1809:

"Before the year 1754 [sic] the best horses for the draft or saddle in Carolina were called the Chickasaw breed. These were originally introduced by the Spaniards into Florida and in the course of time had astonishingly increased. Great numbers ranged wild in and near the Apalache old field. Many of them were caught and tamed by the Indians and sold to the traders. They made use of them for pack horses to bring their peltry to market and afterwards sold them in the low country. These horses in general were handsome, active and hardy, but small; seldom exceeding thirteen hands and a half in height. The mares in particular, when crossed with English blooded horses, produced colts of great beauty, strength and swiftness."

A further statement of interest is that of William Bartram, in 1791, with reference to the Seminole horses, of the same general family as the other Indian or Choctaw horses, as follows:

"The Seminole [sic] horses . . . are the most beautiful and sprightly species of that noble creature perhaps any where to be seen: but are of a small breed and as delicately formed as the American roe buck. A horse in the Creek or Muscogalge tongue is echoclucco, that is the great deer (echo is a deer and clucco is big). The Seminole [sic] horses are said to descend originally from the Andalusian breed brought here by the Spaniards when they first established the colony of East Florida. From the forehead to their nose is a little arched or aquiline. . . .

"The fine Choctaw horses among the Upper Creeks are said to have been brought thither from New Mexico across the Mississippi by those nations of Indians who emigrated from the west beyond the river. These horses are every way like the Seminole [sic] breed, only being larger and perhaps not so capricious".

The history of Carolina and its horses shows that there were no first-class saddle horses in this state before 1740, at which time the Choctaw or Chickasaw horses were introduced into Carolina and became the main source for saddle and racing purposes after 1740. It is reported that the following tabulation represents the horse service in Carolina from a breeding and usage standpoint:

(1) From 1682-1740, the Narragansett (or Rhode Island pacer).

(2) From 1740-1786, the Chickasaw (or Spanish Plains) horse.

(3) From 1755, the English bred horse.

Racing in South Carolina is of great importance in the history of the blood horse in America, and one publication that has given much attention to this subject is the book by Dr. John B. Irving entitled, "History of the Turf in South Carolina" (1857), containing the racing calendars from 1792-1857.

While the Fenwicks, with their John's Island Stud, were the most important and widely known breeders of racing horses in Carolina, several other studs became more or less prominent in the racing field. These were made up of largely native-bred horses from Virginia and other breeding areas. Because the Virginia and Maryland Arabian-bred horses will be mentioned in greater detail in the list of horses making up the pedigree foundations for the American Stud Book, the individual animals need not be listed here.

Chapter 3

Stallions Of Arabian Breeding Imported To America From 1730 To 1830

THE native American horses in Virginia and surrounding states at the time the importation of English horses started in 1730, were chiefly of Chickasaw breeding or what would commonly be known as Indian ponies. By careful selection and breeding of the best to the best, there was considerable improvement in these ponies over several generations, but they were still small and their owners felt sure that through breeding them to imported English stallions, they would achieve the desired larger size and running ability. The small size of the Chickasaw and Seminole horses, which were for all practical purposes but large ponies, was because for many generations since their introduction by the Spanish explorers and colonists they had run wild and bred in the natural state, and had subsisted on inadequate feed.

Racing at the time of the first importations and for many years afterward was generally over short distances, usually one-fourth of a mile or less, and was known as quarter racing. It became a sport of the first magnitude, in the Southern states. No special tracks were available and the races were held wherever a suitable place could be found. Large sums of money were wagered on these races and every effort was made on the part of the planters and breeders to produce superior quarter running horses. There was a marked improvement both in the size and the speed of these horses after the Chickasaw mares were cross-bred with English stallions.

The description given of the following Arabian-bred stallions is that used by Fairfax Harrison in his book entitled "Early American Turf Stock 1730-1830":

"S.C. 1762

"Arabian Horse, called Hushang, Gulliver's. Not in ASB*. The evidence is an introductory Carolina advertisement, (1762, May 1, South Carolina *Gazette*) viz:

" 'Hushang, a famous horse just arrived in the Banjamin, Capt. Gulliver, from London. He was bred by Muley Acshmudt, governor of Bender Raach [sic], a seaport town in Persia, out of a fine leopard-coloured mare belonging to the governor of Balsiria [sic] in Arabia.

" 'Muley Acshmudt made him a present to the Dey of Algiers, and [he was] afterwards sold to Capt. Grandiwort, from whom Capt. Gulliver had him. He is esteemed as compleat a horse as ever came out of that part of the world, and of the highest blood in England.

" 'He will cover this season at ten guineas a mare, at Morgan-Hall, Port-Royal Ferry [South Carolina].

" 'Bred in Persia and sent thence to Morocco; whence he was brought to Carolina, by a merchantman.

" '1762 at Morgan-Hall, Port Royal, S. C. [last record]'.

"Mass. 1770[?]

"Arabian Horse, called Joe Miller, Ruggles'. Not in ASB.

"The fragmentary evidence collected by Battell is that about 1770 Timothy Ruggles (1711-1795) of Hardwick, Worcester Co., Mass., a large figure in the civil and military history of Massachusetts before the Revolution, imported from England a black horse so bred that he was called an 'Arabian'. This might be interpreted as meaning no more than that he was got in England by a horse of Oriental breeding, did not the earliest of the testimonies explicitly state that he was 'imported from Arabia', viz:

---

*See end of Chapter for symbols used.

"1784 [Battell, ii, p. ccxxiii; i, 693] Worcester, Mass.: John Green's bl. c. [age not recorded] 'got by the beautiful Black Horse imported from Arabia and formerly owned by Timothy Ruggles of Hardwick'.

"1795 [ibid, ii, p. cclxvii] Sharon, Conn.: A. Taylor's Romeo, c. 1790, got by Roebuck, a son 'of Brigadier Ruggles' noted imported Arabian horse, Joe Miller.

"1797 [ibid., ii, p. clix; i, 638] St. Johnsbury, Vt.: Arnold's Cuthullin, b. c. 1793, by Roebuck of Hardwick, Mass., a son of 'the noted Joe Miller imported from England by Brigadier Ruggles'.

"Mass. 1800

"Arabian [?] Horse called Dey of Algiers, Swan's. ASB, i, 143, derived from Edgar [who had the Virginia advertisement in 1803], is an adequate but incomplete record of the evidence. The horse was introduced in America by the following advertisement: [1801, April 8, Thomas' Massachusetts *Spy* or Worcester *Gazette;* whence Battell, ii, p. ccxxv]

" 'Dey of Algiers, an imported Arabian [sic] is only seven years old [i.e., foaled 1794] . . . Proofs of his being a real Arabian imported into Prussia are to be seen in the hands of Mr. Jelley, the groom.

" 'Charlestown [Mass.], April 1, 1801.   HENRY JACKSON'."

In 1835 (ATR, vii, 67) James Smock of Fredericksburg, Virginia, had occasion to distinguish this horse, which had died in his possession in 1807, from the Black Sultan (q. v. post, Md. 1806); and then quoted the following extract "from the orginal papers which accompanied the horse to this country and which were sent to me [Smock] with him by General [John] Mason [of Georgetown, D. C.]":

"In 1798 the Emperor of Arabia [sic], having received some signal service from the late Grand Bailiff Fromm of Prussia, tendered to him the choice of any of his stud. The Bailiff procured the assistance of one Frederick Lipentine, the Grand Selector [as he was called], who chose for him from the Emperor's stud, consisting of several hundred genuine and superior Arabian horses, the noble Dey [of Algiers] and two mares, one called Latonia and the other Cappadocia.

"They were taken to Lithuania in Poland, from which place they were taken to Prussia. After the decease of the Bailiff, at the sale of his stud at Fehrbellin in the year 1799, the Dey, then five years old, together with the two mares, were purchased by Lieutenant General Frederick Baron von Diemar; by whom they were afterwards sold to Colonel [James] Swan [1754-1831], an original member of the 'Boston tea party' of Massachusetts, then in Europe; and by him were shipped from Hamburg to Boston to General [Henry] Jackson [1747-1809] of that city."

To this narrative Mr. Smock added:

"In the beginning of the year 1802, Gen. Jackson sent Dey to Gen. Mason of the District of Columbia, by whom he was sent to the subscriber at Fredericksburg in 1807, where he died before the conclusion of the season. He had made several successful seasons in Maryland, and stood one or two seasons in lower Virginia, under the direction of the late Col. John Tayloe."

It will be noted that nowhere is the place of origin of the horse definitely stated. In the Virginia advertisements, as in the Swan certificate, he is called an "Arabian;" but his name suggests that the "Emperor of Arabia," in whose stud he was bred, was the Dey of Algiers. This deduction does not inhibit Arabian blood, for the Algerian potentate undoubtedly had Arabian horses in his stud, but it leaves a doubt as to whether the horse was not what is called in the older English pedigrees a "natural barb."

In the introductory Maryland advertisement (1802) the description of the horse, echoed in all subsequent advertisements, was as follows:

"The Dey is of full stature for his race: he measures exactly fourteen hands two inches and a half. His colour is nearly white, with a few brown spots dashed over his neck and shoulders. In figure and bone, it is believed, he will stand the test of the best judgment. He is only eight years old the coming spring [i.e., foaled 1794], of fine presence and carriage, remarkably vigorous and active."

The evidence contained in extant advertisements is that his life history was as follows:

1794 foaled possibly in the stud of the Dey of Algiers.
1798 brought to Poland and thence to Prussia by the Grand Bailiff Fromm.
1799 purchased at Hamburg by James Swan and sent to Massachusetts, where he arrived in the autumn of 1800.
1801 at Gen. Henry Jackson's, Charlestown, Mass.
1802 sent to John Mason of Georgetown, D. C., and covered at Charles C. Jones', Montgomery County, Md.
1802 Dec., advertised for sale by John Mason, but not sold.
1803 at E. Edelin's, in Prince George's County, Md.
1804 at John Tayloe's quarter, Gwynfield, Essex County, Va.
1805 at William Bronaugh's, Loudoun County, Va.
1806 at John Tayloe's, Petworth, Md.
1807 at James Smock's, Fredericksburg, Va., where he died before the end of the season.

The significant evidence on Selim "Barron's, later Tayloe's — [ASB 1, 147 derived from Edgar [p. 71]" — is scattered through the extant Virginia and Kentucky advertisements of 1803-1810 and is here arrayed in such order as to state the history of the horse chronologically (1805, March 12, Petersburg Virginia *Republican;* being the certificate which Capt. James Barron (II, 1769-1851), U. S. N., brought with the horse to Virginia) :

"Selim, a thoroughbred Arabian horse seven years old [i.e., foaled 1794], 14 hands and a half high . . . was got by Achmet a favourite horse of the Mameluke chief Murad Bey: out of an Abyssinian mare.

"He was procured and presented to the late general Sir Ralph Abercromby [1734-1801] by the [Turkish] Grand Vizier on his [Gen. Abercromby's] arrival in Egypt. Sir Ralph gave him to an officer of high rank; of whom I obtained him.

" (Malta) 1802. N. Ramsay."

(1810, April 21, Kentucky *Gazette;* being the certificate which Capt. Barron furnished to John Tayloe III in 1807):

"I do certify that the horse Selim was landed at Malta from Egypt in the year 1802, at which time I was at Malta in the [U. S.] frigate Philadelphia; and that Major Ramsay of the Queen's regiment was the proprietor of said horse and was a passenger with me from Syracuse to Gibralter, from whom I learned the following particulars, viz: that Selim was one of several horses presented to Gen. Abercromby by [sic] the Mameluke chief, Murad Bey, in Egypt and that in consequence of the death of Gen. Abercromby the horse fell into the hands of [another] general officer from whom he was obtained by Major Ramsay. Several officers who were with me in the ship can attest the facts to which I here subscribe.

"['Pembroke', Hampton, Va., March 1807] James Barron.'

(1803, May 25, Richmond *Examiner*):

"Selim, a thoroughbred Arabian horse . . . just landed at this place.

"For further particulars apply to the subscriber who is empowered to dispose of him by sale or otherwise.

" 'Pembroke' near Hampton (Va.), May 23, 1803. Thomas Jones."

(1809, March 13, Kentucky *Gazette;* being the certificate sent to Kentucky with the horse by John Tayloe III):

"I do certify that I have bred two years [1807-1808] from the genuine and uncommonly fine Arabian horse Selim. . . .

"Major Ramsay, a British officer . . . sold a part of him to Commodore Barron, who brought him to America.

"For half of this horse I later [i.e., in 1807] gave Commodore Barron

$1,500 and have now [1808] sent him out to Major Benjamin Graves, near Lexington, Ky.

"Mount Airy, Virginia, November 10, 1808. John Tayloe (III)."

The life history of Selim was evidently as follows:

1801, March. Bred in the Egyptian stud of the Mameluke chief, Murad Bey, this Selim was presented by the Turkish Grand Vizier to General Sir Ralph Abercromby commanding the British forces in the Mediterranean.

1801, August. After the evacuation of Egypt by the French, purchased by Major N. Ramsay, of the Queen's Regiment, and taken to Malta;

1802 where a half interest was purchased by Capt. James Barron, U. S. N.;

1803, May, who took the horse to America in the U. S. frigate *Philadelphia,* and landed him at Hampton, Virginia, where he was advertised for sale by Thomas Jones.

1804 at William Stark's in Dinwiddie County, Va.

1805 at Robert Rivers' in Greenville County, Va.

1806 at Capt. Barron's, Hampton, Va.

1807 at John Tayloe's, Mount Airy, Va.

1808 at Richard Foote's, in Prince William County, Va.

1808, November, sent to Kentucky.

1809-10 at B. Graves', Lexington, Ky. (last record).

"N. Y. 1804

"Arabian Horse called Grand Seignor, Hazard and Thompson's. ASB has no historical entry."

Lacking an advertisement to speak for the horse the evidence is the following statement, (1839, ATR, xi, 47) viz:

"The Arabian horse Grand Seignor was presented by the Grand Seignor of Arabia to his late majesty [George III] King of Great Britain, was brought to the province of Nova Scotia [1799] by his [fourth] son the Duke of Kent [1767-1820, the father of Queen Victoria], who sold him to his friend Col. Campbell of Windsor; and was purchased from him by Messrs. Hazard and Thompson, by whom he was imported into the City of New York on the 4th October 1804.

"Hunterdon Co., N. J., December 15, 1839. David D. Schamp."

1805-1809 covered in New York and New Jersey (last record).

"Va. 1805

"Arabian Horses (2) called Ishmael and Taurus, William Eaton's."

GASARKIN No. 3992, a 3-week-old filly.

ASB, i, 145 and 148 [derived from Edgar, pp. 69 and 72] s. v. Ishmael and Taurus, are uninformative entries and, moreover, are misinterpretations in that they attributed the importation to Gen. Thomas Eaton, a well known North Carolina horseman.

The evidence for these horses is the letter of December 24, 1805, addressed by General William Eaton of Massachusetts to John Tayloe III of Virginia which was published by Skinner in 1835 (ATR, iv, 120; quoted s. v. Eaton's Arabian-mare called Diana, ante, vol. i, p. 317). There it appears that on his return to America from his African service in the Tripolitan war in the autumn of 1805 Gen. William Eaton brought with him two horses and a mare, and sent all three to Col. Tayloe. The horses were described as follows:

"The Gray horse, called Ishmael, is an Arabian, four years old; came from the neighbourhood of Mecca, was broke in the Mameluke camp, rode by the Kerchief of Demerah, who was a bey in that army, but who came over and took command of the Turkish troops in the province of Jefara about eighteen months ago; and by him [was] presented to me. I wish he may have the benefit of your stables and groom, but not to stand unless you wish to make an experiment among your own horses. The march through the desert, and a long voyage at sea, have very much reduced him; a year's good keeping I trust will restore him.

"The dun horse called Taurus [here followed a description equivalent to that of Ishmael, which was illegible when Gen. Eaton's letter came into Skinner's hands]. I wish him also to have the benefit of your groom; and if occasion offers he may be used at a stand."

B. O. Tayloe noted (ATR, iv, 120) that his father "did not think favourably of the horses" and returned them to Gen. Eaton; and it was later noted by R. L. Allen (*American Agriculturist,* May 1843; whence Battell, i, 695) that they were taken to Gen. Eaton's estate at Brimfield in Massachusetts, where they covered "many years."

The only contemporary evidence for these horses in New England which has come to light is a single Connecticut advertisement which does not identify which of the two it refers to (1811, Hartford *Courant;* Battell, ii, cccxvi) viz:

"The noted stud horse imported from Arabia by Gen. William Eaton, will stand at the stable of the subscriber the present season.
"East Hartford, Conn., May 8, 1811. JOB BECKWITH."
The history of Ishmael and/or Taurus is evidently as follows:
1805 acquired in Egypt by Gen. William Eaton of Massachusetts and used by him in his march across the Libyan desert in his expedition against the Bashaw of Tripoli.
1805 brought to Virginia by General Eaton and sent to John Tayloe III.
1806 sent to Massachusetts.
1807 ff. at Gen. William Eaton's, Brimfield, Mass.
1811 one of the two at East Hartford, Conn. (last record).

"Md. 1814

"Arabian Horse called Arab and Barbarossa and, eventually 'Winter's Arabian', E. I. Winter's. ASB, i, 148, was derived from Edgar, p. 79, who had Skinner's note of Md. tradition [ATR, ii, 377]."

The evidence consists of a series of documents collected by Elisha I. Winter (1781-1840), a Member of Congress from New York 1813-1815 and later a resident of Kentucky, in his Kentucky advertisements of 1824-1825. It will be noted that the place of the horse's origin is nowhere recorded, (1814, September 10, Niles Weekly *Register*, Baltimore, concerning prizes taken by United States ships during the war with England, 1812-1814) viz:

"1142, His Britannic Majesty's transport brig Doris, No. 650, captured by the *Grampus* [privateer] of Baltimore and sent into Marblehead, Mass.

"The *Doris* was from Senegal [in West Africa] bound to Portsmouth, and had on board 30 or 40 soldiers, also two [sic, the second being specified by Mr. Winter in ATR, i, 578, as 'a filly', which suggests that she may have been the Arabian mare which was advertised for sale in Kentucky in April 1815, described as then recently 'imported into New Orleans'] elegant horses [probably taken on board at Gibralter], one hyena, two jackalls, etc., presents for the Prince Regent [afterwards George IV]."

From the 1817, April 5, Richmond *Enquirer*:

"The elegant horse Arab stands at the stable of John Wooden at Govanstown, four miles from Baltimore on the York Road.

"This horse is considered as of the first blood of the Arabian horses. He was taken by the privateer *Grampus* in the year 1814 in the British transport brig No. 136 [sic] bound for London and was said to be sent as a present to the Prince Regent.

"He is a beautiful dappled grey, four years old [i.e., foaled 1812]; and by judges [sic, indicating lack of papers] is said to possess every mark of the blooded horses of Arabia.

"[Govanstown, Baltimore Co., Md.] MARK ANTHONY, groom."

From the 1824, February, Lexington Kentucky *Reporter*:

"The thoroughbred and imported horse known as the Winter Arabian . . . was captured during the late war, viz, in 1814, by the privateer *Grampus* of Baltimore, on board the brig *Doris*, H. B. M.'s transport No. 650, on her passage from Senegal in Africa to Portsmouth in England; and was landed at Marblehead [in Massachusetts]. He was intended as a present to the Prince Regent, now King [George IV] of England [see Niles' "Register," vol. vii, p. 16]. He was then between one and two years old [i.e., foaled 1812], was sold as part of the prize cargo at that age for $1,000. and was bought in for account of the privateer's owners; from whom I purchased him. . . . The only possible objection which has been taken to him is his size, being about four feet nine or ten inches [say 14.2 hands], which is one which will apply to the whole [Arabian] race.

"Lexington, Ky. E. I. WINTER."

In 1825, January 14, a letter was exhibited by Mr. Winter in his description of the horse in ATR, i, 578, and subsequently calendared in his advertisement of March 21, 1825, in the Lexington Kentucky *Reporter.*

"We have now obtained the necessary information for your friend respecting the Arabian horse which was captured in the year 1814 on board H. M. transport *Doris* on her passage from Senegal to Portsmouth. Mr. Aspinwall, nephew to our Mr. Duncan, is acquainted with Col. Bloomfield and Mr. Douglass, who have the management of the King's stud at Hampton Court. He has seen both of those gentlemen on this subject; who state to him that a present was sent to his majesty of a thoroughbred Arabian horse, which was shipped in the transport brig *Doris,* but unfortunately captured; that they did not receive any pedigree [nor do they ever receive pedigrees of thoroughbred Arabians] but they believe him thoroughbred.

"Liverpool, January 14, 1824. W. M. DUNCAN AND SONS."

The life history of Winter's Arabian is evidently as follows:

1814 captured at sea from a British transport by the Baltimore privateer *Grampus* and bought in by the owners of that privateer at the prize sale, who eventually sold him to E. I. Winter.

1816-17 at John Wooden's, Govanstown, Baltimore County, Md.

1818-22 no record, probably still in Maryland.

Edgar (p. 67, whence ASB, i, 142) has an entry, s. v. "Barbarossa, gr. c., 14 hands 3 inches, James R. Jones," which suggests Maryland stud bill for which there is no evidence. It will be noted that the coat, height and date attributed to that Barbarossa all fit the record of the Winter Arabian.

1822 at Spencer Cooper's, Lexington, Ky.

1823 at W. T. Banton's, Lexington, Ky.

1824-26 at E. I. Winter's, Lexington, Ky.

1827 at William Buford's in Woodford County, Ky.

1828 at E. I. Winter's, Lexington, Ky.

1829 at Samuel Davenport's, Danville, Ky.

1831 at John Tucker's, Harrisville, Va. (ATR, ii, 349; last record).

"N. Y. 1819

"Arabian Horse called Bussorah Arabian, Ogden's. ASB, i, 143, was derived from Edgar, p. 68, who had the version of the Van Ranst statement, quoted below, which was exhibited in the Va. advertisement 1824."

AMIR SELFAN A.H.C. No. 5859. Chestnut Arabian stallion at 1 month of age.

The importation papers for this horse were deemed "too long for insertion in an advertisement" and in consequence have been lost; but there has survived a calendar of them by the experienced New York horseman who acquired an interest in him immediately on his importation, (1831, October, ATR, iii, 55) viz:

"The truly elegant and valuable horse known as the Bussorah Arabian was foaled in 1813 at Bussorah [sic in "The Arabian Nights," but now Basra] on the banks of the Euphrates at the head of the Persian Gulf; and was reared under the eye of Dr. Colquhoun, now of Bombay, for many years the East India Company's resident at Bussorah.

"He was purchased of that gentleman (Dr. Colquhoun) and imported into this country by Abraham Ogden, Esqr. [of New York] in the autumn of 1819. He is of the 'Germany' [sic, perhaps intended for Kochlani] breed, a caste held in the highest estimation by the Arabs, as well for their beautiful symmetry of form as for the flinty hardness they evince in the endurance of fatigue. His elegance of form with the beauty of his colour, being a handsome chestnut, his fine movement and the exhibition of those points found only in the blood horse, afford ample evidence of the purity of his descent.

"I bought a share of him in 1820 and in the fall of that year he took the premium of the New York County Agricultural Society as the best stud horse in the state. . . .

"From that period [1820] he stood severally in New York, Virginia and elsewhere, till 1830, when I became the sole owner; since which he has remained in this state [of New York].

"14 Beekman Street, New York. C. W. VAN RANST."

From the 1824, June 11, Richmond *Enquirer*: (After reciting the history of the horse substantially in the language of the Van Ranst statement quoted above, and noting that he had stood successfully in New York for three seasons and had been procured for service in Virginia "for one season only.")

"The original documents proving the genealogy of this horse, too long for insertion in an advertisement, are in my possession and will be shown to those interested.

" 'Curles', Henrico Co., Va., February 19, 1824. Wade Mosby, Jr."

The extant detailed evidence of advertisements of the stands of the Bussorah Arabian is incomplete, but suffices to control the Van Ranst statement, viz:

1821-1823 at Mr. Deyo's, near Harlem Bridge, N. Y.

1824 at Wade Mosby's, "Curles," Henrico County, Va.

1825-29 no record except pedigrees, which indicate stands in New Jersey and New York.

1830-31 at C. W. Van Ranst's, New York.

1832 at Geneseo, N. Y. (Battell, i, 406; last record).

"Pa. 1820

"Arabian Horse called Grand Sultan, Richard B. Jones'. ASB, i, 144, was derived from Edgar, p. 69, who had the Pennsylvania advertisement 1821." The evidence is as follows, (1821, March 9, Philadelphia *Democratic Press*) viz:

"The elegant full blooded Arabian horse Sultan . . . is a beautiful iron gray, 5 years old last autumn, fifteen and a half hands high and for elegance of form, as well as power and activity, not surpassed by any horse ever imported into the United States.

"Grand Sultan was imported into the United States during the summer of 1820, from Tripoli, and selected with the greatest care and attention from the best stock of the Bashaw, and is declared by the certificate of the Bashaw's Public Secretary, Signior Abraham Sercise, to be of the finest and highest Arabian stock ever reared in all Barbary. His sire, Billah, was imported from Syria; his dam Caulah, from Egypt.

"At the sign of the Lamb on the Lancaster Turnpike, one mile from Philadelphia, March 9, 1821. John Elliott."

From a letter dated 1865 to John H. Wallace, published in *Wallace's Monthly* and cited by Battell, ii, cx:

"Grand Sultan was imported by me at the same time [with Grand Bashaw, q. v. next above]. He stood one if not two seasons at Salem, N. J., under charge of Michael Hackett, Esq., about 1822 or 1823, and had many colts and fillies there. He was an iron grey of the Arabian stock.

"Philadelphia, April 25, 1865. RICHARD B. JONES."

1821 at John Elliott's, near Philadelphia.

1822-1823 at Michael Hackett's, Salem, N. J. (last record).

In 1823 Grand Sultan was exhibited at the show of the Pennsylvania Agricultural Society and was placed second to Grand Bashaw (ATR, ii, 483).

"Pa. 1820

"Arabian Horse called Saladin, Richard B. Jones'. ASB, i, 147, was derived from Edgar (p. 71), who had the N. C. advertisement 1823." The evidence is as follows (1823, from an otherwise lost N. C. advertisement preserved by Edgar, p. 71, and controlled by A. J. Davie in ATR, iii, 275) viz:

"Selladin [sic], an elegant and full blooded Arabian horse, was imported during the summer of 1821 from Tripoli by his owner, Richard B. Jones, Esq., late American Consul to that place.

"He was foaled 1815; his sire Kaled was imported [into Tripoli] from the kingdom of Senvaar: his dam Garrind was selected from the stables of the Emperor of Morocco and sent as a present to the Bashaw of Tripoli.

" 'Newhope', Halifax Co., N. C., March 1823. J. S. Shepherd."

(1865, from a letter to John H. Wallace, published in *Wallace's Monthly* and cited by Battell, ii, cx)

"Saladin was imported by me at the same time [as Grand Bashaw and Grand Sultan, q. v. next above]. In my opinion he was superior in purity of blood, size and form to either of the others.

"I sent him to North Carolina, where he improved the stock; and from thence to Georgia, where he died.

"Philadelphia, April 25, 1865. RICHARD B. JONES."

"N. Y. 1822

"Arabian Horse called Bagdad, George Barclay's. ASB, i, 142, derived from Edgar, p. 66, was based on the importation papers cited below.

[1822, from the papers taken with the horse from New York to Nashville, Tenn., and published by W. Williams 'Panton' in ATR, i, 275. The original certificate of the Tripolitan Minister to England, sent to America, was in Arabic and had attached to it the French version which Mr. Williams exhibited; of which the text here given is, in turn, a translation.]

" 'I, Hassana d'Gris, the undersigned, declare and certify by these presents that the brown horse called Bagdad, now in the possession of Mr. George Barclay, merchant in London, is a true Arab. He was included in a consignment of twelve horses of that breed which I myself saw landed at Marseilles in the year 1819 from a ship coming from Aleppo in Syria; of which horses six were purchased for account of the French government for use in its state stud. The horse herein mentioned was one of the six remaining (in my hands), of which three were sent to this country (England).

"London, March 12, 1822. HASSANA D'GRIS, Ambassador of the Bashaw of Tripoli accredited to His Britannic Majesty'."

" 'I, George Barclay, do hereby certify that Bagdad was purchased by me from Hassana d'Gris, Minister to England from Tripoli, who assured me he was imported by him into England as a horse of peculiar value and the purest Arabian blood, for which 1,000 pounds was refused in France; and that Bagdad was his favourite and by far the most valuable of all his six horses.

"New York, November 22, 1823. GEORGE BARCLAY'."

" 'Bagdad is nearly 15 hands high, well shaped in general, but rather light in his hind quarters. He was landed [sic] at Nashville in the winter [say December] 1823, being purchased by a company at $8,000, to be paid in annual installments of $2,000 each.

"Nashville, Tenn. WILLIAM WILLIAMS, Secretary of the (Bagdad) Company'."

"Va. 1824

"Arabian Horse called Syphax, Stith's and Bolling's. ASB, i, 148, derived from Edgar, p. 72, is inadequate." The following is from the 1824, November 16, 1824 Raleigh *Register*:

"The Arabian horse Syphax is a handsome sorrel, beautifully marked, with red mane and tail, upwards of 15 hands high, eight years old [i.e., foaled 1816].

"He was landed at New York in May 1824 from the *U. S.* frigate *Constitution* [and was immediately sent thence to Robert Bolling at Petersburg, Va., ATR, iv, 343], having been purchased from an Arab of distinction [the detail of the romantic story is rehearsed in ATR, vi, 272] by Major Townsend Stith [of Virginia] late American Consul at the Regency of Tunis.

"Sharpsburg, Ky. P. R. Beans."
1824 aet. 2, imported into New York.
1827-29 near New York (ATR, iii, 281).
1830-31 at Barnum's Stables in Baltimore (ATR, iv, 301).
1832 at S. S. Thompson's, Lewisburg, Va., — "where he covered more
    than 100 mares" (ATR, iii, 281; iv, 361).
1833-34 at P. R. Beans', Sharpsburg, Ky. (ATR, iv, 370; v, 394; last
    record).

"N. Y. 1830

"Arabian Horses (4) called Stamboul, Yemen, Kochlani & Zilcaadi,
Charles Rhind's. ASB, i, 70, 145, derived from Edgar, pp. 70, 72, conforms to the contemporary records published by Skinner in ATR, ii,
465; iii, 112, 571; iv, 105, 169."

Charles Rhind, of New York, was U. S. Minister to the Sublime Porte
for several years prior to 1830. On his departure from Constantinople
the Sultan presented to him the four horses here in question, described
as desert-bred Arabians, and Mr. Rhind shipped them to Smyrna and
thence (in August 1830) to New York. Mr. Rhind testified (in a letter
of May 16, 1830, to H. Clay, exhibited with the introductory Kentucky
advertisement of Stamboul in August 1831, and printed also in ATR,
iii, 113, that after they arrived in America the Congress "claimed the
animals by what rights I have yet to learn." He was apparently without
knowledge of the Constitutional precedent with respect to gifts to official
representatives of the United States which had been set by Mr. Jefferson
in 1806 with reference to the horses sent him while President, by the
Bey of Tunis. (See Black Sultan, Va. 1806.) They were sold at auction
in New York in May 1831 for account of the United States.

Although Mr. Rhind valued the horses at $2,000. each, the prices real-
ized averaged $497., or less than the importation and sale costs.

The report of the sale (ATR, ii, 465) described the origin of the
horses and named the eventual purchasers, as follows:

"Stamboul, 'of the tribe called Uegdi, from the neighbourhood of
Bussorah', E. W. Berryman & H. Clay, of Kentucky.

"Kochlani, 'of the tribe on the borders of Syria,' H. Clay & Co. (including several New York & New Jersey horsemen).

"Zilcaadi, 'of the same tribe as Kochlani', Josias S. Johnston (1784-
1833), U. S. Senator from Louisiana. See portrait, p. 470.

"Yemen, 'of the tribe of the desert nearest Aleppo', Shannon &
McDowell, Camden, S. C."

As shown by extant advertisements, three of these horses were duly introduced to American breeders for the season of 1833, viz: Kochlani at E. W. Hockaday's, Winchester, Clark County, Ky. (ATR, iv, 371; v, 395); Stamboul at J. N. Payne's, Mt. Sterling, near Lexington, Ky. (ATR, iv, 372); Yemen at Shannon & McDowell's, Camden, S. C. (ATR, iv, 107; v, 396; vi, 367); while Zilcaadi seems to have covered in Louisiana, where his portrait was painted, standing on the bank of the Mississippi river (ATR, iv, 105).

After 1835, however, they all dropped out of Skinner's stallion lists, thereby indicating that they had not lived up to expectations of improving turf stock with which they had been introduced and which A. J. Davie had eloquently argued (ATR, iv, 107, 169) on their behalf. The names of only two of them (Stamboul & Zilcaadi) have survived, and those only in the literature of controversial theology of trotting horse pedigrees. See the characteristic remarks in Wallace, *The Horse of America,* pp. 416, 418.

The following are the most common symbols found in describing the Arabian-bred animals imported to America. Symbols for newspapers of a limited circulation and available only in the locality where published, are not given. Any reader or student of the Arabian horse who wants to pursue further the study of the breed can secure a complete list of the symbols used in describing these horses by referring to Fairfax Harrison's two books entitled, "Early American Turf Stock." In these books a complete and detailed explanation of the various symbols used is given.

The symbols that most readers would have access to are as follows:

(ASB) *The American Stud Book* — 1868

(ATR) *The American Turf Register* — 1829-1844

(BRUCE) *The Thoroughbred Horse* — 1892

(COTTOM) *The Gentleman's New Pocket Farrier,* by Richard Mason

(CULVER) *Blooded Horses of Colonial Days* — 1922

(EDGAR) *The American Turf Register* — 1833

(FRANK FORSTER) *Horses and Horsemanship of the United States,* 2 Vols., 1857-1858.

(GERRY) *The Matriarchy of the American Turf* — 1931

(GSB) *The General Stud Book* — Weatherby, 1791 to date.

(IRVING) *History of the Turf in South Carolina* — 1857.

Chapter 4

Mares Of Arabian Breeding
Imported To America
From 1730 To 1830

I N the selection of the Arabian breeding mares imported into America during the hundred years dating from 1730 to 1830 the practice has been followed of selecting mares that were so largely of Arabian breeding that they were later designated as Arabs. This simply means that in most instances they were probably only half-bred Arabs while in other instances they have been as much as three-quarters to seven-eighths blood Arabs.

Because all horses then designated as Arabs, Barbs, Turks and Spanish horses were so closely related, and also because it was impossible in many instances to show any great difference between the various so-called types, this compilation includes all of these horses, under the designation of Oriental horses.

Mr. Fairfax Harrison in making up a complete list of the mares imported into the United States between 1730 and 1830 in his aforementioned book, "Early American Turf Stock," has divided the hundred years from 1730 to 1830 into four periods. These, of course, are only arbitrary divisions, and other compilers might have preferred a different grouping, but there were and are very good reasons for Mr. Harrison's method.

KAMAN A.H.C. No. 2738, as a 4-year-old mare.

The first division mentioned by him is from 1730 to 1774. This was a period of unusual and great prosperity, particularly in Virginia and the other tobacco-raising colonies, and continued to the beginning of the Revolutionary War.

The second period is given as from 1775 to 1783. The horses of Arabian breeding that came to America during this period were largely those brought over by British cavalry officers. Many of these horses, in fact, most of them, remained in America.

The third period dates from 1784 to 1805. Due to the changes brought about by the Revolutionary War there was a great deal of difference in conditions surrounding the importation of horses after the war compared with those before the war. Quite a large number of very creditable horses were imported during this period and it is reported that in England so many Americans were trying to buy blood horses that they forced the price up so high that it was difficult to attempt to import them in great numbers during this period.

From 1806 to 1830 is the fourth period given by Mr. Harrison in his compilations. This period is very important in the history of the blood horse because of the fact that during these few years horse racing caught on in the American colonies, and developed quite rapidly.

An exhaustive study of the blood mares imported into this country from 1730 to 1830 made by Robert Livingston Gerry shows that fifty-five mares were imported before 1830, and 253 were imported after 1830, and all influenced heavily the blood horse in America. Of these horses, of course, many of the original fifty-five imported before 1830 were largely of Arabian breeding and were designated and known as Arabian-bred mares.

The figure following many of the names of mares refers to the family number to which this animal belongs, as worked out by C. Bruce Lowe who made a thorough study of the various families of blood horses which he grouped by numbers.

The following quoted descriptions of Arabian-bred mares are those used by Fairfax Harrison in "Early American Turf Stock 1730-1830."

"Va. 1733

"Godolphin-Arabian-Mare, Alexander Clarke's [not identified and probably half bred].

"Because the tradition relating to this mare makes her out to be entitled to two priorities, to have been one of the first crop of the get of the Godolphin Arabian and the first English mare in America got by an identified sire of turf stock, it is historically unfortunate that her record, like that of Bully Rock, the first English bred-horse in America, should have been preserved only in the refracted form of an entry by Edgar.

"Interpreted in its simplest terms, the evidence for this tradition is that Edgar [p. 170] had before him a note by Randolph of Roanoke, formulated after a conversation with Alexander White, a Revolutionary worthy of Berkeley Co., Va., to the effect that Mr. White's father, John White of Richmond Co., Va., was the owner in 1746 of a ch. c. known in the Rappahannock valley as White's Dabster, and that that colt was by Dabster out of 'a mare got by the Cooke [sic read Coke], called afterwards Godolphin, Arabian . . . imported in the year 1773 by Mr. Alexander Clarke and the first foal [sic] of that Arabian's get'.

"So far, this interesting testimony is historically convincing, by reason of (a) the description of the Godolphin Arabian as 'Cooke's Arabian', and (b) the fact that the Alexander Clarke referred to is authenticated by the inventory of his estate, filed in Richmond Co. in 1744. It is therefore unnecessary to strain credibility by invoking Edgar's entry of an extension of the breeding attributed to the Clarke's mare, which makes her out to have been produce, not recorded by GSB, of the dam of Ld. Godolphin's Whitefoot [GSB, i, 77]. As there is no evidence in the MS. stud books of either Edward Coke or Ld. Godolphin [now penes C. M. Prior, Esq.] that Whitefoot's dam was ever mated with the Godolphin Arabian, Edgar's entry to that effect may fairly be adjudged not to have been a part of the original Virginia tradition.

"There are three positive deductions from the record which may, however, be ventured: (a) that the Clarke mare was got while the Godolphin Arabian was in Edward Coke's stud, at Longford in Derbyshire, where the Godolphin stud book shows that he covered from 1731, when he got the colt [Ld. Godolphin's, later, in the stud, the D. of Devonshire's, Lath, b.c. 1732] which GSB [i, 175, 392] recognises as 'the first of his get', to August 1733, when Mr. Coke died; (b) that she was imported as a yearling; and (c) that, considering her date [before the Godolphin Arabian had established his reputation as the sire of turf stock] and the lack of any record of her dam, she was half-bred.

"Md. 1750

"Selima, 21, [Ld. Godolphin's] Tasker's & eventually Tayloe's, b.m. 1745, by the Godolphin Arabian: Ld. Godolphin's Shireborn ['Sister to Sherborne', 1739, GSB, i, 102] by Hobgoblin: Bajazet's dam by Whitefoot: Leeded: Moonah Barb-mare.

"ASB, i, 126, derived from the Va. adv. 1777 of Galloway's Selim, and thence transferred to GSB, i, 99, s. v. Large Hartley-mare, has been disproved, and should be amended.

"No certificate of the breeding of Selima under the hand of either Benjamin Tasker, Jr., her importer, or of John Tayloe II, who eventually owned her, has come to light to speak for her provenience at the American source. The earliest extant American testimony for the mare is of the equine generation following her death; and, so far as it went was convincing because it came from two Maryland horsemen who had

LANA No. 1950. Champion Arabian mare.

known her in the flesh and had bred from her stock. Both Samuel Galloway [1767 s. v. Hector] and Thomas Hamilton [1777 s. v. Stella] certified publicly that Selima was 'by the Godolphin Arabian'; but neither of these confessors named the mare's dam; nor did Judge Duvall [ATR, ii, 458] when he recorded what he had heard on the Maryland turf during his boyhood.

"The consequence of this silence was that after the American Revolution the Maryland tradition of Selima's breeding had become eclectic Some pedigrees then recorded that her dam was 'one of Ld. Godolphin's best mares'; others that [like Kitty Fisher] she came out of Ld. Granby's stud; while still others were content with obviously mythological decorative detail; e.g. [ATR, vi, 157], that Selima was 'presented to Col. Tasker in England upon the express condition of her exportation and that she should not run in the Kingdom'.

"Thus it became possible for Virginia horsemen to originate and bruit four contradictory theses, viz:

" (a) That Selima was out of Shafto's Snapdragon [GSB, i, 192).

"This thesis was first recorded in 1796 by John Tayloe III in the first stud adv. of his Bellair II of Medley. For a generation thereafter it was accepted and repeated throughout Virginia, until Advocate [in "Annals of the Turf" 1826] applied to it the argument from dates, and the genealogists agreed [ATR, iii, 599; v, 643] that it was thereby discredited.

" (b) That Selima was 'Sister to Babraham' [GSB, i, 99].

"This thesis had its origin in the 1777 advertisement by Henry Anderson of Amelia Co. which introduced Galloway's Selim in Virginia and identified the dam of that horse [Selima] as 'Sister to Babraham'. There are precedents in other provincial certificates which suggest that this was intended to be no more than a statement that Selima and Rogers' Babraham were got by the same sire; but when, fifty years later, the collectors of material for ASB were unable to turn up any more authoritative clue to Selima's dam they fell back on the Anderson ctf. Advocate recorded it twice [1826 in "Annals of the Turf," and 1828 in AF, x, 143, No. 82]; Judge Duvall echoed it doubtfully with a qualifying 'it is said' [ATR, 1830, i, 480; 1832, iii, 488]; and in 1832 Gen. George Gibson of Washington [ATR, iii, 599, and cf. iv, 100] first advanced the pro-

GASARA No. 1039 (shown broadside, head and neck view) and her daughter GASARKIN No. 3992.

posal that Selima might be identified with Ld. Craven's anonymous 1746 filly listed by GSB among the produce of the Large Hartley-mare. That specification was, however, then received doubtfully. An unidentified Maryland horseman [1834, ATR, v, 643] admitted that the suggestion was ingenious and possible, but called attention to the fact that it remained conjecture; that the 'Sister to Babraham' thesis had 'only lately' been advanced and did not come from Maryland.

" (c) That Selima was sister to Ld. Godolphin's Daphne [GSB, i, 88].

"This was the thesis of Randolph of Roanoke. It was first recorded and later abandoned by Advocate [in "Annals of the Turf" 1826]. Later, Randolph himself elaborated and stoutly argued it in his adv. of Rinaldo 1832; and was answered by Gen. George Gibson [ATR, iii, 599], who pointed out that GSB entered no Sister-to-Daphne, an argument which was anaesthetic, if not lethal, among American horsemen of the eighteen-thirties. Randolph's thesis has persisted nevertheless. It was reproduced in all the editions of Cottom from 1833-48, and has since reappeared periodically. The most recent avatar was in an unexpected place [cf. the notice of the Selima Stakes in Thoroughbred Record, October 26, 1929].

" (d) That Selima's dam was Sister to Keck's Aura, the dam of Juniper [GSB, i, 24].

"This was 'Panton's' contribution to the Selima debate. In 1832 Robert Livingston of New York noted [ATR, iv, 100] that 'in the pedigrees of Mr. DeLancey's imported horse Lath it is stated that the grandam of Lath [Bay Basto, GSB, i, 32, 59] by Flying Childers was the grandam of Selima'.

"This must have been derived from a pedigree of Lath current among New York horsemen while he was on the American turf [1768-72]; for it does not appear in the pedigrees published after Lath was retired to the stud [1773]; and so what Mr. Livingston reported in 1832 was merely a tradition. But it was such an attractive tradition that the ingenious 'Panton' felt justified in making a play with it. The identification he tentatively proposed [ATR, iv, 264) was, however, purely 'literary' and has never been seriously considered.

"The significance of the Randolph and 'Panton' theses as to Selima is that they were both attempts to specify an old tradition; which, reduced to its elements, was in effect that Selima came out of the D. of Devonshire's stud at Chatsworth and brought with her to America a Flying Childers cross. That this tradition was pre-revolutionary in its origin appears from its relation to Lath; and there has survived another vestigial testimony that it was current in Maryland even before the day of Lath.

KIFFAH No. 1333. Arabian mare nearly 15.3 hands in height. One of the largest Arabian mares in America.

"In a New Jersey adv. of 1779 of Sharpe's Pastime [b. c. 1772, described as by Othello, and if so his last foal] John Ridout [1731-1797] of Annapolis, to whom was committed the duty of dispersing the Whitehall stud after Governor Sharpe had retired to England, is made to certify that the dam of Selima was by Flying Childers out of a Bolton Sloven mare of the No. 4 Family which cannot be identified in GSB. The significance of this is that it apparently represented the opinion of Governor Sharpe; for Mr. Ridout was not himself a horseman and must have founded whatever he said of Selima on Governor Sharpe's stud papers.

"The deduction which the critic is compelled to draw from the cumulative confusion of these records is that in the eighteen-thirties the dam of Selima was unknown. In 1857 'Frank Forester' was considered a heretic for publishing his judgment to that effect; but as the diligent research of the subsequent nineteenth century equine genealogists failed to bring to light any new evidence, the unhappy negative remained constant.

"In 1868 Bruce was unwilling to accept this conclusion. He plumped for the 'Sister to Babraham' thesis and the subsequent identification with Ld. Craven's f. of 1746 and, without suggestion that there was any doubt of the identification, entered Selima, by the pedigree which Gen. Gibson had first extended [ATR, iv, 102] as a member of the No. 15 Family.

"This entry had an unexpected repercussion. On Bruce's authority the 1891 edition of GSB revised its entry of the Large Hartley-mare by describing her previously anonymous filly of 1746 as 'Selima . . . sent to the United States of America' [sic].

"At long last, in 1933, the proof of Selima's breeding came to light, contradicting all the American hypotheses and confirming the earliest Md. tradition that her dam was 'one of Ld. Godolphin's best mares'. The private MS. stud book kept by Lord Godolphin's stud groom from 1734 to 1763 then reached the hands of Mr. C. M. Prior and revealed entries which substantially modify and expand the GSB records of Ld. Godolphin's breeding operations.

"Among the brood mares in Ld. Godolphin's stud, at Babraham in Cambridgeshire, from 1744-1754, the Godolphin stud book lists

RODA A.H.C. No. 886. Mare.

" 'Shireborn [b.m. 1739, being the younger 'Sister-to-Sherborne' of GSB, i, 102] was got by Hobgoblin: her dam by Whitefoot: her grandam by Leeds: and out of Queen Ann Moony [sic] Barb mare at Hampton Court'.

"This mare was entered by GSB as the younger of two 'Sisters to Sherborne' and is there [as in Pick, i, 144] credited with producing Martindale's Shepherdess 1743, Greville's Noble 1744, as well as, among other colts, Ld. Godolphin's Chub 1748 and Entrance 1749. The Godolphin stud book corrects these credits by showing that there were in the Godolphin stud four [not two] 'Sisters to Sherborne', viz: 'Hobgoblin-mare' [bay, 1736], 'Brown Betty' [bay or br. 1737], 'Miss Dutton' [neither coat nor age recorded] and 'Shireborn' [bay 1739 and named from the fact that she came out of the Dutton stud at Sherborne in Gloucestershire], and by listing their respective produce at the source. On analysis of those original entries Mr. Prior notes that 'in GSB several of the produce [of these four mares are] indiscriminately apportioned between the two' [of 1737 and 1739] which GSB entered. What is here of immediate concern in relation to this historical confusion is not so much that the 'Shireborn-mare' has been credited with produce of her sisters [e.g., Martindale's Shepherdess, which was a daughter of the eldest sister of 1736, one of the mares unknown to GSB], as that, if she is shown to have been dam of Chub 1746 and Entrance 1749, several of her other produce were omitted by GSB; including in that omission a filly foal of 1745 by the Godolphin Arabian, which is proved by the detail of the following entry in the Godolphin stud book to have been Selima, viz:

'Stallion	Foles in 1745	Mares
Arabian	April ye 30th: A Bay Filly with a Small Star & a Little of ye near hind Heell white. This Filly sold to Mr. Tasker into Mary Land. She was cover'd by ye Arabian [sic] in 1750 & was sent from here Sepr. following'.	Shirebornmare

"Thus, at the English source, the pedigree of Selima is extended into a family [No. 21] of better quality than that of Babraham [No. 15] to which she has been attributed; and it is proved that she reached Maryland in the autumn of 1750.

"As there is no American evidence that Selima produced a foal imported in utero, an interpretation of the entry in the Godolphin stud book, so far as it concerns the identity of the horse to which the mare was put before she left England, is, happily, academic. It is difficult to believe that that horse was her own sire.

"The earliest American evidence for Selima is that she raced in Maryland in Col. Tasker's colours, in 1752 [Culver, p. 56] unbeaten, and was then retired to the Bellair Stud in Prince George's Co., Md.; where she teemed with six foals before Col. Tasker's death. At the ensuing dispersal of the Tasker stock [see the adv. in MG, May 14, 1761] she was offered for sale, described as 'the noted bay mare called Selima and four of her foals' [Sharpe's Traveller-mare, Stella, Selim and Ebony]. The foals were scattered and the mare herself, then sixteen years old, migrated to the Mount Airy stud of John Tayloe II in Virginia [see the adv. 1783 of Willis' Rockingham] where she lived out her life, producing four more foals.

"On this record the following is a summary of the life history of Selima, viz:

"1745 foaled in Ld. Godolphin's stud.

"1750, April 18, aet. 4 (Cheny, pp. 9, 10) paid forfeit in a Sweepstakes run at Newmarket (when she was described as 'bay filly of the earl of Godolphin's').

"1750, September, aet. 5, 'sold to Mr. [Benjamin] Tasker [junior] and sent to Maryland'.

"1752, aet. 6 & 7, raced in Maryland and Virginia.

"1753-60 in the Tasker stud at Bellair in Md.

"1761, May, aet. 16, sold to John Tayloe II at the dispersal of the Tasker stud.

"1761-65 in the Tayloe stud at Mount Airy in Va.

"1766 (?), aet. 21, died at Mount Airy.

"Va. 1756

"Lonsdale-Arabian-Mare, alias 'Monkey-mare' [Sir J. Ramsden's] W. Nelson's [neither coat nor age recorded, but foaled ante 1751] by [Meredith's] Monkey [son of the Lonsdale Bay Arabian?]: Lonsdale Black Arabian [mare not in GSB]: Lonsdale Bay Arabian [i.e., either the Lonsdale Spider-mare or a sister. See Heber 1758, p. 157; Pick, i, 38; GSB, i, 383]: Coneyskins: Lowther Bay Barb [sic, not the 'Whitelegged Lowther Barb' which was mated with the Vintner mare and is an early cross in the pedigree of the No. 9 Family, for that colt was chestnut]: Dodsworth: Ld. Lonsdale's Royal mare by Spanker [not a Figure Family].

"ASB, i, III, derived from the Va. adv. 1777 of Nelson's Lonsdale, needs amendment, if only to advertise the lack of control of such little evidence as has survived; for this mare, known in pedigrees as 'Lonsdale's-dam', is the crux of the searching observation by William Williams

Side view of head and neck of GASARKIN No. 3992, a 4-year-old mare.

['Panton'] to Skinner in 1832 [ATR, iii, 480] that 'if your Virginia friends would publish the stud . . . of Mr. Secretary Nelson . . . some transpositions in pedigrees might be made to advantage and some long ones probably shortened'. Unfortunately, Skinner was unable to satisfy that requisition and it has since been established by iterated search that all primary evidence for the Nelson stud disappeared early in the nineteenth century and is now apparently lost beyond hope of recovery. William Nelson's MS. Letter Book undoubtedly contained such evidence, but in the form in which it has survived [in the Virginia State Library and cf. *W. & M. Quarterly,* vii, 25] covers only the period [1766-1772] at the end of Mr. Nelson's life, after his importations of horses ceased.

"The historian must, therefore, rely on secondary evidence for the breeding operations of the Nelson family. In respect to Lonsdale's dam that secondary evidence, missed in part by all the collectors of material for ASB, is as follows: 1773 [John Tayloe II in ATR, vi, 159 s. v. Fauntleroy's Nonpareil II, ch. c. 1767, by Tayloe's Nonpareil I; controlled by W. Scott's ctf. 1784 a Va. advt. s. v. A. Spotswood's Sempronius, ch. c. 1775, by Fauntleroy's Nonpareil II]. ' (Tayloe's) Nonpareil (I) . . . was lamed at Leedstown the first time he started as he was running hard against (Lightfoot's) Partner: he was bred by the Hon. William Nelson, Esq., and sold to me a colt for 125 pound bill of exchange.

53

Front view of KHIFFKIN No. 3974 and GASARKIN No. 3992, both 4-year-old mares.

" 'He was got by Joseph Morton's [imported] Traveller: out of a mare imported by Mr. Nelson that was got by the Lonsdale Arabian, and was the dam of Secretary Nelson's fine running horse Lonsdale. . . .

" 'Mt. Airy, Richmond Co., Va., September 20, 1773. John Tayloe (II)'.

"[1777, March 28, VG; whence Advocate in AF, x, 71, 142, Nos. 22 and 72; whence "Annals of the Turf" (1826) s. v. Jolly Roger; Cottom 1830, p. 338; ATR, 1831, ii, 360; 1832, iv, 160; and Bailie Peyton of Tennessee (s. v. his Sir Henry Tonson, gr. c. 1824, by Jackson's Pacolet) in ATR, 1835, vi, 317. All of these entries read the 'Jolly' of the Byrd ctf. of 1777, here in question, as a specification that Lonsdale was by Jolly Roger, and therein followed a tradition which had been previously voiced in explanation of Lonsdale crosses in a series of Virginia advts., viz: 1783 John Edmondson of Essex (s. v. his Leskard, ch. c. 1776, by Tayloe's Yorick) ; 1795 Robert S. Coleman of Spotsylvania (s. v. Berkeley's Gimcrack, infrs); and 1801 Paul Thilman of Hanover (s. v. his Lamplighter, b. c. 1788, by Medley.]

" '[Secretary Nelson's] Lonsdale [b. c. 1759?] was got by Jolly [sic]: out of a mare bought of Sir John Ramsden, bart., late Ld. Lonsdale's; she was got by Monkey: her dam by Ld. Lonsdale's Black Arabian: Ld. Lonsdale's Bay Arabian: Coneyskins: ["Lowther Bay Barb," here introduced by the Spider pedigree]: Dodsworth: out of the younger of the two Royal Mares bought of Mr. Darcy by the first Ld. Lonsdale. Mr. Darcy was Master of the Horse to King William.

" '[Westover] Charles City Co., Va., March 27, 1777. John (Carter) Byrd'.

"[1795, April 9, Fredericksburg, *Virginia-Herald*. This ctf., controlled by a similar advt. of 1797, was missed by all the collectors of material for ASB and in consequence neither Advocate, Edgar nor ASB knew the colt here in question to distinguish him from P. S. Randolph's Roan Gimcrack, ro. c. 1786, q. v. with an erroneous date in ASB, i, 755.]

" 'The noted thoroughbred horse [Berkeley's] Gimcrack, a fine grey [age not recorded, but say 1790] was bred by the late Nelson Berkeley of Hanover. He was got by the imported horse Medley: his dam by Specimen: his grandam by Lonsdale: his g. grandam by Babram: his g. g. grandam by Nonpareil.

" 'Specimen was got by Col. Baylor's Old Fearnought: out of Jenny Dismal.

" 'Lonsdale came from a full bred imported mare and was got by Old Jolly Roger.

" 'Babram was a thoroughbred imported horse, got by Old Babram, and Old Babram was got by the Godolphin Arabian [this Babraham, unknown to ASB and not otherwise identified, is shown by a few pedigrees to have covered in the Nelson stud during the early seventeen sixties and so may have been imported with Lonsdale's dam, as Janus was with Bonny Lass.]

" 'Nonpareil was got by Morton's Old Traveller: out of Lonsdale's dam.

" 'Spotsylvania [Co., Virginia], February 28, 1795. Robert S. Coleman'.

"Although technically it contradicts the Tayloe certificate of 1773, the pedigree certified in 1777 by John Carter Byrd [eldest son of William Byrd III of Westover] when he stood the veteran Lonsdale aet. 18 is convincing of derivation at first hand from the certificate Lonsdale's dam brought with her to America. Back of the Lonsdale Bay Arabian cross this certificate is controlled by the pedigree of the mare Spider, bred by Ld. Lonsdale and recorded when she was included in the dispersal of the Bilton stud, advertised in 1759 [Heber, 1758, p. 157; the source of GSB, i, 383]; but the Racing Calendar, Pick and GSB are all silent so far as concerns a control of any of the later crosses or even a clue to an identification of the Monkey entered as the sire of the imported mare; and Mr. C. M. Prior's diligent search for the stud papers of Sir John Ramsden, which might supply this lack, has drawn blank.

"Left to interpretation, the critic must, then, be content with a series of deductions from the extant evidence, viz:

" (a) that Lonsdale's dam was foaled before 1751; because she was described as 'late Ld. Lonsdale's' and the third and last Ld. Lonsdale of the creation of 1696 died in 1751;

" (b) that the sire of Lonsdale's dam was the Monkey [b. c. 1741, by the Lonsdale Bay Arabian, GSB, i, 132] bred in Ld. Lonsdale's stud [and reproducing the name of the earlier Lonsdale Monkey sent to America in 1737] which was on the turf 1746-47 as Meredith's [Cheny's entries correct the GSB foaling date]. This colt of 1741 does not appear in any published stallion list. On his retirement from the turf he must have returned to Lowther and there covered privately until Ld. Lonsdale's death and thereafter in the stud of his nephew Sir John Ramsden. On this thesis may be reconciled the American evidence [supra] that Sir John Ramsden sent to America a 'Monkey-mare' of the Lonsdale-Arabian family with the English evidence that in 1759 [Heber, p. 36] he introduced on the turf another Monkey, b. c. 1755. That colt of 1755 is not otherwise identified in the Calendar, but his name and dates suggest that he was got by the same horse which got his contemporary Lonsdale's dam.

" (c) that Lonsdale's dam was imported by William Nelson of York-town, who is shown by the Tayloe ctf. to have bred her earliest recorded foal [Nonpareil I];

" (d) that as Lonsdale's dam derived from the Ramsden stud and had a Virginia floruit contemporary with Booth's Bonny Lass [q. v. next above] and as the evidence is that Bonny Lass, imported by a neighbour of William Nelson, also came from the Ramsden stud it is probable that the two mares were imported together in 1756; whence that date is here tentatively proposed in respect to Lonsdale's dam in the lack of a categorical record of her importation date.

"Va. 1762

"Wilson's Arabian-Mare, 12, [Holme's] Ld. Stirling's, ch. m. 1754, by Wilson's Chestnut Arabian: dam of Holme's Old Rock and Smith's Hero [GSB, i, 184] by Panton's Slipby, son of Old Fox: Holme's Meynell [GSB, i, 96, 126] by Crofts' Partner.

"ASB, i, 138 is a lucid interpretation of the breeding as recorded in the Va. adv. 1762; but needs amendment to show the subsequent American history of the mare.

"GSB, i, 184, omitted this mare from its roster of the produce of Old Rock's dam, as it did also her uterine brother Smith's Hero, who was sent to America with her.

"She was one of the consignment in the summer of 1762 by John Holme of Carlisle to John Carlyle of Alexandria, Virginia, and was offered for sale by the following adv.: [1762, July 29, MG; ATR, iv, 55]

" 'Imported by Carlyle & Dalton in the ship *Christian,* Captain Stanly, and for sale, three horses [Thorne's Starling: Smith's Hero, and Leary's Old England] and three mares [the other two being the Rock-mares Nos. 1 and 2] of full blood, viz:

" 'A ch. m. with a star and two white heels behind, eight years old:

" 'Got by Wilson's Chestnut Arabian: her dam by Slipby, brother to Snap's dam: and out of Menil [sic] the dam of Trunnion.

" 'Menil was got by Partner: out of Sampson's-Sister, which was got by Greyhound: her grandam by Curwen's Bay Barb: her g. grandam by Ld. D'Arcy's Arabian: her dam by Whiteshirt: out of a famous mare of Ld. Montagu's.

" 'Alexandria, Va., July 1762. John Carlyle'.

"The purchaser of this Wilson's-Arabian-mare was William Alexander [1726-1783], born in New York, son of a Scottish refugee after the '15, who began life as a merchant, saw active service in the Seven Years War as Aide-de-Camp to Governor Shirley of Massachusetts; and later [1760], while in England with Shirley, propounded a formal claim to the Scots earldom of Stirling, then in abeyance. Though his petition failed in the House of Lords, thenceforth Alexander styled himself Ld. Stirling and so he was called when later he was a Major General in Washington's Revolutionary army. In 1761 he returned from England to resume his New York affairs and then established the country place at Basking Ridge in New Jersey, where he stood his Falstaff [q. v. N. J. 1761].

"The evidence for the Wilson's Arabian-mare in Ld. Stirling's stud is the following adv.: [1774, April 14, Rivington's N. Y. *Gazette;* not known to ASB]

" '[Ld. Stirling's] Americus, br. c., age not recorded, was got by [Ld. Stirling's imported] Falstaff out of a chestnut mare by Wilson's Arabian; her dam by Slipby, own brother to the dam of Snap: her grandam by Old Partner: Greyhound: Curwen's Bay Barb: Ld. D'Arcy's Chestnut Arabian: Whiteshirt: out of the famous Old Montague mare . . .

" 'Americus was bred by the earl of Stirling at Basking Ridge in New Jersey.

" 'Rocky Hill, N. J. Peter Vanderveer'.

"S. C. 1762

"Wilson's-Arabian-Mare called Camilla [Charles Wilson of Yorks?] B. Waring's, ch. m. [age not recorded], by Wilson's Chestnut Arabian: dam not certainly identified. Not in ASB. This mare is not identified in the English books. The American evidence for her consisting of advts. of several of her produce is that she was imported into South Carolina 'at the same time' as Drayton's Pharaoh, i.e., in 1762, as is proved by the introductory advt. of Pharaoh; and that she was thenceforth throughout a long life the property of Benjamin Waring of 'Cypress Meadows', St. George's Dorchester, one of the conspicuous members of the first South Carolina Jockey Club [q. v. JIS], who at various times stood Pharaoh, Friar, Whig alias Partner and other good horses.

LHASA. Yearling filly.

"The two extant testimonies which come nearest to supplying an identification of the mare's origin are as follows: [1778, March 26, S. C. and American General *Gazette;* not known to ASB].

" '[Hayne's] King Herod, ch. c., rising six years old [i.e., foaled 1772] is a great grandson to the Godolphin Arabian and grandson to the Wilson Arabian, from the best running mares'.

" 'St. Bartholomew's parish, S. C. Stephen Careful, groom'.

"This pedigree, intended for neighbours who were not horsemen, is elucidated by the following entry in the Plantation Book [MS. penes Langdon Cheves, Esq., of Charleston, S. C.] of Col. Isaac Hayne [1745-1781], the Revolutionary worthy who suffered a tragic fate at the hands of the British in the last year of the war, viz:

" '75. King Herod, a chestnut stallion, got by [imported] Centinel [son of the D. of Ancaster's Blank and he by the Godolphin Arabian]; out of a running mare by Wilson's Arabian. He was foaled in Carolina 1772 and cost 735 pounds (currency)'.

"[1779, March 11, S. C. & American General *Gazette;* not known to ASB]

" '[Hervey's Young] Centinel covers this season at Capt. Peter Bocquit's plantation near Dorchester [South Carolina] . . . He was got by the famous horse Centinel [imported 1766 by Edward Fenwick of John's Island and] late the property of John Gibbes: out of an Arabian mare called Camilla. William Harvey'.

"The clues to identification afforded by these testimonies are that the imported mare was by the Turkish horse known in English pedigrees [GSB, i, 394] as Wilson's Chestnut Arabian, was called Camilla, and came of racing stock. Meagre as they are, these facts suggest that the mare derived from the Yorkshire stud of the Charles Wilson who owned and stood [at Oran in Yorks. 1754-1761] the Chestnut 'Arabian' which bore his name. The argument is that the imported mare, being called Camilla, was described [s. v. Waring's Cephalus, infra] as 'a full blooded mare of the race breed'; that Charles Wilson is shown to have had on the turf 1753-54 a racing galloway mare called Camilla [unknown to GSB but identified by Heber 1753, p. 170, as a ch. m. 1747 by Cade: Bald Galloway]; that that Camilla had opportunity for mating with the Chestnut 'Arabian' after she was retired from the turf; and so may have been the dam of the imported mare here in question. But proof of such a specification is lacking; which is historically a pity, because she is shown to have been a brood mare of unusual quality. During a prolific stud life she produced the best race colts which were credited to the several high bred English horses with which she was mated.

"Va. 1763

"Cullen-Arabian-Mare (Apollo's dam) called Diana, 12, [D. of Kingston's] Bernard Moore's, later A. Spotswood's and W. Fitzhugh's gr. m. 1754, by Ld. Cullen's Arabian: Grisewood's [later 'the Duke' and eventually Hammond's] Lady Thigh [GSB, i, 112] by Crofts' Partner: Routh's Crop, alias 'Sister to Sampson', by Greyhound [Prior, Early Records, pp. 60, 34, 45]: 'Sister to Little George' [Sophonisba's dam] by the Curwen Bay Barb [GSB, i, 73]. ASB, i, 81, s. v. 'Dutchess [Bland's, called also Diamond]' needs revision.

"By this complicated and in consequence much debated entry Bruce, following Edgar, combined the evidence for Apollo's dam [the mare here in question] with that for two other English mares also imported into Virginia in 1763; namely, 'English' John Bland's Babraham-mare, which was called Dutchess, and Benjamin Harrison's Cullen Arabian-mare [for both of which separate entries will be found infra]; made play with a Kentucky tradition that Apollo's dam was 'called Diamond'; and, ignoring the specification of that tradition that Apollo's dam was 'imported by

Gen. Spotswood of Virginia', added gratuitously a statement that the mare so 'constructed' was 'imported into South Carolina before the Revolution', a deduction apparently derived from a tradition of still another mare, Mayrant's Dutchess [q. v. S. C. 1760].

"The source material for Apollo's dam is limited but quite definite, viz:

"1758 (Heber, p. 124) Nominations for a Sweepstakes for fillies to be run at Newmarket in Easter-week 1759.

" 'D. of Kingston's by Ld. Cullen's Arabian: out of Hammond's-mare'.

"The summary of the race [Heber 1759, p. 5] for which this nomination was made indicated that the D. of Kingston did not start. [1777, March, VG; Advocate (AF, x, 119, No. 68) recorded this, whence Edgar and ASB as to breeding on the dam's side].

"[Spotswood's] 'Apollo was got by Fearnought: his dam by the Cullen Arabian: her dam was the noted mare called Lady Thigh got by Partner: her grandam by Greyhound: her great grandam by the Curwen Bay Barb, which mare was the dam of Sophonisba, remarkable for her high form and great speed.

" 'This pedigree of Apollo's dam was attested by His Grace the Duke of Kingston.

" 'Brunswick County, Virginia. Richard Elliot'.

FARZIKA A.H.C. No. 4585.

"[1798, March 24, Augusta *Chronicle;* not known to Advocate or subsequently reported to AF or ATR; hence unknown to Edgar and ASB]

" '[Fitzhugh's] True Whig was got by [Fitzhugh's] Regulus: his dam was Diana [the dam also of the celebrated Apollo], an imported mare.

" 'Augusta, Ga. N. Durkee'.

"These certificates serve (a) to identify Apollo's dam with the Cullen Arabian filly which GSB [i, 112] lists among the produce of Grisewood's [later 'the Duke's', and eventually Hammond's] Lady Thigh, without date or coat, but with attribution to the D. of Kingston; and which filly may [on that lead] be supplied with both coat and age from Heber's record of her single appearance on the turf, viz:

"1758, October 10. [H., p. 76], at Newark, 'D. of Kingston's gr. f.' [no name or breeding recorded] unplaced in a Sweepstakes for 4 years old.

" (b) to prove that Apollo's dam was known in Virginia as Diana. The Georgia certificate for True Whig which supplies that name is borne out by the fact that in four successive generations of the immediate descendants of Apollo's dam there were fillies called Diana [ASB, i, 340].

"When it comes to naming the importer of Apollo's dam the primary evidence is silent. The Kentucky tradition, above referred to, that the importer was 'Gen. Spotswood of Virginia'; i.e., Alexander Spotswood [1746-1818], is contradicted by the date [1763] of the importation of the mare; for in that year Alexander Spotswood was a boy at Eton [*William & Mary Quarterly*, ii, 13]. Nor could the importer have been Gen. Spotswood's father, the John Spotswood [1725-1758] who was a proven importer [of two horses and a mare, Jolly Roger and Creeping Kate in 1751; Diamond alias Jack of Diamonds, son of Y. Hautboy and he by Fox, in 1758]; for he was dead five years before 1763. The tradition which has related Apollo's dam to the Spotswood stud cannot, however, be ignored and it is, happily, possible to give it a reasonable explanation. The evidence being that the mare came out of the Duke of Kingston's stud, whence John Spotswood, in partnership with his brother-in-law [later also his executor] Bernard Moore [1720-1772] of 'Chelsea' in King William, had drawn Jolly Roger in 1750, Bernard Moore is indicated as the importer of the mare and the breeder of Apollo [foaled 1767]; and the deduction follows that it was from that uncle that Alexander Spotswood acquired Apollo and perhaps Apollo's dam also, after his return to Virginia from his education in England.

"The earliest primary evidence of ownership of Apollo's dam in Virginia is of 1774 in the hands of William Fitzhugh [1741-1800] of 'Chatham', when he mated her with his Regulus [son of Fearnought] to produce True Whig. As Col. Fitzhugh is proven also to have been the owner of Apollo's full sister [Diana II, by Fearnought, to which the tentative date 1770 is here assigned], it may be further deduced finally that William Fitzhugh acquired both that filly and her dam either from the Moore estate after Bernard Moore's death in 1772, or from A. Spotswood.

"Va. 1763

"Cullen-Arabian-Mare [breeder not identified] Benjamin Harrison's [neither coat nor age recorded, but foaled not earlier than 1760], by Ld. Cullen's Arabian: dam not identified.

"ASB, i, 79, needs limitation and interpretation.

"The statement published in 1833 [ATR, v, 100] for the stud of Dr. William Cutler of 'Mount Pleasant', Dinwiddie County, Virginia, which is the source for the importations of 'English' John Bland, says that with his Dutchess [q. v.] there was brought to Virginia also another English filly which Mr. Bland

" 'sold to Mr. Harrison of Brandon [i.e., Benjamin Harrison, 1743-1807, who is best remembered by horsemen for his production of the Aristotle mare, Meade's Brandon], the father of [George Evelyn Harrison, 1797-1839] the present [1833] proprietor of that estate'.

"The substance of this statement is confirmed by an authenticated pedigree of a colt sent to Georgia from the Brandon stud, viz: [1799, March 9, Augusta *Chronicle;* not known to Edgar or ASB]

" '[Harrison's] North America, b. c. 1792, by [Harrison's] Soldier [alias Y. Selim, son of Galloway's Selim]: [Wormeley's] King Herod [who stood in Dinwiddie, near Brandon, 1778-80]: Fearnought: an imported mare of Col. [Benjamin] Harrison's [of Brandon].

" 'Augusta, Ga. William Tyler',

"and is elucidated by Edgar's entry of a traditional Southside pedigree, viz: [Edgar, p. 153; whence ASB, i, 79]

" '[Harrison's] Claudius, br. c. [date not recorded, but not 1762, as entered by Bruce, because Fearnought was not in Virginia until 1764], by Fearnought: imported thoroughbred mare got by the Cullen Arabian. Wm. Maxwell'.

"This pedigree was discredited in Edgar's day by the other collectors of material for ASB by confusion of the colt therein recited with a later colt of a similar but not the same name. Andrew Meade's Clodius [b. c. 1777, by Janus: Meade's Brandon by Aristotle] was authenticated by stud advs. 1782-83 but, unhappily for Edgar's reputation, was entered by Advocate [AF, x, 151, No. 93] s. v. Claudius.

"On the record thus assembled it may therefore be now deduced that the imported mare which 'English' John Bland sold to Benjamin Harrison of Brandon was by the Cullen Arabian; i.e., the historically un-explained mare entered by Bruce [ASB, i, 79].

"Edgar's extension of the Claudius breeding back of the Cullen Arabian, which Bruce adopted, need detain no one. On its face it was borrowed from Harrison's Monkey [GSB, i, 73] and was tacked on to a traditional certificate for Claudius, ending in the Cullen Arabian, which came into Edgar's hands. The suture remains visible.

"Md. 1764

"Panton-Arabian-Mare, called Young Daphne, 4, [Ld. Godolphin's] Dulany's, gr. m. 1755, by Panton's Grey Arabian: Ld. Godolphin's, later D. of Ancaster's, Daphne [b. m. 1751, GSB, i, 193, 94, s. v. Sister-to-Markwell, erroneously attributed to the Godolphin Brown Barb] by the Godolphin Arabian: Ld. Godolphin's, later D. of Richmond's, Child [m. 1746, GSB, i, 198, 193, s. v. Snip-mare, Markwell's dam] by Snip: Panton's Spinster alias the Widdrington-mare by Crofts' Partner. ASB, i, 66, s. v. 'Arabian-mare' needs amendment.

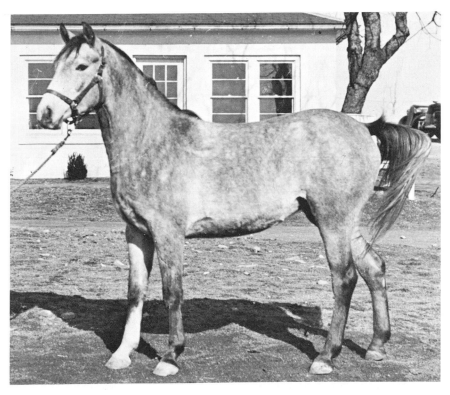

RAFAYA A.H.C. No. 2692. Gray Arabian mare. Twin to the stallion RAFAYL No. 2693.

"This mare was never on the turf and so missed entry among the produce of her dam in GSB, with the consequence that, like Selima, she was not identifiable either in England or America until Ld. Godolphin's MS. stud book came into the hands of Mr. C. M. Prior in 1933.

"As he lacked the evidence for Galloway's Silvertail, Bruce was unable also to identify the importer and he weakened his entry by changing to 'Snap' the 'Snip' cross of his sources, i.e., Gen. Forman and Edgar.

GASARAFF No. 4246. A 6-year-old daughter of Champion INDRAFF No. 1575.

"She was one of two mares [the other being Bladen's Gower-Stallion-mare, q. v.] imported into Maryland about 1764 by Daniel Dulany of Annapolis, the eminent Maryland lawyer, and seems to have been sold by him to Samuel Galloway; for all the extant American evidence for her comes out of the Galloway stud at 'Tulip Hill' in Anne Arundel Co., Md., viz: [1782, April 6, Pennsylvania *Packet;* not known to ASB]

" '[Galloway's] Silvertail, b. or br. c. [1776], bred by Samuel Galloway, and got by Wolstenholme's Tanner out of [Galloway's] Tulip.

" 'Tulip was got by Old Selim [son of Othello]: out of a mare imported by Daniel Dulany.

" 'Warwick, Cecil Co., Md. Charles Heath'.

"[1783, April 3, Maryland *Gazette;* not known to ASB]

" '[Galloway's] Silvertail, rising seven years old [i.e., 1776] by Tanner: out of Tulip by Selim: her dam by Panton's Arabian: Godolphin Arabian: Snip: Panton's Widdrington-mare.

" 'Tulip Hill, Anne Arundel Co., Md. Mark Roughed [groom]'.

"[1827, Gen. T. M. Forman of Md. in AF, ix, 263; whence Edgar, p. 108, and ASB, i, 66]

" '[Dulany's] Belmont [neither coat nor age recorded, but say 1775] was got by Tanner: his dam by Selim: out an imported mare bred by Ld. Godolphin, she was by Panton's Grey Arabian: her dam by the Godolphin Arabian: her grandam by Snip: out of Mr. Panton's famous Widdrington mare.'

"The original advertisements of Silvertail 1780-81 [ATR, iv, 99] lacked the Snip cross; but the breeding in that respect was corrected in the advs. 1783 [here cited] and 1784; and that correction is confirmed by the certificate for Belmont which Gen. Forman preserved in his collection; as well as by advs. of Thomas' Ariel [1782, April 11, MG] and Conaway's Godolphin [1784, April 6, Md. *Journal*].

"The progressive entries in Ld. Godolphin's MS. stud book [penes C. M. Prior, Esq.], serving to identify the mare, which the testimonies cited above show was imported by Mr. Dulany, and to check the breeding attributed to her in Maryland, are as follows:

" 'Mares at his Lordship's stud at Babraham . . .

" 'Child [unnamed in GSB, i, 198] was got by Snip: her dam [the Widdrington mare] by Partner: her gr. dam by Bloody Buttocks: her g. grandam by Greyhound: her g. g. grandam by Makeless.

" 'My Lord had her in 1749; [and] sold [her] to Ld. Eglington for ye D. of Richmond, 25th of April, 1756.

	'Foales in 1751	
Arabian	21st April. A bay filly with a Starr, ye off fore foott white.	Child
	This Filly put into ye Studd in 1754 and called Daphne.	

	Foales in 1755	
Mr. Panton's	19th April. A gray filly	Daphne*
Grey Arabian	The dam of this Filly sold to the Duke of Ancaster, 23rd of April 1756.	

*" (Note by Mr. Prior: 'Daphne's foal of 1755 appears to have been retained in the stud and known as Young Daphne . . . No foalings are recorded for the years 1757 and 1758 so presumably the stud was given up on the sale of the Brown Barb in November 1756, only the filly Young Daphne being retained, and foals entered in the five subsequent seasons were each the produce of this mare'.)"

	1759	
(Ld. Godolph-in's) Doctor (br. c. 1749 by Crab: Y. Whiteneck, g. dam of Aristotle and Gower Stal-lion mare, by the Godolphin Arabian)	12th April. A grey Filly This Filly my Lord gave me (i.e., the Stud Groom). I sold her to Mr. Girdler in 1763.	Daughter of Daphne

	1760	
Doctor	13th April. A Brown Colt fole with a few white Hairs in his forehead.	Young Daphne

	1761	
Doctor	6th April. A bay Filly, no white.	Young Daphne

	1762	
D. of Devon-shire's cht. Arabian	13th April. A grey Filly, the off fore foot and two hind feet white.	Young Daphne

	1763	
D. of Devon-shire's Hector (son of Lath)	27th April. A Bay filly.	Young Daphne' "

"Thus it appears that the imported mare here in question was the last mare reserved in Ld. Godolphin's stud after 1756; that she there produced five foals 1759-1763; and that the record of her in the God-olphin stud book ends in April 1763. As the American record picks her up as 'sent to Maryland' with the Gower-Stallion-mare which came out of Thomas Bladen's stud, it may be deduced that Mr. Bladen purchased her from Ld. Godolphin in the autumn of 1763 for Mr. Dulany's account.

"Mass. 1800

"Two 'Arabian' Mares, called Latonia and Cappadocia, sent by James Swan from Hamburg to Boston. Not in ASB.

"In 1835 [ATR, vii, 67] James Smock of Fredericksburg, Va., recorded the history of the imported Arabian horse Dey of Algiers [wh. c. 1794] which had died in his possession in 1807; and then quoted the following extract 'from the original papers which accompanied that horse to this country and which were sent to me [Smock] with him by General [John] Mason [of Georgetown, D. C.]' viz:

" 'In 1798 the Emperor of Arabia [sic], having received some signal service from the late Grand Baliff Fromm of Prussia, tendered to him the choice of any of his stud. The Baliff procured the assistance of one Frederick Lipentine, the grand Arab selector [as he was called], who chose for him from the Emperor's stud, consisting of several hundred genuine and superior Arabian horses, the noble Dey [of Algiers] and two mares, one called Latonia and the other Cappadocia.

" 'They were taken to Lithuania in Poland, from which place they were taken to Prussia. After the decease of the Baliff, at the sale of his stud at Fehrbellin in the year 1799, the Dey, then five years old, together with the two mares, were purchased by Lieutenant General Frederick Baron von Diemar; by whom they were afterwards sold to Colonel [James] Swan [1754-1831, an original member of the "Boston tea party"] of Massachusetts, then, in Europe; and by him were shipped from Hamburg to Boston to General [Henry] Jackson (1747-1809] of that city .

"It will be noted that this statement fails categorically to indicate the place of origin of this stock. As none of the several extant advts. of Dey of Algiers supplies that lack, and as no 'Emperor of Arabia' can be identified in 1798, while the imported horse was called by the title of one of the potentates then known as the 'Barbary Powers', the weight of the evidence is that this stock was derived immediately from North Africa and not direct from Arabia. Technically they must therefore be classed as 'natural barbs'.

"The horse Dey of Algiers was advertised for the season of 1801 to stand at Charlestown, Mass., [Battell, ii, ccxxv] before he was sent to General John Mason of Georgetown, D. C., to live out his life in Maryland and Virginia [see the full record among the imported horses]; and the evidence is that during that season of 1801 he got, on one of the Arab mares imported with him, a colt whose scant historical record supplies the only American testimony which has come to light for either of those mares [1806, May 31, Columbian *Centinel,* Boston; whence Battell, ii, ccxxx] viz:

" 'Young Dey of Algiers is a full blooded Arabian colt, nearly 15 hands, dapple gray, 4 years old [i.e. foaled 1802].

" 'His sire was the noted Dey of Algiers, imported by Col. James Swan in the year 1800; his dam the gray Arab mare imported at the same time with the horse.

" 'Brush-Hill' [Milton, Mass.], Eliphas Packard, May 27, 1806'.

"Va. 1805

"Arabian Mare, called Diana, Eaton's, later Tayloe's. Not in ASB.

"Although this m. left no produce in America, she is interesting as the only authenticated native Arabian mare known to have been in America before 1830 and also because of the romantic adventure which lead to her importation.

"William Eaton [1764-1811], born at Woodstock, Conn., served in the ranks of the Continental army throughout the Revolution, thereafter graduated at Dartmouth College [1790], secured a commission as Captain in the U. S. Army [1792], and after duty in various parts of the U. S. was sent [1799] to the Mediterranean as Consul at Tunis. In 1801, in order to prey on American commerce, the Bashaw of Tripoli declared war on the U. S. and Eaton went home to secure support for an ingenious plan to checkmate him. Returning to the Mediterranean in September 1804 with a commission as 'U. S. Naval Agent to the Barbary States', Eaton sought out a previous Bashaw of Tripoli, who had been ousted from his throne and was then living in exile in Egypt, and, persuading him to an attempt to recover his heritage, organized at Alexandria a motley army of 500 Arabs, Greeks and Americans and lead them 600 miles across the Libyan desert to attack the usurper who was at war with the U. S. The expedition reached and, with the aid of two U. S. gunboats, captured [April 1805] the important Tripolitan seaport fortress of Derne [see Whittier's poem of that name] and was about to move on the capital when [July 1805], to Eaton's chagrin, the U. S. government concluded with the reigning Bashaw what Eaton deemed a premature treaty of peace, and so abandoned the exile.

"Eaton returned to America in November 1805, bringing with him to Washington an Arabian mare and two horses which he had acquired during his Mediterranean adventure. They arrived at the time when John Tayloe III of 'Mount Airy' in Va. was in the midst of an experiment with oriental stock in the hope of finding another Lindsey's Arabian [see Swan's Dey of Algiers, 1800; Barron's Selim, 1803; and Jefferson's Black Sultan, 1806] and Gen. Eaton offered his importations to Col. Tayloe in the following letter, [1805, December 24, ATR, iv, 120] viz:

" 'I have left at Mr. Stell's in Washington City, three horses, two Turkish saddles and bridles, and one English saddle and two bridles, all of which he is to deliver to your order.

" 'The mare is [of] the first blood of Arabia; was presented about seven years ago to a relation of the Emperor of Morocco, by the chief Mufti at Mecca, where the young prince was on a pilgrimage. She was brought to Tripoli, and given to the Bashaw of that Regency in the expression of gratitude for attentions paid him [the young prince] in sickness at Tripoli. She was given by the Bashaw to a French Ambassador; by the latter sent to Tunis; where she came into my hands about five years ago [1800]. I believe her about [blank] years old. If you will take her, let her produce and divide with me the profits, it would be agreeable to me. If, on proving her, you should choose to purchase, we will arrange the price on my return to the seat of government. . . . ' " (See further quotes under "Ishmael and Taurus" Chapter 3.)

" 'The mare is called Diana; the grey horse Ishmael [see the confused attribution of this horse to Thomas Eaton of North Carolina in Edgar, p. 69; ASB, i, 145]; and the Dun Taurus.

" 'I have the honour to be, with great respect and esteem, sir, your obliged and obedient servant, William Eaton'.

"When this document came into Skinner's hands and was published by him in 1832 he was informed, probably by B. O. Tayloe, that the Eaton mare and the two horses were sent by John Tayloe III to his stud at Mount Airy in Virginia; that the mare

" 'was most beautiful and Col. Tayloe thought highly of her; unfortunately she died suddenly not long after her arrival at Mount Airy, without produce. Of the horses he did not think favourably and they were returned to General Eaton'.

"Sent to Massachusetts, the two horses were established on Gen. Eaton's estate at Brimfield; and there they covered 'many years', justifying Col. Tayloe's estimate of them by leaving 'no marked improvement in the horses of Massachusetts' [R. L. Allen in *American Agriculturist,* May 1843; whence Battell, i, 695]."

See list of symbols at the end of Chapter 3.

CASSANDRA A.H.C. No. 3831. Mare.

Chapter 5

Imported Barb Mares And Horses

L ITTLE or no distinction is usually made between the several different species of Oriental horses such as Arabians, Barbs, Turks, etc., but it does seem proper to devote some attention to a short description of the most prominent and widely known Barb mares and stallions imported into this country between 1730 and 1830.

In the development of the light horse breeds, the Barb horse, after an influential beginning, gradually became less and less of a factor in the American and English breeding picture. The Oriental, or Arabian is now, of course, recognized as the source of all the foundation animals from which the American and English Thoroughbreds have sprung and, as we know, all such stock — plus other light breeds in the United States — is directly descended from the Byerly Turk, the Darley Arabian and the Godolphin Arabian.

The following quoted information on the subject of Barb mares and stallions is taken from Fairfax Harrison's "Early American Turf Stock, 1730-1830":

"African Barb Mare (from the stud of the Bey of Tunis) — J. W. Eppes' of Virginia. ASB, i, 150, and the ensuing entries conform general-ly, but not in detail, to the evidence.

"In the early spring of 1806 Melli Melli, an ambassador from the Bey of Tunis, reached Washington to negotiate a settlement of claims of his master arising out of American activities during the war with Tripoli. He brought with him an African barb horse and two mares and on behalf of his master presented them to Thomas Jefferson, then President of the United States. After the ambassador had departed these horses were sold for account of the United States, as will appear from the following contemporary documents: [1806, April 24, Universal *Gazette,* Washington; not known to ASB]

" 'The superb barb Black Sultan, presented by the Bey of Tunis to the government of the United States, and lately brought to this country by the Tunisian ambassador [Melli Melli] will stand the ensuing season at Petworth, the farm of John Tayloe [III], Esq., near Rock Creek Church and within two miles of the city of Washington . . .

" 'This Royal present being one of the most choice animals of the Regency of Tunis and full 16 hands high, a desire has prevailed that so valuable a race should be extended as much as possible and it has therefore been directed that he be placed at a low price [of $20] . . .

"Petworth, D. C., April 4, 1806. Chester Bailey, manager for John Tayloe, Esq.'

"1806, October 17, *National Intelligencer,* Washington; not known to ASB]

" 'For sale. On the second day of the Washington Races which are to commence on Tuesday the 28th inst. there will be offered for sale at auction the elegant Barbary horse and two mares which were brought from Tunis by his Excellency the Tunisian Ambassador and intended as a present to the Executive of the United States'.

"[1806, December 15, *National Intelligencer,* Washington; not known to ASB]

" 'The horse Black Sultan and the two mares brought to the United States by the late Ambassador of Tunis will be disposed of at private sale.

" 'Both the mares are in foal to the horse and all three are in good condition.

" 'Application to be made to the subscriber at the office of the Secretary of State.

" 'Washington, December 15, 1806. Daniel Brent'.

"A diligent search has failed to turn up in the archives of the United States any report or other record of the sale or sales so advertised. What is known of the subsequent history of the stock is gleaned from breeding records, viz:

" (a) From South Carolina newspapers it appears that Black Sultan was sent thither, and covered the season of 1807 at Elias Earle's in Greenville District and the season of 1808 at John Gallant's in York District, S. C. As this Elias Earle [1762-1823] was in Washington in December 1806 as a Member of Congress from South Carolina, it may be deduced that he was the purchaser of the horse at the government sale; but what is more significant is that the S. C. advts. prove that the horse was separated from the mares which came with him to America, after he had covered them both in Washington during the season of 1806.

" (b) From a note by Bruce [ASB, i, 150], which does not disclose its source, it seems that one of the mares was sent to Louisiana [from which it may be deduced that she also was purchased by a Member of Congress] and that she there produced, from the cover by Black Stallion in 1806, a colt known as Beau Laquaise, of which nothing more is known.

"As he did not know that Melli Melli brought to America two imported barb mares Bruce described this colt as 'full brother to [Eppes') Sultana' [q. v. infra], an attribution which is shown to have been impossible by the evidence that before Sultana was foaled the sire and dam of Sultana were separated, never again to meet.

" (c) The records of the subsequent history of the second of the Melli Melli mares here immediately in question are, however, explicit if eventually confused in ASB. Following the evidence already cited that in December 1806 this mare was in foal to Black Sultan there are the following testimonies for her and her immediate descendants: [1830, ATR, i, 419; and cf. A. J. Davie in iii, 277; whence ASB, i, 150; ii, 338; i, 601]

" 'Lady Burton, m. 1813, bred by John W. Eppes of Eppington, Chesterfield County, Virginia, got by the celebrated horse Sir Archy out of the full blooded mare Sultana; she was out of the mare and got by the horse sent as a present by the Bey of Tunis, by his ambassador Melli Melli, to Thomas Jefferson, President of the United States.

" 'Halifax Co., N. C. H. G. Burton, Alex. Henderson'.

"[1833, ATR, iv, 546; whence s. v. Clarion, Edgar, p. 153; ASB, i, 719]

" 'Report of blood stock of H. G. Burton, Halifax Co., N. C.

" 'Judy O'Flannigan, ch. f. 1830, by Clarion: her dam by Carolinian, son of True Blue.

" 'Clarion was by Gen. Chamberlain's Tiptop, son of Lightfoot's Oscar: his dam by Citizen: out of the mare sent by the Bey of Tunis to the American government.

" 'Attest: H. G. Burton'.

"[1834, ATR, vi, 131, s. v. Chance]

SELFRA No. 1034. Arabian mare and foal TAKA No. 2735.

" 'I well remember that in the fall of 1815 I purchased of the late John W. Eppes of Virginia (who had married my wife's sister) the mare now called Lady Burton, the dam of Coutre Snapper [b. g. 1817, by Chance, q. v. ATR, i, 433, and what Bailie Peyton said of him, ATR, vii, 285, s. v. Ellen Douglass].

" 'This name was given her after I parted with her [to Alexander Henderson of N. C., who eventually gave her in 1833 to Bailie Peyton of Tenn., in whose stud she was still producing in 1837, aet. 24. See ATR, vi, 263; vii, 285; viii, 527].

" 'Halifax, N. C., August 23, 1834. H. G. Burton'.

"From these testimonies it may be deduced that one of the two imported Barb-mares reported in December 1806 to be in foal to Black Sultan [viz, the one here in question] was then purchased by Mr. Jefferson's son-in-law, John Wales Eppes [1773-1823] who was in Washington at the time as a Member of Congress from Virginia, and was sent to his seat in Chesterfield Co., Va.; that after she had produced [1807] her filly

"Mr. Samuel C. Potter, brother-in-law to Major Stith, certifies that Syphax was raised near Mecca in the Kingdom of Yeman in Arabia Felix; crossed the Red Sea to Derra in Nubia; from thence [was taken] through a part of the desert to Toanlia in Teran; thence through the Regency of Tripoli to Beledugerid; and from thence to the American consulate in the city of Tunis.

" 'Greenwood', Warren Co., N. C., November 10, 1824. Robert Ransom."

1823 purchased at Tunis by Townsend Stith, U. S. Consul, as a desert bred Arab.

1824 sent to America (with the Jones Arabian, q. v. next below) in the U. S. S. *Constitution,* landed in New York in May and sent to Petersburg, Va.

1825 at Robert Ransom's, Warren County, N. C. (adv.).

1826 in Nottoway County, Va. (ATR, iv. 343).

1827-30 in Monroe County, Va. (ATR, iv, 343).

1831-34 at Staunton, Va. (ATR, iv, 343 & iii, 375).

1835 at Xenia, Ohio (ATR, vi, 367; last record).

"N. Y. 1824

"Arabian Horse called Amurath, Wolcott Chauncey's. ASB, i, 142, was derived from Edgar, p. 66, who had the importer's certificate quoted below." The evidence is the following statement by Commander Wolcott Chauncey (1784-1835), U. S. N., (1831, ATR, iii, 281) viz:

"The Arabian horse Amurath I bought at Tripoli [Barbary] in 1823 of Col. Warrington, the English Consul at that place. He was then one year old [i. e., foaled 1821] and had been purchased [by Col. Warrington] a short time previous from the Arabs who had accompanied the caravan from Nubia to Tripoli. From the well-known character of Col. Warrington as an experienced judge of horses and with the assurances of many Arabs, I am convinced that Amurath is a true Arabian horse.

"On my arrival in this country [1824] I placed the colt in charge of an experienced man near New York who thoroughly broke him. Since then he has stood for mares parts of three seasons and proven himself a sure foal getter.

"New York, October 1, 1831. Wolcott Chauncey." An 1832 note by Skinner in ATR, iii, 281 states:

"Amurath was for some time in Baltimore [cf. ATR, iv, 361] and certainly came nearer in appearance to the Godolphin Arabian than any we have seen.

"Baltimore, February 1832. J. S. Skinner."

From the March 14, 1833 Lexington Kentucky *Observer*:

"The fine Arabian horse Amurath . . . is a beautiful black, five feet and three-eighths of an inch [say rising 15.1 hands] high.

Sultana by Black Sultan Mr. Eppes bred her to Citizen [who stood in Chesterfield Co., Va., 1809] to produce another filly; and that that Citizen-mare and a daughter of Sultana [Lady Burton] eventually found their way into the stud of Mr. Eppes' brother-in-law [by his second marriage to a daughter of Willie Jones of N. C.], Hutchins Gordon Burton [1774-1836] of Halifax Co., N. C., sometime Governor of North Carolina.

"Md. 1740

"Andalusian Horse, called 'Barb', Ogle's. Not in ASB.

"The evidence that this horse was introduced into Maryland by Governor Samuel Ogle [1694-1752] is the series of pedigrees cited below. There is no extant primary evidence for his origin, but as the testimonies quoted indicate that he was a contemporary of Nelson's Spanker and suggest that he, too, was a Spanish 'barb', it may be reasonably deduced

Champion NABIKA No. 653 and CASSIM No. 2556 at 4 months of age.

SLIPPER No. 442 with foal RIPPLES No. 818.

that he was imported 'from the Mediterranean' with Spanker and about 1740 [1752, July 30, MG] viz:

" 'To be sold very reasonably at the plantation of the late Rev. Mr. Henderson, deceased, in Prince George's County [Maryland], two very fine breeding mares of the Barbary breed [sic meaning got by Governor Ogle's "Barb"] with two young mare colts foaled this spring; also two promising horse colts a year old, not cut, which were got by the Governor's fine English horse Spark'.

"[1762, April 15, MG]

" '[Tyler's] Driver, c. [neither coat nor age recorded], by [Tasker's] Othello: his dam by [Ogle's, later Tasker's] Old Spark: his grandam by the late Governor Ogle's Barb.

" '[Prince George's Co., Md.] Robert Tyler'.

"[1763, April 28, MG; whence ATR, iv, 55. This testimony is controlled for the breeding by a Pa. advt. 1769 of Barnsley's Exotic, son of Jolly Chester]

" '[Yeldell's] Jolly Chester, c. [neither coat nor age recorded], by [Tasker's] Othello: [Ogle's, later Tasker's] Spark: Digges' Stallion [not identified]: his [third] dam by Governor Ogle's Barb.

" 'Prince George's Co., Md. William Yeldell'.

"[1767, March 31, Pennsylvania *Chronicle*]

" '[Sharpe's] Bohemian, gr. c. 1759, by Othello: Governor Sharpe's mare by Col. Colvill's Horse: out of a mare of the blood.

" 'Col. Colvill's Horse was got by a Barb: out of a mare [Colvill's, later Tasker's, Miss Colvill] imported from England, bred by Lord Tankerville.

" 'Kensington, near Philadelphia. Thomas Hopkins'.

"[1781, March 20, Maryland *Journal*]

" '[Sim's] Wildair [b. c. 1765], bred by Col. Joseph Sim of Prince George's County . . . was got by Mr. DeLancey's [imported] Wildair: [Tasker's, later Brent's] Ariel [son of Spark]: Othello: his [third] dam [by] a Barb.

" 'Baltimore Co., Md. Richard Jones'.

"[1789, March 13, Philadelphia *Independent Gazette* or *The Chronicle of Freedom*]

" ' [Bates'] Atlas, b. c. 1786, by Bates' Eclipse, son of Waters', later Haynes', King Herod: Ulster Lass [sister to John Allen's Pantaloon] by Perkins' Granby, son of the Belsize Arabian: Diana by DeLancey's Wildair: Hunt's Bully Rock, son of Spark: her [i.e., Ulster-Lass'] grandam was by Governor Ogle's Barb, imported.

" 'Point-no-Point, Pa., March 12, 1789. Jacob Bates'.

"[1821, from Gen. T. M. Forman's collection of pedigrees in ATR, iii, 583]

" '[Matthews', later Knight's] Palafox [b. c. 1805], the property of William Knight, Esq., was got by the celebrated horse [Gen. A. W. White's] Express: Matthews' Cubmare by McCarty's Cub: Heath's Childers: Heath's Traveller: Dove: Othello: Spark: 'his seventh dam [sic, but query was there here lost the cross of "Digges' Stallion" noted in the ctf. for Jolly Chester, supra?] by Governor Ogle's Barb.

" 'Cecil County, Md., May 2, 1821. Charles Groom'.

"1740 imported into Md. by Governor Ogle.

"1741-1750? at 'Bellair' in Prince George's Co., Md. [no record of death].

"S. C. 1762

"Barbary Horse, called Abdullah, Raines'. ASB, i, 142, derived from

INDAIA No. 813 and INDRAFF No. 1575 as a colt.

the S. C. advt. of 1767 and misinterpreting it, needs amendment.

"The evidence consists of two Carolina stud advts. [1762 and 1767], neither of which recorded age or coat. The introduction was as follows [1762, April 24, South Carolina *Gazette*] viz:

" 'To cover this season, at Mr. Mullryne's plantation near Beaufort, Port-Royal, at twenty pounds [currency] each mare, Abdullah, a fine high-blooded barb, got by a famous stallion belonging to the Emperor of Morocco: out of a grey the property of Muley Mustarnoi, King of Arzeyla, in West Barbary.

" '[The horse was] sold by the King to Gen. Crauford at Gibralter, and is just arrived from thence in the *Harrietta,* Capt. Raines.

" 'Port Royal, S. C. John Vann'.

"Irving [iii, 35] has a pleasant anecdote of how Col. Frank Huger, then aet. 11, backed this Abdullah, '16 h. [sic] never ridden', when he first arrived in Carolina.

"Bred in Morocco and brought thence to Carolina by a merchantman.

"1762 at Mr. Mullryne's plantation near Beaufort, S. C.

"1767 at Mr. Thomas Hartley's plantation, S. C. [last record].

"Pa. 1766

AADRAFFA A.H.C. No. 2075. Gray Arabian mare with her 4-month-old colt RAFFLIND No. 4319.

"Barbary Horse, called Bellsize Arabian, Samuels and Footman's. ASB, i, 143, derived from Edgar, who had the Pa. adv. 1768, conforms to GSB, i, 396, which, however, did not note that the horse was 'sent to America'.

"From the English advts. cited below and the ctfs. which he brought with him to America [ATR, vii, 95] it appears that this horse was bred in Morocco by the Governor of Wazan; that his sire was an 'Arabian' and his dam 'one of the most beloved mares' of the stud of the Emperor of Morocco; that he was purchased in Morocco by Jonathan Welch, H. M. Vice Consul at Tetuan; who sent him to England in 1759, where he covered for seven years before he was acquired by Admiral Sir Charles Saunders [1713-1775] who, being a 'lover of America', sent the horse to Pennsylvania consigned to a firm of merchants [Samuels & Footman] to be placed where he might 'improve the breed'.

"The American evidence is the introductory Pa. advt., [1766, July 10, Pennsylvania *Gazette*] viz:

" 'Bellsize Arabian, known in England to most sportsmen, just arrived from England, is kept at Jacob Hiltzheimer's stable [in Philadelphia].

" 'He is a fine upstanding silver grey, with a black mane; is near 16 hands high, with strength in proportion. . . . [After a summary of the

Moroccan breeding certificate, quoted subsequently at length in ATR, vii, 95, and a disquisition on the advantage of fresh crosses of "Arabian" blood, the history of the horse is resumed and continued by the statement that]

" 'in England 1,000 gns. has been refused for him more than once [cf. J. Simpson's ctf. 1764 cited ante s. v. Evans' Sterling, Va. 1765] nor would this sum at any time have parted him from his owner [Mr. Welch] had not the death of the latter separated them forever. . . .

" '[After Mr. Welch's death] his present owner [Sir Charles Saunders] being a lover of America, purchased him and sent him over with a public spirited intention of improving the breed amongst us.

" 'Philadelphia, Pa. Samuels & Footman'.

"Bred in Morocco and sent thence to England.

"1760H. 153 at Bellsize in Middx.

"1761H. 163 at Bellsize in Middx.

"1762H. 122 at Bellsize in Middx.

"1763H. 130 at Bellsize in Middx.

"1764H. 153 at Bellsize in Middx.

"1765H. 145 at Bellsize in Middx.

"1766H. 178 at Bellsize in Middx.

"1766 sent to Pennsylvania.

"1766 at J. Hiltzheimer's in Philadelphia, Pa.

"1766 at J. Wing's in Philadelphia, Pa.

"1768-72 at J. Perkins' in Philadelphia, Pa.

"1772 for sale by J. Perkins (last record).

"Conn. 1766

"Barbary Horse, called Ranger and Lindsey's Arabian, gr. c. 1762, Wyllys' & later Lindsey's. ASB, i, 145, derived from Edgar, followed the statement of the early history of this horse and of his purchase in Connecticut, during the Revolution, to be sent to Virginia, made by Gen. T. M. Forman of Md., and first published in 1827 [AF, ix, 223; ATR, i, 67].

"The significant extant American evidence is as follows [1770, Connecticut *Courant;* calendared in Battell, i, 113]:

" 'Ranger stands near Hartford: of a fine dapple gray colour, rising 15 hands high and allowed by competent judges to be the compleatest horse ever brought to America.

" 'He is a horse of fine strength and beauty, equal perhaps to any in America, of the true Barbary [sic] breed.

" 'He is the same horse that was in my keeping last season.

" 'Hartford, Conn. James Nichols.'

"[1777, May 9, Connecticut *Gazette*]

" 'The public are hereby informed that the full-blooded Arabian [sic] horse called Ranger, formerly the property of Col. Wyllys of Hartford and which has been kept there for several seasons past by Capt. Nichols, is now owned by Charles C. Chandler, in Woodstock, Conn., and will cover at $5. the season or 15 shillings the single leap'.

"[1779, March 19, VG]

" 'Ranger, an imported Arabian horse, stands at my farm two miles from Port Royal, and will cover mares at 30 l. [Virginia currency] the season.

" 'Port Royal, Caroline Co., Virginia. William Lindsey'.

"1766, aet. 4, presented by the Emperor of Morocco to the Captain of a British frigate, who carried him to the West Indies, where he was injured, sold to an American merchantman, and thereafter sent to Connecticut.

"1766-68 at S. Wyllys', Hartford, Conn.

"1769-76 at J. Nichol's, Hartford, Conn.

"1777 at Chandler's, Woodstock, Conn.

"1778 at Howard's, Windham, Conn.

"1779 purchased by Col. Harry Lee and Capt. W. Lindsey and sent to Virginia.

"1779-80 at Lindsey s Mill, Port Royal, Caroline Co., Va.

"1780 adv. for sale by W. Lindsey.

"1781 at W. Lyle's in Prince George's Co., Md.

"1782 at E. Edelin's, Prince George's Co., Md.

"1783-84 at Gilpin's, Alexandria, Va.

"1785 died in Virginia, aet. 23 years.

"N. Y. 1766

"Barbary Horse, called Somerset, gr. c. [age not recorded], Platt's. Not in ASB. The evidence is the following N. Y. advts., [1767, May 4, New York *Mercury*] viz:

" 'Somerset, a beautiful gray Barb, will cover at E. Platt's, North side of Hampstead Plains [Long Island]'.

"[1769, June 5, New York *Mercury*]

" 'Arabian Horse: A very fine Arabian horse to be sold at the Merchants' Coffee House [in New York] on Friday next at public sale. He is very good for the saddle and has produced a number of fine colts since he has been in this country. The owner of him being at sea, and no person here to take proper care of him is the only reason of his being sold. He is to be seen at Caleb Hyet's at Fresh Water. Any person living in the country may doubtless clear a great deal of money by the purchase of him'.

"Bred in Morocco and brought thence by an unidentified American merchantman.

"1766-68 at Platt's, Hempstead Plains, L. I., N. Y.

"1769 adv. for sale in New York (last record).

"N. Y. 1767

"Barbary Horse, called Bashaw, Van Wyck's. Not in ASB. The evidence is the introductory N. Y. adv., [1768, June 16, N. Y. *Journal* or *General Advertiser;* ATR, iv, 610] viz:

" 'The fine Arabian horse Bashaw is about 15 hands high and was bred by the Emperor of Morocco who sent him a present to the Dey of Algiers; and he gave him to the Swedish consul there, who presented him to the Grand Duke of Tuscany. Whilst his royal highness had him he won in the same summer the plates at Sienna, Florence, Pistoia and Spoleto, beating a famous English horse at Florence called the Grand Diavolo [cf. Shafto's b. c. 1764, by Marske, GSB, i, 140] and many others of no inferior note.

" 'Little Neck', Flushing, L. I., N. Y. Stephen Van Wyck.'

"This c. was later confused with DeLancey's Bashaw [b. c. 1768, by Wildair out of the Cub-mare] in a statement published 1831 in ATR [iv, 609] with the consequence that DeLancey's Bashaw was entered in ASB as imported. Bred in Morocco and sent thence to the Grand Duke of Tuscany.

"1764-66 on the turf in Italy.

"1767 sent to New York.

"1768 at Van Wyck's, Flushing, L. I., N. Y. [sole record].

"N. C. 1771

"Barbary Horse, called Emperor of Morocco, Maurice Moore's. Not in ASB. The most informing evidence is a Va. advt., [1779, March 26, VG] viz:

" 'The Emperour of Morocco, a most beautiful Barb, 15 hands high, will stand this season at my house near Hanover town, and will cover mares at 20 l. the season.

" 'The Emperour of Morocco was imported to Cape Fear from Barbary by Judge Moore, and from thence to this place. As the Barbs is in as high repute as any horses in England, this horse must shortly be deservedly esteemed as one of the finest horses that ever was in America.

" 'Hanover Co., Va. Richard Burnley'.

"Bred in Morocco and imported thence 'to Cape Fear in North Carolina by Maurice Moore and Peter Melatt'.

"1771-75 on Cape Fear, N. C.

"1776-78 at J. Alston's, Waccamaw, S. C.

"1779-80 at R. Burnley's, Hanover Co., Va. (last record).

KISHTA A.H.C. No. 1820 with colt.

"Md. 1806

"Barbary Horse called Black Sultan, Thomas Jefferson's, later Elias Earle's. ASB, i, 150, derived from Edgar, p. 73, is an adequate statement of the origin and importation of the horse, but did not follow his career in America. The extant documents are as follows [1806, April 24, Universal *Gazette,* Washington; not known to ASB]:

" 'The superb barb Black Sultan, presented by the Bey of Tunis to the government of the United States and lately brought to this country by the Tunisian ambassador [Melli Melli], will stand the ensuing season at Petworth, the farm of John Tayloe [III], Esq., near Rock Creek Church and within two miles of the City of Washington . . .

" 'This Royal present being one of the most choice animals of the Regency of Tunis and full 16 hands high, a desire has prevailed that so valuable a race should be extended as much as possible and it has therefore been directed that he be placed at a low price [i.e., stud fee] of $20. . . .

" 'Petworth, D. C., April 4, 1806. Chester Bailey, manager for John Tayloe, Esq.'

"[1806, October 17, *National Intelligencer,* Washington; not known to ASB]:

" 'For sale. On the second day of the Washington Races which are to commence on Tuesday the 28th inst. there will be offered for sale at auction the elegant Barbary horse and two mares which were brought from Tunis by his Excellency the Tunisian Ambassador and intended as a present to the Executive of the United States'.

"[1806, December 15, *National Inteligencer,* Washington; not known to ASB]:

" 'The horse Black Sultan and the two mares brought to the United States by the late Ambassador of Tunis will be disposed of at private sale.

" 'Both the mares are in foal to the horse and all three are in good condition.

" 'Application to be made to the subscriber at the office of the Secretary of State.

" 'Washington, December 15, 1806. Daniel Brent'.

"[1807, March 14, Charleston *City Gazette*]

" 'The superb barb and much admired stallion Black Sultan . . . was presented by the Bey of Tunis to the government of the United States and brought to this country by the Tunisian Ambassador last year . . . He is full 16 hands high, six years old [i.e., foaled 1800] possessing great bone, with fine shape and symmetry: has stood but one season in America and proved to be a sure foal getter.

" 'Greenville District, S. C. Elias Earle'.

"From these testimonies it appears that the purchaser of the horse at the sale by the Department of State was Elias Earle [1762-1823] of South Carolina, who was in Washington in 1806 as a Member of Congress.

"1800 foaled in the stud of the Bey of Tunis.

"1806 sent to Washington, D. C., as a gift to Thomas Jefferson.

"1806 covered at John Tayloe's farm 'Petworth' in the District of Columbia.

"1806 sold by the U. S. to Elias Earle of S. C.

"1807 at Elias Earle's, Greenville District, S. C.

"1808 at John Gallant's, York District, S. C. [last record].

"Md. 1810

"Barbary Horse called Arabarb, Tobias Lear's. ASB, i, 143, derived from Edgar, p. 67, [who had an otherwise lost N. C. stud bill] entered this horse s. v. 'Black Arabian Barb' and classified him as 'Arabian'. The extant evidence is a calendar of a letter from Dr. William Thornton of Washington to Thomas Branch of Chesterfield Co., Va., exhibited in the introductory Va. adv., [1811, February 22, Richmond, Virginia *Argus*] viz:

" 'The noble Black Arabian Barb was sent [to me] by Col. [Tobias] Lear [1762-1816], our Consul General to the Barbary powers, and arrived in America about five months ago [July 1810].

" 'Col. Lear says he was bred in the Mountains of Algiers, whence the stud of the Dey [of Algiers] is largely recruited, and he has reason to believe that he possesses as much of the true Arabian blood as any

FALOUMA A.H.C. No. 1507 with filly FARNYMA.

horse in the Regency [of Algiers]; that he does not send a pedigree as the people of Barbary do not keep them. The horse is all of 17 [sic] hands high, black [being the favourite colour among the Barbs] and [was] so famous as a foal getter that Col. Lear was desirous of obtaining some of his stock.

" 'The robe I [Dr. Thornton] received with the horse I am ashamed to send, as it seems fitter for an Empress than a horse; being a rich crimson satin, splendidly woven with gold flowers, surrounded with a deep fringe of crimson and gold, and lined with rich damask.

" 'On arriving at Baltimore his tail swept the ground; but I am sorry to say that a groom was so officious as to shorten it.

" 'Washington, D. C., January 1811. William Thornton'.

"1811, s. v. 'Black Arabian Barb', at Thomas Branch's in Chesterfield Co., Va.

"1812-14, on the Roanoke River in N. C. [Edgar, controlled by the Washington advt. 1815 which recites that the horse had then 'returned from Carolina'].

"1815-18, s. v. 'Arabarb', at Dr. William Thornton's in Washington, D. C.

"1819-23 in Virginia.

"1824, s. v. 'Arabarb', at Coleman Lewis', Georgetown, Ky. [last record].

"N. J. 1815?

"Barbary Horse called Coxe's Arab, Charles D. Coxe's. Not in ASB. Lacking a stud adv't, the extant evidence for this horse consists of incidental references to him in several New Jersey pedigrees, [1824, ATR, i, 367; whence ASB, i, 202]:

" 'Chihoangti, c. [neither coat nor foaling date recorded], is by the imported horse Arab which stood at $50. the mare: his dam [Van Mater's] Aurora by Honest John: [Hunt's] Zelipha by Messenger: Dido by Bay Richmond: [DeLancey's] Slamerkin by Wildair: [DeLancey's] Cub-mare.

" 'New Jersey. Joseph Johnson'.

"[1837, ATR, viii, 524; whence ASB, i, 254]

" '[Frost's] Rosebud, ch. m. 1829, by Long's Henry, son of Sir Archy: Arab, imported by Charles D. Coxe, U. S. Consul at Tunis, which stood at $50. the mare in New Jersey: [Lowndes'] Maid of Northampton [ASB, ii, 10] by Thornton's Clifden: Jane Powndes by Thornton's Driver: [Lowndes'] Modesty by Hall's Union, son of Eden's Slim: Galloway's Madge by Galloway's Selim, son of Othello: Sharpe's Spotmare [q. v. ante, vol. i, p. 190].

" 'This mare [Rosebud] I have run in New Jersey and Illinois with considerable success, having started her six times and been winner five.

" 'Jerseyville, Green Co., Illinois. John Frost'.

"These ctfs. for Coxe's Arab are controlled by crosses in pedigrees of American trotting horses; e. g., American Star [q. v. in Brown, "The Horse of the Desert," p. 138], whose papers record that 'Coxe's Arabian' was presented to Mr. Coxe by the Bey of Tunis.

"The archives of the Department of State show that Charles D. Coxe of New Jersey was in the Barbary States in North Africa during two periods separated by a sojourn in the United States, viz: 1807-1813 and again 1824-1830. On the official record he was designated as 'in charge of the Consulate at Tunis' during the first period, and during the second as 'Consul at Tripoli', and it is noted that he died in Italy in 1830, without return to America.

"Reading these dates with the tradition that Coxe's Arab came out of the stud of the Bey of Tunis, it seems probable that Mr. Coxe brought the horse home with him when he returned to the United States from Tunis after 1813.

"1815? brought to New Jersey by Charles D. Coxe from Tunis.

"1815? ff. covered in Middlesex Co., New Jersey.

"Pa. 1820

"Barbary Horse called Grand Bashaw, Joseph C. Morgan's. ASB, i, 144, derived from Edgar, p. 69, is based on the Pa. advt. 1822. The evidence is as follows, (1822, March 27, Philadelphia *Aurora* & *General Advertiser*) viz:

" 'The elegant imported Arabian horse Grand Bashaw . . . is an iron grey, rising 6 years old, 15 hands 1 inch high, and was imported from Tripoli in August 1820, by Mr. Joseph C. Morgan, who resided there several years, and who selected him from the best stock of Arabian horses extant. He is allowed by judges, as to symmetry, speed and action, superior to any horse ever imported into the United States.

" 'Certificates of pedigree, and two of Bashaw's colts, now about 5 months old, to be seen at his stand.

" 'Lower Merion Township, Montgomery Co., Pa., March 6, 1822. John Elliott'.

"[1823, from "Memoirs of the Pennsylvania Agricultural Society," Philadelphia 1824, p. 310; whence Judge Duvall in ATR, ii, 483, and Battell, ii, p. cx]

"At the first Annual Meeting of the Pennsylvania Agricultural Society, held at Paoli, Chester Co., Pa., October 25, 1823, the Committee on Horses reported:

" 'That they are of opinion that the Arabian horse Grand Bashaw, owned by Joseph C. Morgan, is entitled to the premium of 50 dollars for the best thoroughbred [sic] stallion'.

"His pedigree is as follows:

" 'I, John A. Carstenson, his Danish Majesty's Consul General at Tripoli-in-the-West, do hereby certify that on the 24th of May 1819 J. C. Morgan, Esq., of the United States of America, purchased from me an iron grey Arabian [sic] horse, rising four years old [i.e., foaled 1816].

" 'This horse is of the very best blood to be obtained here. He was begotten by the late Bey's favourite horse Khasnadger, celebrated in this place for his beauty and other excellent qualities: from a fine mare of the country.

" 'Tripoli-in-the-West, May 24, 1819. J. A. Carstenson'.

" 'I do hereby certify that I am fully acquainted with all the facts stated in the [above] certificate relating to the famous horse called the Grand Bashaw; and that [that certificate] is entitled to full faith and credit.

" 'Tripoli, May 24, 1819. Richard B. Jones, U. S. Consul'.

"1865, from a letter to John H. Wallace, published in *Wallace's Monthly,* and cited by Battell, ii, cx]

" 'In 1818 (at Tripoli) I loaned to some Danish officers a very valuable Arabian horse. By accident they killed him [and] on the following morning I found Grand Bashaw in my stable to replace him. I declined under the circumstances any compensation, and suggested to Mr. [Joseph C.] Morgan, [then] residing with me, to purchase [Grand Bashaw] and by virtue of my official influence would assist him to facilitate his embarkation to America. In 1819 he took [the horse] to Italy and from there to Marseilles, where Mr. Morgan joined me on my way to the United States. We sailed from there to Boston and arrived the 20th of August 1820. From there Grand Bashaw was taken to Lower Merion, Montgomery Co., Pa., and stood there several years.

" 'Grand Bashaw was a beautiful black with a small white star and snip [sic; whence Wallace in "The Horse of America," p. 322; but as Grand Bashaw was recorded in the contemporary records as "iron grey" it is possible that Mr. Jones, here writing from memory after 45 years, was thinking of his favourite Saladin (q. v. infra) the only one of the three horses he imported in 1820 whose coat was not contemporaneously recorded].

" 'He was a Barb of the finest quality in every respect; but their pedigrees are not kept with the care of the Arabians. I have no personal knowledge of the mares bred to him, but have seen many of his descendants, all showing a resemblance to the original sire . . .

" 'Philadelphia, April 25, 1865. Richard B. Jones'.

"1821-22 at John Elliott's, on the Lancaster turnpike near Philadelphia.

"1823-45 near Philadelphia.

"In 1831 Judge Duvall noted [ATR, ii, 483] that Grand Bashaw had covered at Whitemarsh Township, near Philadelphia, in 1827, and 'it is believed, is still in Pennsylvania'; which record was extended by Wallace's note [in "The Horse of America"] that the horse died at Newton, Pa., in 1845, having stood all his long life 'near Philadelphia'.

"Md. 1824

"Barbary Horse called 'The Jones Arabian', Jacob Jones'. ASB, i, 145, was derived from Edgar, p. 69, who had the Pa. advt. of 1828, cited below. The evidence is [1828, a Pa. advt. from Gen. T. M. Forman's collection of pedigrees in AF, x, 127; and cf., to the same effect, the comments on the horse by Gen. Forman and J. S. Skinner in AF, viii, 319; ATR, ii, 327]:

" 'The Jones Arabian is a dapple grey horse eight years old this spring [i.e., foaled 1820]. . . . He was selected with great care by Major [Townsend] Stith, the American Consul at Tunis, and by him purchased for Commodore Jacob Jones [1768-1850], U. S. N., by whom he was imported in the frigate *Constitution* in 1824.

" 'Previous to his importation he ran a trial race at Gibralter, at the solicitation of the Governor, the Earl of Chatham, against one of his Lordship's blood horses. Although the Jones Arabian had but little preparatory training, was very young and just taken from on shipboard, it was admitted he made an excellent race, manifesting fine speed, wind and bottom.

" 'The Jones Arabian has stood for mares but a few seasons [1825-27] in Cecil [cf. AF, viii, 319] and Kent Counties, Maryland, with distinguished reputation and success. Some thoroughbred mares are in foal to him [i.e., in 1827 Duckett's, later Wallis', Equa, ch. m. 1815, by Chance, ATR, ii, 356; vi, 308, 368, 484; ASB, i, 197]. His oldest colts are but two years old this spring [i.e., foaled 1826].

" 'Harrisburg, Pa., April 1, 1828. W. B. Donaldson'.

"1824, aet. 4, imported by Commodore Jacob Jones, U. S. N., at New York and sent to Md.

"1825-26 in Cecil Co., Md. (AF, viii, 319).

"1827 in Kent Co., Md. (AF, x, 127).

"1828 at W. B. Donaldson's in Harrisburg and Carlisle, Pa. [AF, x, 127; last record].

"N. J. 1826

"Barbary Horse called Numidian, Shaler's. ASB, i, 146, derived from Edgar, p. 71, is a skeleton entry, s. v. Numidia [sic] to the effect that 'nothing is known of this horse except his name'. The evidence is as follows [1833, Fessenden's "New England Farmer"; whence Battell, ii, p. ccxxxii):

" 'The full blooded Arabian horse Numidian was captured by the Dey of Algiers while warring against the desert Arabs during the winter of 1823-24, was purchased by Mr. [William] Shaler [1778-1833], American Consul General at Algiers and was imported in 1826.

" 'Since 1827 he has been kept at Mount Holly, N. J.

" 'Ten Hill', near Boston. Samuel Jacques'.

"1826 'sent to America' from Algiers.
"1827-1832 at Mount Holly, N. J.
"1833 at Samuel Jacques; near Boston, Mass. (last record).

"Field's Barb. ASB, i, 150, ii, 99, both derived from Edgar, are traditional entries, (a) among the imported Barb horses of 'Barb, a white horse formerly the property of the late Mr. Thomas Field of Mecklenburg County, Va. He was an excellent foal getter'; and (b) among the American-bred mares of 'Miss Alsup [sic] by Janus [sic] dam by Fearnought: [Whittington]: Jolly Roger: Shock: Sober John: [Secretary Carter's Slyboots]', described [by Edgar] as 'a famous quarter [sic] runner bred [sic] by the late Mr. Thomas Field of Mecklenburg County, Virginia, foaled in 1772 [sic]. She was purchased from Mr. Field by the late Mr. John Goode, Sr., at an enormous price'.

"When these entries are read with the note by Randolph of Roanoke in his *Register* [TF&F, ii, 199] that Speaker Nathaniel Macon had told him that 'Field's Barb [was] by Lindsey's Arabian out of Miss Alsop by Fearnought' it is apparent that the tradition which reached Edgar from the stud of John Goode of Mecklenburg [noted quarter racer and amateur of Janus blood] was a cumulative misinterpretation, and particularly that the Janus cross in the pedigree was a 'Southside' intrusion. From the extant evidence here arrayed it may be deduced

" (1) that Field's horse was named Barb and was Virginia-bred, not 'imported';

" (2) that the dam of that horse was the Miss Alsop [b. m. 1771 by Fearnought] which was a winner on the Rappahannock in 1774 in the colours of Moore Fauntleroy [Culver, pp. 119, 120];

" (3) that Miss Alsop was bred in the Baylor stud and was a member of the family of John Baylor's first brood mare described in pedigrees as 'by Secretary Carter's horse Slyboots' [unidentified but fl. 1740, and query by Beau]; which family is shown by pedigrees to have produced also the Fearnought colts John Nelson's Macaroni [b. c. 1770, ASB, ii, 432, a confused double entry which may be controlled by a Va. advt. 1776]; Peyton Randolph's Careless [ch. c. 1771?, ASB, i, 712, corrected by a Va. advt. 1779]; Spotswood's Sempronius [ch. c. 1775, by Fauntleroy's, formerly Tayloe's, Nonpareil II, not in ASB but attested by a Va. advt. 1784]; and Wyllie's Patsy Walthall [gr. m. 1791?, by Medley, ASB, ii, 181, extended to Carter's Slyboots by a Va. advt. 1808, whence ASB, ii, 436, of her son Wyllie's Marsk];

"(4) that Miss Alsop remained in the Fauntleroy stud until 1779, when she was mated with Lindsey's Arabian [q. v. ante, Conn. 1766] on the arrival of that horse in Virginia; and subsequently was sold, with her Lindsey's Arabian foal [Field's Barb, gr. c. 1780?], to Thomas Field of Mecklenburg; and

"(5) that Mr. Field retained the colt but sold Miss Alsop to his neighbour John Goode, Sr."

WARDAT BADIYA A.H.C. No. 2577 with filly.

Chapter 6

The First Listing Of Arabian Horses In A Printed Stud Book In America

I N 1826 there appeared in a Virginia newspaper, the Petersburg *Intelligencer,* a column or department known as "Annals of the Turf," by an Advocate for the Turf, which had to do with the breeding and pedigrees and the leading turf annals of that period. This department became very popular, and while it was written by an anonymous individual, it later developed that the author was George Washington Jeffreys, the son of a rich planter and land owner in Person County, North Carolina. J. S. Skinner, who published *The American Farmer* at Baltimore, Maryland, secured permission to reprint these "Annals" in his paper and for some time they were so published. It is quite evident that information in "Annals of the Turf" was largely the source material for much of the information to be found in the first two attempts to produce a stud book in printed form by Richard Mason, M.D., formerly of Surry County, who by 1830 had published the fifth edition of the "Gentleman's New Pocket Farrier." This edition carried the first published stud book on the blood horse in America. The list of blood horses given covers several hundred animals, and a total of eighty-eight pages.

Much of the information is very limited, but a great deal of it is sufficient to permit the tracing of complete breeding, ownership and race records, if any, of these animals. No attempt has been made to go through this entire list and select animals of known Arabian breeding, but details concerning nine Arabian animals together with an introduction by Dr. Mason entitled, "Annals of the Turf," are offered, as follows:

"ANNALS OF THE TURF. — 'The transcendent consequence of the horse to man in every possible stage of human existence, has been the invariable theme of writers on the subject from the earliest records of time. Indeed it is impossible to conceive any other, out of the vast variety of animals destined by nature to human use, which can, with the least prospect of success, dispute with the favourite horse the palm of his master's predilection and attachment. It is an attachment of a truly rational nature, and to a most worthy object. The very idea of being supported at ease by an auxiliary and borrowed animal power, and of being safely borne from place to place, at will, with a pleasant and gentle motion, or with the rapidity of lightning, must have impressed the mind of the first discoverers of the mighty benefits of the horse, with ineffable delight. Such sentiments and feelings respecting this noble animal have been constantly entertained and handed down to us from the earliest ages. The general beauty, the harmony of proportion, the stateliness and delicacy of the superior species of this paragon of brute animals, could not fail of inspiring admiration in the breasts even of savage and untutored men. Time and the improving faculties of man, gradually developed the various uses and qualifications of the horse. Endowed by nature with a portion of intellect, with a generous pliability of disposition and fortitude of heart, with vast and energetic bodily powers, he was found capable of bearing a sort of social part in all the pleasures and labours of man. He was associated with his master in the pleasures of the journey and the chase; he shares willingly and with ardour in the dangers of the martial field; and with a steady prowess partook in the humble labours of cultivating the soil for mutual subsistence. By the most illustrious nations of either ancient or modern times, the horse has ever been esteemed of the highest worth and consequence, and treated with a distinction and attendance befitting his rank as the first of domestic animals, approximating in society and service to human nature. It is among the most savage and debased tribes of men only, that the breed, condition, and comforts of this noble animal have been neglected.'

"Arabian Lindsay's or Ranger, presented by the Emperor of Morocco to the captain of an English vessel, and landed in the West Indies;

92

there he broke three of his legs, and was made a present to a gentleman from Connecticut, where he went by the name of Ranger. Captain Lindsay was sent by General Lee, in 1777-8, who purchased him and brought him to Virginia. See *American Farmer,* vol. 9, page 223.

"Jones'. A dapple grey 15 hands high, black legs, mane and tail. Selected in Tunis by Major Stith, American Consul there, and purchased for Commodore Jacob Jones of the United States Navy. See *American Farmer,* vol. 10, page 127.

"Selim, g. h. presented by Murad Bey to the late Gen. Sir F. Abercrombie, and after his death he became the property of Commodore Barron, of whom he was purchased, and afterwards sold and carried to Kentucky. 1815, John Tayloe.

"Winter's. Was captured during the last war, [1814] then one year old, by the privateer *Grampus,* of Baltimore, on board the brig *Doris,* his Majesty's transport, No. 650, on his passage from Senegal in Africa, to Portsmouth, England, and was intended as a present for the then Prince Regent, late king of England. This horse was sold, and purchased by E. J. Winter, member of Congress, from the State of New York. This Arabian is now white, and about four feet nine inches high.

"Bagdad. Was purchased by George Barclay, Esq. of New York, from Hassana de Gris, Minister to England from Tripoli, who imported him to England, as a horse of the purest Arabian blood: he was purchased by a Company in Nashville, Tennessee, for $8,000. — 1823.

"Bussora, [imp'd] from the land of Job, for which $4,000 was paid. Stood at New York.

"Ballesteros, dk. br. formerly the property of Ferdinand King of Spain, and still bears the Royal Mark. When the French Army got possession of Madrid, the steed belonging to the King of Spain, was taken by the Spanish nobles, carried to Cadiz and there sold. Amongst others was young Ballesteros — he became the property of Richard S. Hackley, Esq. Consul at that place, who disposed of him to Captain Singleton, of Philadelphia, who brought him to this country, and sold him to Thomas Guy of Richmond, Va. he got some colts in the State of Delaware.

"Broad Rock, Va. 1816, William Ball.

"Arabarb, bl. [imp'd] by Col. Lear, a large strong horse, well proportioned but not handsome; he was the sire of the dam of Fairfax. Col. Lear.

"Arabia, bl. h. by Old Janus, from a blood mare by an [imp'd] Horse.

"Cumberland Cy. Va. 1777, Thomas Moody.

"Felix, ch. m. by Arab, dam by Shylock. Thomas T. Tabb."

Chapter 7

Arabian Horses In The American Race-Turf Register

IN 1833, Volume I of a proposed two-volume stud book entitled, "The American Race-Turf Register, Sportsman's Herald and General Stud Book," under the authorship of Patrick Nisbett Edgar, of Granville County, North Carolina, was published in New York. This was the second printed book in America purporting to be a general stud book, and while much of the information in it needed clarification, it is regrettable that the second volume was never finished.

Because methods of communication were very primitive in that era, it is evident that the work involved was very great. It is reported that Mr. Edgar spent years riding horseback through the colonies gathering information from all available sources for the stud book. Some students of the horse are inclined to state that Edgar was a faker. This is questionable. He did, after all, have the confidence of, and secured information from, many of the leading colonists such as John Randolph, of Roanoke, and others.

One distinct advantage of Edgar's stud book is that it supplies the source for a more detailed study of many blood horses because in many instances the pedigrees of numerous animals are given in great detail.

While Edgar's stud book contained the pedigrees of all blood horses covering the period for which it was compiled, only that section of the book devoted to Arabian horses (pages 66 to 72) is herewith quoted:

"Arab: His color or character is unknown.

"Amurath: 'Was brought from Tripoli, in Barbary, and imported into New York in the year 1823, then one year old. He was brought from Nubia to Tripoli. 1832. Wolcott Chauncey'.

"Arab Barb: Vide Black Arabian Barb.

"Arabian: A cream colored horse.

"Bagdad: A beautiful brown bay horse, precisely one fourth of an inch under 15 hands in height; imported into Tripoli, from the city of Alleppo; well shaped in the general, but rather light in the hind quarters. He was landed in England, being the property of Hassana D'Gris, Minister from Tripoli to that place, who sold him to George Barclay, Esq. of New York, who gave the following certificate of his being a genuine Arabian horse, together with the French attestation of the said Tripolitan Minister, Hassana D'Gris:

" 'I, George Barclay, do hereby certify, that Bagdad was purchased by me from Hassan D'Gris, Minister to England from Tripoli, who assured me he was the one imported by him, into England, as a horse of peculiar value, and of the purest, real Arabian blood, for which "one thousand pounds" were refused in France, and that Bagdad was his favorite, and by far the most valuable of all his six horses.

" 'New York, Nov. 22nd, 1823, George Barclay'.

"Here follows the attestation of Hassana D'Gris, written in French; taken from the Arabic language, which accompanied Bagdad, when he was shipped from the City of Aleppo.

" 'Bagdad. — Je soussigné déclare et certifie par la présente que le cheval appellé Bagdad, coleur brun, maintenant en possession de Monsieur George Barclay, Négociant de cette Ville, est véritablement cheval Arab, et faisant partie de douze chevaux de menue race que j'ai vu débarquer à Marseille en l'année 1819 d'un Bâtiment venant des côtes d'Alleppo d'Arabie; que six des dits chevaux ont été achetés pour le compte du gouvernment Français, pour le service des haras, et que celui mentionné plus haut des six autres, dont trois ont été amenés dans ce pays.

" 'Hassana D'Gris, Fils du Ministre de S. A. R. C.

" 'Pacha De Tripoli, son beaufrère Son Ambassadeur auprès S. M. B. Londres le 12 Mars, 1822'.

"Ballasteros: 'A beautiful dark brown Arabian horse, 8 years old, formerly the property of "Ferdinand, King of Spain," and still bears the Royal Marks: when the French army got possession of Madrid, the stud belonging to the King of Spain, was taken by the Spanish Nobles, carried to Cadiz, and there sold, and among the rest was young Ballasteros; he was alternately the property of the Duke of Wellington and R. S. Hackley, Esq. our Consul General at that place, who disposed of him to Capt. Singleton, of Philadelphia, who brought him into the United States, and from whom he was purchased by the late Mr. Thomas Guy, of Richmond, Va.

" 'He stood in Granville County, North Carolina, several seasons, and proved himself to be a sure and a very good foal getter. 1816'.

"Barbarossa: 'A grey horse, (it is believed) and a horse of fine form, action and shape; 14 hands 3 inches high. 1819, James R. Jones'.

"Belsize Arabian: 'Imported (we have been informed) into Pennsylvania; a grey horse. He has been much admired, by the best judges, for his beautiful form, and elegant carriage, which, with his strength and size, renders him equally qualified for mixing his blood with American Racing Mares, as well as those kept for other purposes, the Arabian horses being remarkable for stamping their figure and other qualities on their stock. He stood in Philadelphia, in 1768. Pennsylvania *Chronicle,* 1768, John Perkins'.

"Black Arabian Barb: 'Called also "Arab Barb," a black horse, imported by Col. Lear. He was a large, strong horse, well proportioned, but not handsome. He was a horse of an unusual size for an Arabian, being 17 hands high, of great bone and muscular powers, with uncommon activity.

" 'This noble animal was sent to America on the account of Col. Lear, our Consul General to the Barbary Powers, resident at Algiers, and though many of the horses in the stables of the Dey are immediately descended from Arabians, we have just reason to believe that this horse possesses as much of the true Arabian blood as any in the Regency. No pedigree came over to America with him, as the people of Barbary do not register them, but we are assured, by those who knew the horse, that he is of the first and highest Arabian blood, and that he was highly valued, as possessing many of the points the most in estimation among the Arabs.

" 'General Ridgely, of Hampton, who has possessed some of the best Running Horses in America, wishes to breed from him, and declares he never saw a horse with so many, and such extraordinary running points combined. I am of the same opinion. (From a printed Advertisement). William Thornton, M. D.'

"Bussorah Arabian: 'So called, (but was evidently a Persian horse,) because he was bred at Bussorah, on the Euphrates River, at the head of the Persian Gulph, and reared under the eye of Dr. Colquhoun, of Bombay, for many years the East India Company's Resident Agent at that place — from whom he was puchased by (the agent of) Abraham Ogden, Esq., and imported into New York in the fall of 1819, in the ship *Horatio,* from Bombay.

" 'He is of the "Germany" breed; a caste of Arabian horses always held in the highest estimation, as well for their beautiful symmetry of form, as for the flinty hardiness they evince in the endurance of fatigue.

" 'His elegance of form together with his beauty of color, (a handsome sorrel,) fine movement and the exhibition of all those points which we seek in vain for except in the "thoroughbred horse," of themselves evidence that he is of the first blood, and afford the strongest assurances that his Stock will tend to improve the American breed of thoroughbred horses. (From a printed advertisement, N. Y. 1824.) Corns. W. Van Rantz'.

"Cardozo: A chestnut horse imported into Boston, in June 1832, by Messrs. R. D. Tucker & Son, in the Brig *Caroline* from Gibralter. Certifcate of his Arabian owners:

" 'We, the undersigned, do hereby certify that the Chestnut Horse five years old, with a white spot on the forehead, was sent from Oran to Consul Cardozo, and that said horse is of the purest Arabian breed. In testimony whereof, we give the present in Gibralter, this 3d day of Del Hogia, year of Elgira, 1247. (Signed in Arabic) Faquih Hamet Bengusef, Mostafa Bengaly.

" 'Certified to be the true signatures of Faquih Hamet Bengusef and Sidi Mostafa Bengaly, by A. CARDOZA, Vice Consul of the Bashaw, Bey of Tunis. Gibralter, May 4th, 1832'.

"Croucher: 'An Arabian horse of the most beautiful kind. Va. 1825. N. & T. Nelson, John Nelson.'

"Dey of Algiers: 'He was an elegantly formed horse, possessing both beauty and strength; most of his points are equal and some of them very superior to any horse on the Continent; he is fully fourteen hands two inches and a half high; (a height by no means usual in the genuine Arabian race) — he is nearly of a white colour with a few brown spots dashed over his neck and shoulders; he is of fine presence and carriage, and remarkably vigorous and active.

" 'This beautiful animal was procured from Arabia in the year 1798, at four years of age, by the late Grand Bailiff Fromm, of Prussia, and brought to Fehr Bellen, in that kingdom, where he was purchased after the Bailiff's death, at the sale of his stud in 1799, by Lieut. General Frederick, Baron of Diemar, by whom he was sold to Col. Swan, of Mass. (then in Europe,) and by him shipped from Hamburg to Boston, to Gen. Jackson, of that city, who sent him in the beginning of the year 1802, to General Mason, of the District of Columbia. (From a printed advertisement). E. Beasley, Manager for John Tayloe, Esq. at Gwinfield'.

"Grand Bashaw: 'An elegant Arabian Horse; imported from Tripoli, in August, 1820, by Mr. Joseph S. Morgan, of an iron-grey colour, foaled in 1816, full 15 hands high. He was selected by the importer from the best stock of oriental horses in that country, and (it is believed,) that in point of beauty, action, and speed, he is not excelled by any horse ever imported into the United States.

" 'He arrived in America in 1820, and stood in Lower-Merrion township, Montgomery county near Philadelphia. No pedigree given. (From a printed advertisement). John Elliott'.

"Grand Sultan: 'He was an elegant full blooded Arabian horse; foaled in 1816, a beautiful iron-grey; 15 hands 2 inches high, and for elegance of form, as well as power and activity, not surpassed by any horse ever imported into America.

" 'He was imported into the United States, also from Tripoli, in 1820, and selected with the greatest care and attention from the best stud, of the Bashaw, and is declared by the certificate of the said Bashaw's public secretary, signior Abraham Serrusi, to be of the finest and highest Arabian stock, ever reared in all Barbary. Pedigree — his sire Billah, was imported from Syria, his dam Caulah from Egypt.

" 'Grand Sultan stood one mile from Philadelphia. (From a printed advertisement). John Elliott'.

"Ishmael: A grey horse brought from Mecca, imported by the late General Eaton, of North Carolina.

"The Jones Arabian: He was a dappled grey horse, 15 hands high; black legs, mane, and tail, of fine temper, spirit, and action. In all the points, which constitute the courser, he admits of no superior in this country.

"He was selected by Major Townsend Stilth, the American consul at Tunis; and by him purchased for Commodore Jacob Jones, of the United States Navy, by whom he was imported in the Frigate *Constitution*. Previous to his exportation, he ran a trial race at Gibralter, at the solicitation of the Governor of that place, the earl of Chatham; against one of his lordship's English Blood Horses — Although the Jones Arabian had but little preparatory training, was very young, and just taken from on ship board, it was admitted, he made an excellent race, manifesting fine speed, wind and bottom.

"Kochlani: An Arabian horse of the tribe bred on the borders of Syria — he was a chestnut horse, and selected from the stables of the Sultan Mahmoud, in Constantinople; and presented by him, to Mr.

Rhind, minister plenipotentiary from the United States, to that court: he was sold for the benefit of the said United States in New York, in May 1831, for $450.

"Lindsay's Arabian: Called also 'Ranger'. 'About the year 1777, or 1778, Gen. H. Lee, of the American Cavalry, and his officers, had their attention drawn to some uncommon fine Eastern horses employed in the public service; horses of such superior form and appearance, that the above officers were led to make much enquiry respecting their history, and this proved so extraordinary, that Capt. Lyndsay was sent to examine and make more particular enquiry respecting the fine cavalry which had been so much admired; with instructions, that if the sire answered the description which had been given of him, the Captain was authorized to purchase him, if to be sold.

" 'The Captain succeeded in purchasing the horse, which was taken to Virginia, where he covered mares at an exceedingly high price, and with very considerable success. It was not until this very fine horse became old and feeble, that the writer of these recollections rode thirty miles expressly to see him. He was a white horse, of the most perfect form and symmetry, rather above 15 hands high, and although very old and crippled, appeared to possess high and gallant temper, which gave him a lofty and commanding carriage and appearance.

" 'The history of this horse, as given to me during the Revolutionary War, by several very highly respectable persons from the State of Connecticut, at various times, is —

" 'For some very important service rendered by the commander of a British Frigate to the son of the Emperor of Morocco, the Emperor presented this horse (by far the most valuable of his whole stud) to the captain, who shipped him on board the Frigate with the sanguine expectation of obtaining a great price for him, if safely landed in England. Either in obedience to orders or some other cause, the Frigate called at one of the West India Islands, where, being obliged to remain some time, the Captain in compassion to the horse, landed him for the purpose of giving him exercise. No convenient (securely enclosed) place could be obtained but a large lumber yard, into which the horse was turned loose. Delighted and playful as a kitten, his liberty soon proved fatal to him. He ascended one of the piles, from which and with it, he fell and broke three of his legs. At this time in the same harbor, the English Captain met an old acquaintance from our now Eastern States. To him he offered the horse, as an animal of inestimable value, could he be cured. The Eastern captain gladly accepted of the horse, and knowing he must be detained a considerable time in the Island before he could dispose of his assorted cargo, got the horse on board his own vessel, secured him in slings, and very carefully set and bound up his broken legs. It matters not how long he remained in the harbour, or if quite cured before he arrived on our shore; but he did arrive, and he must certainly have covered mares several seasons before he was noticed as first mentioned. He was landed in Connecticut in 1766, then 4 years of age. His stock was very valuable, and many capital Race Horses, and brood mares descended from him. In Connecticut he was called "Ranger." (Signed) F.'

"From the *American Farmer*.

"Mouse Colored Arabian: Nothing is known of this horse except his name.

"Numidia: Nothing is known of this horse except his name.

"Ranger: (Alias Lyndsay's Arabian.)

"Selim: A grey horse, presented by Murad Bey to the late Gen. Sir Ralph Abercrombie, Bart. of the British Army, who rode him into the field of battle at Aboukir, in Egypt, and got mortally wounded on him. He was afterwards sold to Commodore Baron, of the United States Navy, and by him brought into the United States, and afterwards sold to Col. John Tayloe, of Va. we have been informed. He got some capital formed stock.

"Pedigree. — He was got by Achmet — his dam an Abysinian Mare.

"Selladin: 'An elegant and full-blooded Arabian horse imported during the summer of 1820, from Tripoli, by his owner, Richard B. Jones, Esq. late American Consul to that place; Mr. J. selected him with the greatest care and attention from the whole stud of the Bashaw, and by the certificate of Abraham Serrusi, the Bashaw's public Secretary, was declared to be of the highest Arabian race ever imported into Barbary.

" 'Pedigree. His sire Kaled, was imported from the kingdom of Sennaar; his dam Garrind, was selected from the stables of the Emperor of Morocco, and sent as a present to the Bashaw of Tripoli — foaled in 1815. (From a printed advertisement) Halifax County, N. C. 1823. Richard B. Jones, J. S. Shepherd'.

"Spot: 'Imported by Major Formley, of Va. New Jersey printed Advertisement, 1830'.

"Stamboul: A chestnut horse; an Arabian of the tribe called 'Uegdi'. He was selected from the stables of the Sultan, Mahmoud, in Constantinople, and presented to the late Mr. Rhind, Minister from the United States to that Court. He was sold for the benefit of the United States at $575.

"Syphax: A sorrel horse imported from Tunis in the United States Frigate *Constitution*, 1824.

"Taurus: A dun horse imported by the late General Eaton, of North Carolina.

"Winters' Arabian: A white horse 14 hands one inch high; a superior formed animal and an excellent foal getter. He was sent to the late King of England as a present from the port of St. Louis, on the Senegal River, but got captured on his passage to England by the *Grampus* Privateer, on board the Transport Brig *Doris,* in 1814, and brought into Marblehead, where he was sold to Elisha J. Winter, late Member of Congress and carried out to Kentucky.

"Yemen: A grey horse, an Arabian of the tribe of the Desert nearest Aleppo, presented also by Sultan Mahmoud to Mr. Rhind, and sold for the benefit of the United States in 1831, for $535.

"Yourouk: A mountain Arabian horse. Nothing except his name is known.

"Zilcaadi: A chestnut horse, an Arabian of the tribe on the borders of Syria. He was likewise presented by the Sultan to Mr. Rhind, and was sold for the benefit of the United States, for $430.

Chapter 8

A. Keene Richards, A Kentucky Thoroughbred Breeder, Imports Arabian Horses

A BOUT 1850, one of the leading Thoroughbred breeders in the United States was a Mr. A. Keene Richards of Georgetown, Kentucky near Lexington, the Thoroughbred horse-breeding center of the world.

He was considered a very thorough student of horse-breeding and pedigrees, and from his studies, he became convinced that the Thoroughbred of that day would be improved by an outcross with Arabian stallions. His belief was probably influenced by his knowledge of the breeding history of the Byerly Turk, the Darley Arabian and the Godolphin Arabian. Mr. Richards decided to try using Arabian stallions in his own breeding operations.

At the time, one of the leading racing associations was the New Orleans Jockey Club of which Mr. Richards was probably a member, since he raced his horses at their meetings. He convinced this organization that it would be to the interest of Thoroughbred breeders to procure pure-bred Arab stallions, and the Club cooperated with him when he made the second of two trips to the Arabian desert countries.

A. Keene Richards, A Kentucky Thoroughbred
Breeder, Imports Arabian Horses

Mr. Richards' first trip was made in 1851 to 1853 and the second in 1855 to 1856. He is reported to have been the first American to go directly to the source to import pure-bred Arab stallions to the United States. On his second trip, he was accompanied by Mr. E. Troye, the noted animal painter, by his cousin, M. H. Keene and by a Syrian who was an interpreter and an Arabian horse expert. Soon after their arrival, the Syrian died and Mr. Richards had to spend the next seven months learning Arabic in order to deal with the Bedouins.

His first importation consisted of two stallions and one mare, and the second consisted of three stallions and one mare. The horses were: Sacklowie, a bay stallion bred by the Anayza Bedouin; Sadah, a gray mare; Lulie, an Arab mare in foal to Ahzees Pasha's chestnut Arabian, Bagdad; Fysaul, a chestnut stallion; Hamdan, a gray Arabian stallion; Massoud, a chestnut stallion; and Mokladi, a gray stallion. All are recorded in early American stud books.

The first offspring from the mating of these five stallions with Thoroughbred mares was so impressive that, by 1857, Mr. Richards had decided to offer their services to other owners of Thoroughbred mares. Within a couple of years after this the Civil War threatened and naturally, interest in horse-breeding was greatly curtailed, and Mr. Richards' five stallions never had the great influence they might have had under different circumstances.

Mr. Richards first bred five Thoroughbred mares to the best of his Arab stallions and from the first group of colts came the great race horse, Limestone. Another one became the dam of the famous Dorsey's Golddust. Two or three mares in the highly successful stud of General W. T. Withers of Kentucky were sired by one of Keene Richards' Arabs and Withers considered them to be his finest brood mares.

Mr. Richards' own comments on his experiences in importing these Arabian horses are interesting:

"I determined to import the best Arabs that could be found in the East and cross them with our best mares. I made myself acquainted with the modern importations by going to England, France, and Spain, and examining the best Arabs belonging to these governments, visiting Morocco, and going through the interior of Algeria. I went to Tunis, thence to Egypt, and from Egypt through Arabian Perta and the desert east of Damascus as far as Palmyra. During this tour I selected Mokhladi, Massaoud and a grey mare, the first mentioned bred by the Tarabine tribe in Arabia Petra, and the latter by the Anayza tribe.

"They arrived safely, and I immediately made arrangements to select some of our best mares to breed to them. The result was quite equal to my expectations, and I commenced preparing to make another trip to the East, determining to spare no trouble or expense in procuring the best blood, as well as the finest formed horses in the desert.

"For two years I made this subject my study, consulting the best authors as to where the purest blood was to be found, and comparing their views with my own experiences. I found that most authors who have written on the subject differ materially as to the facts; and that those who have seen the Arab on his native soil know more about the idle legends of the country than about the fine points of a horse.

"The first horse selected was a stallion from Beni-Zahr. This was a horse of superior form and blood, purchased from one of the Sheikhs of the tribe. Determined to have the best, this horse was afterwards exchanged for the bay horse 'Sacklowie' [Seglawi] by giving considerable boot. This last importation consisted of the bay 'Sacklowie, a chestnut "Faysal," ' supposed to be the best young horse in the Anayza tribe, a grey colt two years old, a mare and two dromedaries.

"In making both of these importations I determined not to offer the services of any of the stallions to the public until they had shown some evidence of their merits. The colts of two of them having borne off the prizes last fall [1856] over the best Thoroughbred stock in Kentucky, I was induced by some friends not to wait longer, but to give the breeders of Kentucky an opportunity to try the cross with some of our fine mares."

Chapter 9

Imported Arabian Horses And Mares Registered In The American Stud Book

THE American Stud Book, commonly known as the Jockey Club Stud Book, has been published by the American Jockey Club since 1873. The first compiler of The American Stud Book was S. D. Bruce, editor of *The Turf, Field and Farm,* and the first edition was in two volumes.

The Arabian horses and mares imported into the United States up to 1872 were registered in Volume I. Also registered in Volume I were Barbs and Spanish horses, but as previously mentioned, we are including the Barb and Spanish horses along with the Arabians.

The principal reason that these Arabian horses and mares, as registered, are here listed is because most of them were used by many different owners to improve native horses, their stud records are scattered, and their histories may be lost unless this stock of information is noted. The following is from The American Stud Book, Vol. I, 1873, under the chapter heading "Imported Arab, Barb and Spanish Horses and Mares":

"IMPORTED ARABIAN HORSES.

"Abdallah — An imported Arabian horse, first carried to Gibraltar from Arabia, thence imported into Beaufort, Port Royal, S. C., by Capt. Barnes, in the year 1767.

"Arab — His color and character are unknown.

"Arab Barb — Vide Black Arabian Barb.

"Arabian — A cream-colored horse.

"Amurath — Was brought from Tripoli, in Barbary and imported into New York, in the year 1833, then one year old. He was brought from Nubia to Tripoli, 1832.

"Bagdad — A beautiful brown bay horse . . . [See Chapter 7, under "Bagdad" for further information.]

"Ballasteros — A beautiful dark brown Arabian horse . . . [See Chapter 7, under "Ballasteros" for further information.]

"Barbarossa — a gray horse (it is believed) and a horse of fine form, action, and shape; fourteen hands three inches high. 1819.

"Belsize Arabian — Imported . . . [See Chapter 7, under "Belsize Arabian" for further information.]

"Black Arabian Barb — called also 'Arab Barb' . . . [See Chapter 7, under "Black Arabian Barb" for further information.]

"Bussorah Arabian — So-called, but was evidently a Persian . . . [See Chapter 7, under "Bussorah Arabian" for further information.]

"Cardoza — A chestnut horse . . . [See Chapter 7, under "Cardozo" for further information.]

"Croucher — An Arab horse of the most beautiful kind. Virginia, 1825.

"Dey of Algiers — He was an elegantly formed horse . . . [See Chapter 7, under "Dey of Algiers" for further information.]

"Fysaul — ch. h. Fourteen and three-quarters hands high, an Arab stallion from Nesjd, of the Koheyle and Sacklowie races, foaled 1852; purchased in the desert from the Bedouin who bred him, and imported by A. Keene Richards, Esq., of Kentucky, in 1856.

"Grand Bashaw — An elegant Arabian horse . . . [See Chapter 7, under "Grand Bashaw" for further information.]

"Grand Sultan — He was an excellent full-blooded Arabian horse . . . [See Chapter 7, under "Grand Sultan" for further information.]

"Hamdan — Gray Arab stallion from Nesjd, of the pure Koheyle race, foaled 1854, purchased in the desert from a Sheik of the Rouibah tribe of Bedouins, and imported by A. Keene Richards, in 1856. Stood the season of 1859 and '60 at the stables of Dr. Feris, Richmond, Texas. A gray colt, one year old, the finest that could be found in the tribe, was purchased, and as he is of the Koheylan blood, and the stock from which he came

HANAD No. 489. Famous chestnut stallion doing the Spanish walk.

had been in the family of the Sheik from whom he was purchased for more than three hundred years, the pedigree or certificate is here given as a specimen of the pedigree of the oldest races in the tribe. Died at Dr. Feris', 1861.

Ramadon 21, 1272

" 'This is to certify, That, at the date of this document, Messrs. Keene and Troye bought from Sheik Hammed, Esq., Sohiman, the son of Shalan, the gray horse, even the horse of Hammed, son of Sohiman, who is the son of Shalan, even the Sheik of the Arabs of Anayza. The said horse is Koheylan, the son of the old Koheylan father, and of an old Koheylan mother. We declare this by fortune, to which God, and Mahomed, the Apostle of God, are witnesses. There is no better horse, being from the side of both father and mother a blood horse. He is a Koheylan, the son of a Koheylan, and his mother is Koheylan purer than milk. He was born and brought up in the land of Nesjd.

" 'This is the genealogy of the said horse. God is omnipotent.

" 'The sale was made at the land of Sophira. (Seal.) Hammed Es. Sohiman, the son of Shalan.

" 'Witnesses: The writer of this document, who stands in need of God.
      ARD-ALLAH, the son of Nowphal, the Lecturer.
      MAHAMMAD, the son of Mashial.
      AKHBIEF, the son of Mashaul.
      ISH-SHE-RA-TAH, agent of Fysal-Ish-Shalaa.
                United States Consulate, Beyroot, June 12, 1856.

" 'This is to certify, That the above is a correct and true translation of the original document attached to it. (Seal.) Henry Wood, Consul'.

"Ibrahim Pacha — This beautiful Arab horse was obtained by Commodore Elliott from the Neapolitan Consul at Joppa, Palestine, in the summer of 1835, and imported by him in the corvette *John Adams*, August, 1836. He is a dark iron-gray, with a silvery mane and tail; is fifteen hands high and seven years old; he is closely and compactly formed, with elastic and graceful gait, showing the sinew and muscle so peculiar to the famous Merlano breed. Pedigree: The pedigree of this horse is in the original Arabic, with a translation attested by the Consular Seal of the American Consul at Jerusalem, and is in possession of Commodore Elliott:

CASSIM No. 2556, at 10 years of age.

INDRAFF A.H.C. No. 1575. Champion gray Arabian stallion.

" 'We, the undersigned, do declare that the horse which Mr. Elliott, American Commodore, bought from us, is a Merlano of the Bedouin horses, of the race of Sirbaa, and, in consequence, this declaration is written for the Commodore, so that he may be satisfied that the said horse is really Bedouin; in faith of which we give the present affirmation. (Signed) ACHMED EL SAID MASTIFANI. ACHMED EL EBAB.

" 'I, the undersigned, do testify that the horse above mentioned, which Commodore Elliott bought at Joppa, is a Bedouin horse, of a famous Merlano race, and in consequence I hereby give the present testimonial. (Seal.) MURAD ARTIN, Jucaricato, as American Consul for Joppa and Jerusalem, Joppa, 15 Gerwad Acher, 1252'.

"Ishmael — A gray horse brought from Mecca; imported by the late General Eaton, of North Carolina.

"Jones' Arabian — He was a dappled gray horse . . . [See Chapter 7, under "Jones Arabian" for further information.]

"Kochlani — An Arabian horse . . . [See Chapter 7, under "Kochlani" for further information.]

"Lindsay's Arabian (called also Ranger) . . . [See Chapter 7, under "Lindsay's Arabian" for further information.]

"Maanake Hedgrogi — " 'Consulate of the United States for Syria and Palestine, Beyroot, April 30, 1860

" 'I, the undersigned, Ayoub Bey Trabulsi, hereby declare that the Red Horse sent by me to Hon. W. H. Seward is between seven and eight years old. His offspring is excellent. The Arabs used him, when in their possession, for propagating the race, charging five camels for each time when they allowed him to be used for that purpose. (Signed) AYOUB BEY TRABULSI, Assistant of the Court of Saidei District'.

"Massoud — ch. h. fifteen hands high, an Arab stallion, from the Anayza tribe, foaled 1844; imported by A. Keene Richards, Esq., in 1853; died of lung fever, September 25, 1859.

"Mazyouble (Delight of the Eye) — Imported Arabian stallion; a gray horse, imported in 1836, by Mr. Willshire. His sire was a full-blooded Arabian, his dam the best blooded Barb of the Abdah breed. He stood at Georgetown, Ky., and at Dayton, Ohio.

"Mensor — An Arabian from Cabila, in the territory of Mequina; after the bombardment of Tangier, the Bashaw presented this horse to the Neapolitan Minister. Certified by Thos. N. Carr, Con.-Gen. U. S. at Tangier, Morocco.

"Mokhladi — gr. h., fourteen and a half hands high, an Arab stallion from the Tarabine tribe of Bedouins, in Arabia Petra; foaled 1844; imported by A. Keene Richards, Esq., in 1853.

"Mouse-Colored Arabian — Nothing is known of this horse except his name.

"Numedia — Nothing is known of this horse except his name.

"Ombark (in English, Imcomparable) — Imported by Capt. Jas. Riley, Swearah, in Africa; a black horse, fifteen and a quarter hands high. Ombark was bred in the country of Bled el Tedlah, by Bashaw Cidi Ben, Abd-Allah, south of the Atlas Mountains, near Tunis El Gaarb, and from the purest and most celebrated Arabian blood. His Arabian pedigree is very long, and has been translated into English to go with the horse, when sold. He is a good stallion, and believed to be very swift.

"Sacklowie — A mahogany bay, fifteen hands high, bred by the Anayza Bedouin, foaled 1851, imported 1856. He was the choice of Mr. E. Troye, the celebrated animal painter, over all the stallions he saw in the East. Imported by A. Keene Richards, Esq., Georgetown, Scott County, Ky. Died 1860.

"Sebastopol — A handsome gray, with black legs, mane and tail. Stood

RAFAYL A.H.C. No. 2693. Ch/B Arabian stallion. Twin to the mare RAFAYA No. 2692.

at Thomas J. Holton's, Covington, Ky., 1859. Pedigree: Sebastopol was bred by the Shammar tribe of Bedouins, in that part of Arabia bordering on the valley of the Euphrates; was purchased, when a colt, by Lieut. Wadsworth, of the 12th Royal (British) Lancers, taken to India, and subsequently 'packed' his owner by the overland route across the Desert to the Crimea, where he was bought by Major Robertson, Aid-de-Camp to Lieut.-General Sir William Eyre, K.C.B. He served through the war in the Crimea as Major Robertson's charger, doing a vast amount of severe work, and undergoing great privations. He proved himself a thoroughly game, staunch, hardy horse. After the fall of Sebastopol, Sir William Eyre and Staff were ordered to Canada, and Major Robertson brought Sebastopol with him. He landed at Montreal fresh and hearty. During the spring of 1858, Major Robertson was ordered to England, and the present proprietor of the horse was so pleased with his fine form

111

and spirited action that he purchased him from Major Robertson, under warranty as a thoroughbred Arab of the purest blood and highest caste.

"Selim — A gray horse . . . [See Chapter 7, under "Selim" for further information.]

"Selladin, or Salladin — An elegant and full-blooded Arabian horse . . . [See Chapter 7, under "Selladin" for further information.]

"Sheriff Pacha — In the summer of 1837, being on the coast of Northern Syria, Commodore Elliott, in pursuance of orders from the Navy Department, and prompted by a commendable Zeal to improve the breed of horses in the United States, procured a thoroughbred Arabian of the Nadji breed from an agent of the Governor or Viceroy of Northern Syria, 'Sheriff Pacha'. The horse referred to is a stallion, 5 years old, and of a rich bay color, standing fifteen and a half hands high, of fine bone and finish. He bears a strong resemblance to the high-mettled racer of 'the race-horse region,' and there can be no doubt that he is what he is certified to be, a real Nadji — the most celebrated breed in Syria. The experienced judge of the race-horse will detect at a glance, and be immediately impressed with the idea, and convinced of the purity of his origin. No formal pedigree need be offered to the observer of this superior animal, for, without these, nature has so impressed her seal that they would not be required; but, fortunately, the most authentic are given, attested by the American Consul's seal at Damascus. Mustapha Aga, of Damascus, purchased this horse of Kage Ali, the Alepine, who procured him of an Arab of Atrah. A great many testimonials are given by the Arabs of Dawleh, the neighbors of the Araba of Atrah, each of whom concurs that he is a real Nadji. He stood in Tennessee.

"Siklany Gidran —

" 'Consulate of the United States for Syria and Palestine, Beyroot, April 30, 1860.

" 'I, the undersigned, Ayoub Bey Trabulsi, hereby declare that the light-colored colt sent by me to Hon. W. H. Seward is of the Arab race, and is called Siklany Gidran, being two years and two months old; he requires to be broken and trained. His hind hoofs are, as yet, without shoes, according to the custom of the Arabs in cases of colts. After the 14th of September he should be shod, as he is then to be used for the first time for riding. I think that the Hon. Mr. Seward will have him for his private use. When he gets to be four years old, he could be used for propagating the race, as he is of the best race, as above stated. (Signed) AYOUB BEY TRABULSI, Assistant of the Court of Saidei District.'

"Spot — Imported by Major Wormley, of Virginia.

"Stamboul — A chestnut horse . . . [See Chapter 7, under "Stamboul" for further information.]

"Syphax — A sorrel horse, imported from Tunis in the United States frigate *Constitution,* 1824.

"Taurus — A dun horse, imported by the late General Eaton, of North Carolina.

"Winter's Arabian — A white horse . . . (See Chapter 7, under "Winter's Arabian" for further information.]

"Yeman — A gray horse, an Arabian of the tribe of the desert nearest Aleppo, presented also by Sultan Mahmoud to Mr. Rhind, and sold for the benefit of the United States, in 1831, for $535.

"Yourouk — A mountain Arabian horse. Nothing is known except his name.

"Zilcaadi — A chestnut horse — an Arabian of the tribe on the borders of Syria. He was likewise presented by the Sultan to Mr. Rhind, and was sold for the benefit of the United States, for $430.

"IMPORTED ARABIAN MARES.

"Com. Elliott's Imported Mares. — The following is a list and description of some Arabian mares imported by Commodore Jesse D. Elliott, in the summer of 1838, procured on the coast of Syria during a cruise in the summer of 1837, in the frigate *Constitution*:

"Lady Hester — A bay mare; was got by a Bedouin horse of Gaza, of the Adilia strain of blood; purchased in Joffa in 1836. She was tried in a race at the Island of Minorca, and, in running with one hundred and twenty-eight pounds ten ounces, she distanced the fastest Andalusian horse in the Island of Minorca.

"Lady Mary — A black mare, 5 years old, purchased at Damascus in 1837; was got by the Arabian Selawee Gediawee, named Mehkeeby, out of a celebrated bay mare called El Jilgah, with her filly foal. This mare is stinted to Com. Elliott's full-blooded Arabian Sheriff Pacha.

"Lady Stanhope — Gray mare; is a Merlano of the race of Hegagi, seven years old; purchased at Joffa in 1836; is a dam of the bay horse called Constitution, and the Andalusian filly Miss Catherine, now in foal to Sheriff Pacha, and is the same referred to in the Turf Register of May, 1837.

"Andalusian mare, Spanish blood, iron-gray, four years old, foaled at Herrys, and purchased at Gibraltar in 1838.

"A bay colt, foal of the gray mare Lady Stanhope, foaled 11th of April, 1837, in the Island of Minorca.

"Miss Catherine — The foal of Lady Isabella, got by a thoroughbred Arabian of Damascus; foaled spring of 1838 at Minorca.

"A dark iron-gray filly, Miss Catherine, the foal of the gray mare Lady Stanhope; got by a full blooded Andalusian horse, who was got by a horse that Bonaparte permitted the Queen of Spain, when he took possession of that country, to send to the Island of Minorca.

"The above mentioned animals are now on the estate of Samuel G. Barr, Boonville, Mo., where they will be bred on shares to Commodore and Mr. Barr. 1839.

"Esnea — Bay Arabian mare, imported by Wm. McDonald, Esq., Baltimore, Md.

"Produce: 1860, ch. f. Lady Guilford by Revenue.
         1864, — c. by Burlington (trotter).

"Lulie — Arab mare, imported 1856, by A. Keene Richards, Esq., Kentucky; bred by the Anayza Arabs of the pure Koheyl race. This mare was imported in foal by Ahzees Pasha's Chestnut Arab Bagdad.

"Produce: 1857, lost colt foal by Ahzees Pasha's Bagdad.
         1858, lost foal by Lexington.
         1859, missed to Bonnie Laddie.
         1860, missed to Knight of St. George.
         1861, gr. f. Mahah by imported Arab Fysaul.
         1865, ch. f. by imported Mickey Free.
         1866, gr. f. Hopsie by imported Mickey Free.
         gr. f. Kaffeah by Arab Fysaul.

"Sadah — Gray mare, imported in 1853 by A. Keene Richards, Esq., Kentucky, from the Anayza tribe of Bedouins.

"Produce: 1853, gr. c. Boherr, foaled at sea, between the ports of Liverpool and New Orleans.
         1854, gr. f. Zahah by imported Arab Mokhladi.
         1855, missed to imported Arab Massoud.
         1856, gr. c. Abdel-Kader by imported Mokhladi.
         1857, ch. c. Yusef by imported Arab Massoud, Sam'l Townsend, Mississippi.
         1858, missed to Fysaul.
         1859, missed to Fysaul.
         1860, gr. c. by Knight of St. George.
         1861, gr. f. Haik by imported Arab Fysaul.
         1864, gr. f. by imported Mickey Free.
         1866, — by imported Mickey Free.

"Saieda — Grey Arabian mare, imported by Wm. McDonald, Esq., Baltimore, Md. Produce: 1859, gr. c. Guilford by Revenue.

"Zahah — Grey mare, foaled 1854, bred by A. Keene Richards, Esq.; got by imported Arab Mokhladi, out of imported Arab mare Sadah. Produce: 1860, bl. c. by Knight of St. George."

Volume III of The American Stud Book contained not only those Thoroughbred horses bred in the United States and imported up to the year 1878, but also the registration of a small group of six head of Arabs and Barbs that were imported after Volume II of the Stud Book was completed and up until Volume III was published. A description of the horses imported follows:

"IMPORTED ARABS AND BARBS.

"Black Sultan (now Emperor) — bl. h. foaled 1868, 15 hands high, with white fetlocks behind, three black and one white hoof. Presented to the Emperor of Morocco by the French Ambassador during an official mission at Fez in 1871. Purchased and imported by P. W. Scott, late U. S. Consul at Tangier, who imported him into New York on the steamship *Assyria,* of the Anchor Line, September 16, 1873; owned by John B. Hall, Toronto, Can.

"Cossack (The Noland Arabian) — gr. h., foaled 1850; purchased in the Syrian Desert by Capt. Noland, of the 15th Royal (British) Hussars, from 'Schelas,' of the Serhan tribe of Bedouins; imported by Gen. Eyre; owned by Company of Cincinnati, Ohio, 1858. This horse was of pure Bedouin blood, of the 'Keboyshan' breed, and was considered by Capt. Noland as one of the finest and purest bred horses in Syria.

"Coxe's Arabian — ch. h., of the best caste, called Dashley, 15¼ hands high; imported from Tunis in 1816 by Charles D. Coxe, Consul for the United States for that place, by special permission of the Bey of Tunis. Stood at Cincinnati in 1820. He was the sire of Bey of Tunis, Mahomet, and other winners.

"Ibn Mosk — Bay h., foaled 1875, imported by W. H. Wilson, Kentucky, in 1876. By Chouerman (Arab).

"1st dam Eng. bred mare, Musk by Newcourt.
"2nd dam Marpesia by Annandale.
"3rd dam Margery by Voltaire.
"4th dam Proserpine by Rhadamanthus.
"5th dam by Sir Peter.
"6th dam Eaton Lass by Pot-8-o's.
"7th dam by Highflyer.
"8th dam by Snap.
"9th dam Chalkstone's dam by Shepherd's Crab.
"10th dam Miss Meredith by Cade.
"11th dam Little Hartley Mare by Bartlett's Childers.
"12th dam Flying Whig by Woodstock Arabian.

"13th dam by St. Victor Barb.

"14th dam by Why Not.

"15th dam Royal Mare.

"Koheyl Tajar — br. h., foaled April, 1872, bred by his Majesty King of Wurtemburg. By Tajar 5th, he by Tajar 4th (son of Amurath and grandson of Barakthar), out of Daria by Chaban 2nd (son of Amurath out of Mara 4th), Koheyl Tajar's dam Koheyl by Burun; 2d dam Saida (original Arab) Burun by Amurath out of Beckow 4th (son of Bairaktar (original Arab) out of Saida 3d, Beckow 4th by Harif (original Arab) out of Beckow 3d; imported and owned by Dr. Otto Prisoni, Nebraska.

"Lulie — Arab mare, imported 1856, by A. Keene Richards, Esq., Kentucky, bred by the Anayza Arabs of the pure Koheyl race. This mare was imported in foal by Ahzees Pasha's Chestnut Arab Bagdad.

"Produce: 1857, lost colt by Ahzees Pasha's Bagdad.

1858, lost foal by Lexington.

1859, missed to Bonnie Laddie.

1860, missed to Knight of St. George.

1861, gr. f. Kaffeah by imported Arab Fysaul.

1865, missed to imported Mickey Free.

1866, gr. f. Hopsie by imported Mickey Free.

1867, gr. f. Maha by Arab Fysaul.

"Corrected from Vol. I."

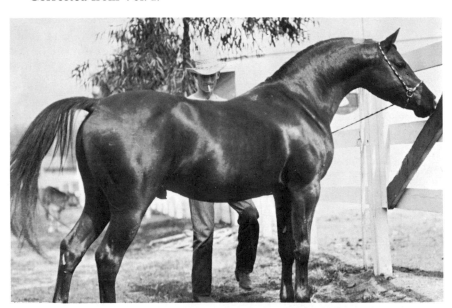

RASRAFF No. 2365. Arabian stallion at 6 years of age.

Volume IV of The American Stud Book, which is principally concerned with registering Thoroughbred horses both native-bred and imported, was published in 1884 and registers horses up to the close of the year 1883. The following five Arabian horses were imported during the interval between the publication of Volume III and Volume IV:

"IMPORTED ARABS.

"Leopard — gr. h., foaled 1872; bred by the Sultan of Turkey, and by him presented to Gen. U. S. Grant; owned by J. B. Houston, New York, 1883.

"Linden Tree — gr. h., foaled 1875; bred by the Sultan of Turkey, and by him presented to Gen. U. S. Grant; owned by U. S. Grant, Jr., New York.

"Peter the Great — gr. Arab, by Sultan; imported by William Easton, New York, 1881.

"Esnea — Arabian mare; purchased in Damascus, Syria, and imported by the late William McDonald, of Guilford, Baltimore; light bay in color, white face, and three white feet, extending above pasterns; owned by J. W. Garrett, Montebello, Md. See vol. 1, page 149.

"Produce: 1860, ch. f. Lady Guilford by Revenue.

        1864, b. c. Young Burlington by Burlington. (Trotter.)

        1866, b. f. Zoe by imported Bonnie Scotland.

        1869, b. c. Saladin by Daniel the Prophet.

        1870, b. c. Selim by Harper's Virginian.

        1874, ch. c. Damascus by Hamlet. (Trotter.)

"Damascus was sent as a present to the King of Italy in June, 1876. Damascus was her last foal. She died in 1876. Her skeleton is in the museum at New Haven, Conn.

"Saieda — gr. Arabian mare; purchased in Damascus, Syria, and imported by the late William McDonald, Guilford, Baltimore, Md.; owned by John W. Garrett, Montebello, Md. Vol. I, page 150.

"Produce: 1859, gr. c. Guilford by Revenue.

        1864, gr. c. Adniack by Burlington. (Trotter.)

        1875, gr. f. Sultana by Bashaw, Jr. (Trotter.)

        1877, gr. f. Gulnare by Saladin.

"Mare died in 1882. Skeleton at Druid Hill Park, Baltimore, Md."

Volume VII of The American Stud Book was published in 1898, and listed registration, description and breeding of four Arabian stallions and four Arabian mares. While some of these horses have already found their way into the Arabian Horse Registry as foundation animals, several of them did not produce any pure-bred offspring, therefore the only information available is that contained in this volume:

"Bekboolat — ch. Arab horse, foaled 1882; bred at the Streletsky Stud, Russia; imported by Grand Duke Dimitry for exhibition at Chicago Fair 1893; owned by William P. Dixon, New York City. By Bacchus, son of Bourny and Obrastzovaya by Obejan Szerebreuny, pure blood Arabian of the Abeyan family. 1st dam Ismennitza (Orloff saddle mare) by Iney son of Ibrahim and Farssa (descendant of Favorit). 2nd dam Dobraya by Jerit, imp. English thoroughbred.

"Gouniad — ch. h., foaled 1889; imported July 27, 1893; owned by H. K. Bush Brown, Newburg, N. Y. By imp. Arab Hussar.

"1st dam Egoistka by imp. Arab Eshref.

"2nd dam Ptashka by Pasha (Obmen).

"3rd dam Belta by Beztsenny.

"4th dam Eureclike by imp. Arab Efir.

RUFFLES A.H.C. No. 3254. Gray Arabian stallion.

"5th dam Manzhetka.

"6th dam Tabauraia by Magmiad Baiarkhan. (Imp. Arab).

"7th dam Opuntsia by Takhteiwan Trukhmiansky.

"Naomi — The Keheilan Arab mare, (a Maneghi-Hedrudj) ch. m., foaled 1877. Naomi was imported to England in utero, from the Euphrates valley, by Capt. Roger D. Upton, of the 9th Royal Lancers. After his death, she was purchased by Rev. F. F. Vidal, of Needham Market, England, from whom she was bought and imported to the United States in 1888, by Randolph Huntington. By Yataghan, pure Arab. See vol. 6, page 1164. 1st dam Haidee, a ch. mare of the Maneghi-Hedrudj family.

"Produce: 1892, b. c. Boaz Clay by Huntington's Young Jack Shepherd.

1894, ch. c. Nejd by Anazeh (Arab).

1895, ch. c. Kahled by Nimr (Arab).

Not bred in 1885-'9. Barren in 1893.

"Nazli — Chestnut Arab mare, foaled 1888; bred by Rev. F. F. Vidal; imported and owned by Randolph Huntington, Oyster Bay, L. I. By Maidan (Arabian). 1st dam Naomi by Yataghan. 2nd dam Haidee Arabian of the Maneghi-Hedrudj family. See vol. 6, page 1164.

"Produce: 1891, ch. c. Nimr by Kismet (Arabian).

1895, ch. f. Naarah by Anazeh (Arab).

"Nedjme — gr. m., foaled 1881; bred by Hadje Memmed, Damascus, Syria. Imported 1893 to Chicago, by the Hamidie Society, owned by J. A. P. Ramsdell, Hamlock Glen, Newburg, N. Y. By a Seglawi Jedran sire, dam a Keheilet Ajuz mare.

"Produce: 1895, b. c. Alhama by imp. Henry.

1896, dk. gr. c. Nogailah by Nimr.

1897, r. f. Alruna by Shahwan.

"Rakusheh — Bay Arab mare, foaled 1889; bred by Miss Dillon; imported 1893, and owned by J. A. P. Ramsdell, Hamlock Glen, Newburg, N. Y. By El Emir (an Arab). See vol. 6, page 1164. 1st dam Raschida (Arab) by Kars (Arab). 2nd dam Wild Thyme, an Arab mare of the Kehileh Rasel Fedawi tribe, and bred by the Beggara tribe of the Euphrates.

"Produce: 1893, b. f. by Maidan (Arab).

1894, b. c. Rahman (imp. in utero) by Jamrood.

1895, b. c. Roala by Anazeh (Arab).

"Seglawi — Chestnut Arab horse, foaled 1881, of the well-known blood of Seglawel Jedran, and bred from Anizeh tribe stock, the breeders living in the desert north of Arabia; sold to Pickering Clark, by Sheik Esan bin Curtas in 1886; owned by William P. Dixon, New York City.

"Shahwan — White horse, foaled 1887; a Dahman Shahwan of the strain of Ibn, Khalifeh Sheykh of Behreyn; bred by Ali Pacha Sherif; dam's gran dam, the mare of Ibn Khalifeh; sire Wazir, the celebrated Seglawi Jedran; bred by Ali Pacha Sherif. Imported and owned by J. A. P. Ramsdell, Hemlock Glen, Newburg, N. Y."

Volume IX of The American Stud Book was published in 1906 and registered in this volume are two stallions and eight mares. These are principally Arabians and represent the importation of Spencer Borden of Fall River, Massachusetts. Some of these will be found in the Arabian Horse Registry, but there seems to be more complete and detailed information about them in this Volume IX of The American Stud Book, therefore this material is herewith quoted:

SARTEZ No. 2500. Chestnut Arabian stallion, son of ANTEZ. SARTEZ has made a greater number of speed trials in record time than any other Arabian stallion owned or bred in the United States.

"IMPORTED ARABIANS — Stallions.

"Seyyid — ch. h., foaled 1894; imported 1903 and owned by Charles Butters, San Francisco, Calif. By El Emir (Sanad). 1st dam Shiboleth by Kars. 2nd dam Sherifa. See English S. B., vol. 18, page 865.

"Imamzada — b. h., foaled 1891; imported 1905 and owned by Spencer Borden, Fall River, Mass. By Imam. 1st dam Kesia 2nd by Heddud Seglawee-el-abd. 2nd dam Kesia. See English S. B., vol. 18, page 865.

"Mares.

"Antika — ch. m., foaled 1902; imported 1906 and owned by Spencer Borden, Fall River, Mass. By Mesaoud. 1st dam Asfura by Azrek. 2nd dam Queen of Sheba. See English S. B., vol. 20, page 937.

"Mahal — b. m., foaled 1904; imported 1905 and owned by Spencer Borden, Fall River, Mass. By Imamzada. 1st dam Raschida by Kars. 2nd dam Wild Thyme. See English S. B., vol. 20, page 1113.

"Najine — b. m., foaled 1899; bred and owned by J. A. P. Ramsdell, Newburgh, N. Y. By Garaveen. 1st dam Nedjme (see vol. 8, p. 940). Produce: 1905, ch. f. Regan by Bekboolat.

"Nedjme — gr. m., foaled 1881; owned by J. A. P. Ramsdell, Newburgh, N. Y. By a Seglawi Jedran Sire, out of a Kehielet Ajuz mare. See vol. 8, page 940.
"Produce: 1900, gr. c. Yaquis by Garaveen.
1901, gr. f. Natick by Garaveen.
1902, gr. f. Nanshan by Garaveen.
1903, gr. c. Negus by Garaveen.
1905, b. f. Nanda by Garaveen.

"Nessa — b. m., foaled 1905; imported 1905 and owned by Spencer Borden, Fall River, Mass. By Hauran. 1st dam Raschida by Kars. 2nd dam Wild Thyme. See English S. B., vol. 20, page 1113.

"Nonliker — gr. m., foaled 1898; bred and owned by J. A. P. Ramsdell, Newburgh, N. Y. By Shahwan. 1st dam Nedjme (see vol. 8, p. 940) by a Seglawi Jedran Sire. 2nd dam a Kehielet Ajuz mare.
"Produce: 1902, gr. c. Yima by Garaveen.
1903, gr. f. Onrust by Garaveen.
1905, gr. f. Arletta by Garaveen.

"Rose of Sharon — ch. m., foaled 1885; imported 1905 and owned by Spencer Borden, Fall River, Mass. By Hadban. 1st dam Rodania. See English S. B., vol. 20, page 943.

"Produce: 1902, ch. f. Rumeliya by Rejeb.
1906, ch. c. Rodan by Harb.

"Rosetta — ch. m., foaled 1902; imported 1906 and owned by Spencer Borden, Fall River, Mass. By Mesaoud. 1st dam Rosemary by Proximo or Jeroboam. 2nd dam Rodania. See English S. B., vol. 20, page 943."

Volume XI of The American Stud Book was published in 1914 or six years after the Arabian horse breeders in the United States organized the Arabian Horse Club which has now become the Arabian Horse Registry. Registered in Volume II of the American Jockey Club will be found four stallions and nineteen mares. These animals are largely from importations by Spencer Borden, of Fall River, Massachusetts, and by W. R. Brown, of Berlin, New Hampshire. The principal reason for giving this information is that several animals on this list did not produce pure-bred offspring and for that reason did not find their way into the Arabian Horse Club Registry:

"Stallions.

"Abu Zeyd — ch. h., 1904; imported [in 1910] and owned by Herbert J. Brown, Graunkar Stud, Falmouth Foreside, Maine. By Mesaoud. [English Stud Book, vol. 22, page 959.] 1st dam Rose Diamond, by Azrek. 2nd dam Rose of Jericho, by Kars. 3rd dam Rodania, a Keheilet Ajuz.

"Halim — b. h., 1906; imported [in 1908] by Spencer Borden; owned by Capt. Frank Tompkins, Fort Huachuca, Ariz. By Astraled. [English Stud Book, vol. 21, page 894.] 1st dam Hilmyeh, by Ahmar. 2nd dam Bint Helwa, a Seglawieh Jedran.

"Hauran — b. or br. h., 1897; imported [in 1910] and owned by Spencer Borden, Interlachen Stud, Fall River, Mass. By Roustum or Jezail. [English Stud Book, vol. 19, page 901.] 1st dam Hagar, a Keheilet Ajuz.

"Jahil — b. h., 1908; imported [in 1910] by Homer Davenport; owned by Spencer Borden, Interlachen Stud, Fall River, Mass. By Berk. [English Stud Book, vol. 21, page 895.] 1st dam Jalmuda, by Mesaoud. 2nd dam Johara, a Seglawieh Jedran.

"Mares.

"Amra — b., 1906; imported [in 1909] by Spencer Borden; owned by Herbert J. Brown, Graunkar Stud, Falmouth Foreside, Maine. By Feysul. [English Stud Book, vol. 21, Page 892.] 1st dam Abla, by Mesaoud. 2nd dam Asfura, by Azrek. 3rd dam Queen of Sheba, by a Managhy Hedruj.
"Produce: 1911 b. c. Aladdin (died 1913) by Segario.
1912 b. f. Amanita (died 1913) by Segario.
1913 barren.

"Antika — ch. 1902; imported by Spencer Borden; owned by W. R. Brown, Berlin, N. H. By Mesaoud. See vol. 10, page 1274. 1st dam Asfura, by Azrek. 2nd dam Queen of Sheba, by a Managhy Hedruj.
"Produce: 1908 ch. c. [geld.] Raisuli, by Segario.
1909-11 barren.

"Arletta — gr., 1905; bred by J. A. P. Ramsdell; owned by Spencer Borden, Interlachen Stud, Fall River, Mass. By Garaveen. 1st dam Nonliker, by Shahwan. [vol. 9, p. 1073.] 2nd dam Nedjme, a Keheilet Ajuz.
"Produce: 1913 gr. c. Omar, by Abu Zeyd.
1914 covered previous year by a trotter.

"Butheyna — b., 1904; imported [in 1908] and owned by Spencer Borden, Interlachen Stud, Fall River, Mass. By Seyal. [English Stud Book, vol. 21, page 892.] 1st dam Bereyda, by Ahmar. 2nd dam Bozra, by Pharaoh.
"Produce: 1910 br. or b. f. Badoura, by Segario.
1911 barren.
1912 b. c. Boabdil, by Hauran.
1913 b. f. Bathsheba, by Hauran.

"Ghazala — wh., 1896; imported [in 1909] and owned by Spencer Borden, Interlachen Stud, Fall River, Mass. By Ibn Sherara. [English Stud Book, vol. 22, page 955.] 1st dam Bint Helwa, by Aziz.
"Produce: 1911 gr. c. Giaour by Segario.
1912 ch. or gr. f. Guemura, by Segario.
1910-1913 barren.

"Jamila — ch., 1887; imported [in 1893] and owned by W. H. Forbes, Neponset Stud, Readville, Mass. By Roala. [English Stud Book, vol. 18, page 879.] 1st dam Jerboa, a Managhieh Hedruj. 1898 b. f. Beulah 2nd, by Meddler.

"Mahal — b., 1904; imported by Spencer Borden; owned by Capt.

Frank Tompkins, Fort Huachuca, Ariz. By Imamzada. See vol. 10, page 1274. 1st dam Raschida, by Kars. 2nd dam Wild Thyme.
  "Produce: 1912 b. or br. f. Yildez, by Hauran.
    1910-11-13 barren.

  "Nanda — b., 1905; bred by J. A. P. Ramsdell; owned by Herbert J. Brown, Graunkar Stud, Falmouth Foreside, Maine. By Garaveen. 1st dam Nedjme, by a Seglawi Jedran. [Vol. 9, p. 1072.] 2nd dam a Keheilet Ajuz mare.
  "Produce: 1912 b. c. Akhmet, by Abu Zeyd.
    1913 b. f. Matina, by Jahil.

  "Narda 2nd — ch., 1902; imported [in 1910] by F. Lothrop Ames; owned by Herbert J. Brown, Graunkar Stud, Falmouth Foreside, Maine. By Rejeb. [English Stud Book, vol. 22, page 958.] 1st dam Narghileh, by Mesaoud. 2nd dam Nefisa, by Proximo or Hadban. 1909 ch. c. Crabbet, by Rijm.

  "Nazlet — ch. 1900; bred by Randolph Huntington; owned by W. R. Brown, Berlin, N. H. By Kahled. 1st dam Nazli, by Maidan. [See this vol.] 2nd dam Naomi, by Yataghan.
  "Produce: 1911 barren.
    1912 b. or br. f. Narina, by Halim.
    1913 b. or br. f. Nazami, by Hauran.

  "Nazli — ch., 1888; imported and owned by Randolph Huntington, Oyster Bay, N. Y. By Maidan. See vol. 7, page 1128. 1st dam Naomi, by Yataghan. 2nd dam a Haidee Arabian of the Managhieh Hedruj family. 1900 ch. f. Nazlet, by Kahled.

  "Nessa — by Hauran [see vol. 10, page 1274] was not covered in 1909-10-12.

  "Risalda — ch., 1905; imported [in 1911] and owned by Spencer Borden, Interlachen Stud, Fall River, Mass. By Daoud. [English Stud Book, vol. 21, page 898.] 1st dam Risala, by Mesaoud. 2nd dam Ridaa, by Merzuk. 3rd dam Rose of Sharon, by Hadban.
  "Produce: 1912 ch. f. Radha, by Berk (Eng.)
    1913 barren.

  "Rosina — ch., 1908; bred and owned by Spencer Borden, Interlachen Stud, Fall River, Mass. By Segario. 1st dam Rosetta, by Mesaoud. [vol. 10, p. 1275.] 2nd dam Rosemary, by Proximo or Jeroboam.
  "Produce: 1912 b. f. Primrose, by Halim.
    1913 ch. c. Rosario, by Rodan.

"Rumeliya — by Rejeb [see vol. 10, page 1275] was barren in 1910, and died in 1911.

"Shabaka — by Mameluke [see vol. 10, page 1275] died in 1910. Her 1910 foal died.

"Shibine — ch., 1899; imported [in 1910] by F. Lothrop Ames; owned by Herbert J. Brown, Graunkar Stud, Falmouth Foreside, Me. By Mesaoud. [English Stud Book, vol. 22, page 960.] 1st dam Shohba, by Shahwan. 2nd dam Shelfa, by Proximo or Jeroboam. 1910 ch. f. by Ibn Yashmak.

"Vashti — b. or br., 1909; bred and owned by Spencer Borden, Interlachen Stud, Fall River, Mass. By Segario. 1st dam Mahal, by Imamzada. [Vol. 10, p. 1274.] 2nd dam Raschida, by Kars. 1913 barren.

"Zem Zem 2nd — br., 1889; imported [in 1910] and owned by Spencer Borden, Interlachen Stud, Fall River, Mass. By El Emir. [French Stud Book, vol. 16, page 1103.] 1st dam Hagar, a Keheilet Ajuz.
"Produce: 1910 b. f. Zobeide, by Hauran.
              1911 barren.
              Mare died 1912."

Because Arabian horse owners in the United States formed the Arabian Horse Club in 1908 and registered as pure-bred Arabians those animals up to that time which had been imported or bred in the United States and which were accepted and listed as foundation animals, it hardly seems necessary to carry on and list any further Arabs registered in the American Jockey Club. The American Jockey Club continued to register pure-bred Arabs as Thoroughbred horses until November, 1943, but the information so registered for the last twenty-five or thirty years is no more complete than that to be found in the registry of the Arabian Horse Club.

In Volume II of The American Stud Book the following Arabian stallions, and a list of the brood mares that they have sired appears. This is an interesting bit of information for Arabian horse breeders:

"Daoud by Mesaoud out of Bint Nura, a Dahmeh Nejib. Risalda.

"El Emir by a Kohel Cheyti out of a Managhieh Ibn Sbeyil. Zem Zem 2nd.

"Feysul, a Kehilan Ajuz, of the Jellabi strain, or Kehilan Jellabi. Amra.

"Garaveen by Kismet out of Kushdil, by Kars. Arletta. Nanda.

"Hauran by Roustum or Jezail out of Hagar, a Keheilet Ajuz. Nessa.

"Ibn Sherara. Ghazala.

"Imamzada, by Imam out of Kesis 2nd, by The Heddud Seglawee-el-Abd. Mahal.

"Kahled by Nimr out of Naomi, by Yataghan. Nazlet.

"Maidan. Nazli.

"Mameluke (a high-caste Arab). Shabaka.

"Mesaoud, a Seglawi Jedran. Antika. Shibine.

"Rejeb by Mesaoud out of Rosemary, by Proximo or Jeroboam. Narda 2nd. Rumeliya.

"Roala by Kars out of Rodania, a Keheilet Ajuz. Jamila.

"Segario by Nimr out of Shabaka, by Mameluke. Rosina. Vashti.

"Seyal by Mesaoud out of Sobha, by Hamdanieh Simri. Butheyna."

Chapter 10

Randolph Huntington Breeds Part-Bred Horses

FOLLOWING the Civil War, Randolph Huntington was a partner in a drug house in New York City. He withdrew from this firm and moved to central New York where he engaged in the buying and selling of fine road and coach horses for the New York trade.

His studies convinced him that the most desirable horses were descended from Standardbred horses rich in Arabian blood lines and for many years he devoted his attention to the breeding of horses particularly suitable for the carriage, coach and roadster trade.

It was only natural then that he would have been interested in the stallions, Leopard and Linden Tree which General U. S. Grant received in 1877 as a present from the Sultan of Turkey. The following is a quotation from Jesse R. Grant's book published by Harper & Bros. in 1925, under the title, "In The Days of My Father, General Grant," concerning these two horses:

"Constantinople in March is not the most delightful city in the world. . . . Upon the invitation of the Sultan, Abdul Hamid, father and I, accompanied by the American minister, visited the Royal stables. I saw nothing in Constantinople that interested me more. Here were Arabian horses, scores of them, with pedigrees antedating Mohammed, if one is to credit the high Turkish official who acted as our escort. As for me, I am ready to believe that only centuries of selection and breeding could have produced such a number of horses so individually perfect and conforming so absolutely to type.

"Father was particularly interested in the stallions, of which there were scores. The Turkish official asked father which pair of stallions he considered the best? After careful examination, father indicated a pair of bays. The official made no comment, but asked father's opinion as to the next best pair. This time father selected a pair of grays.

"Thereupon the official announced 'They are yours, General Grant, by order of the Sultan'.

"Astonished and embarrassed, father protested, but the official was firmly insistent. Father as firmly declined to accept the gift, but to temper his refusal he mentioned the fact that he had no way of getting them to America.

" 'You have a man-of-war, General', smiled the Turk. 'Simply have the guns removed from one deck and there will be abundant space for stalls and exercising room'.

"With no more intention of accepting the gift than of transporting the animals as suggested, father was striving to express his appreciation and yet decline without giving offense, when the American minister intervened. He quickly explained that the gift must not be refused. To do so, no matter what the reason, could only give offense, and to the Sultan it would appear that father was dissatisfied with his gift.

" 'Accept them, General', he urged, 'and then leave the matter to me. I will arrange it somehow, without offending anyone'.

"Glad to be relieved of the responsibility, father accepted the Sultan's gift, and left the rest to the minister.

"About six months after my return home the pair of gray Arabian stallions arrived in New York. Father was still abroad, and I did not know what to do, but I accepted them and arranged for their shipment to the stock farm of General Beal, near Washington. I have no idea what became of the pair of bays, or who paid the shipping charges upon the pair I received. Neither do I recall that father ever mounted either of them, but I know there are many horses in this country with a strain of Arab blood that came from these grays. . . ."

Mr. Huntington immediately contacted General Grant, inspected the two horses and made arrangements to breed some high-class trotting mares of the Clay family to these two Arabian stallions. The mares were bred in 1879 and the first foals arrived in 1881.

In 1884, as a result, Randolph Huntington prepared and had privately printed a book entitled, "General Grant's Arabian Horses, Leopard and Linden Tree and Their Sons, Beale and Hegira."

Many well-known horsemen of the times were curious about the reasons for breeding these fine Standardbred mares to Arabian stallions, and since Mr. Huntington already had three stallions and two fillies, from one to three years old at the time, he outlined details concerning his breeding ideas and spoke of his decision to attempt to develop a national horse. A short description from Mr. Huntington's book, of these five part-bred Arabs, later known as Clay Arabia horses, follows:

"Beale is a golden sorrel, marked with a handsome straight white stripe in the face, gray at the root of the tail, a long white dash under the brisket, two white ankles forward, and nigh hind white sock. He was foaled June 25, 1881; was got by Leopard from Mary Sheppard, a black-roan mare fifteen and one-quarter hands high, by Jack Sheppard by Henry Clay, from his own daughter. Beale is fifteen hands high.

"Hegira is a coal-black, with faint star and white on all four feet. He was got by Linden from Nell Pixley by Henry Clay; was foaled July 9, 1882, and stands fifteen and one-quarter hands high at three years old. Nell Pixley, his dam, was bred by Supervisor Pixley of Monroe County, New York. She is fifteen and one-half hands high, strong.

"Islam is a dark chestnut, with two white ankles behind. He was got from Nell Andrews by Red Bird by Henry Clay; was foaled May 12, 1882, and stands fifteen hands high at three years old. His dam is also a dark chestnut, with two white ankles behind and stripe in the face; and her dam was also a dark chestnut mare inbred to Morgan blood. The dam of Islam is fifteen and one-quarter hands high.

"Clayrabia is an iron-gray without white. She was by Linden from Mag Wadsworth by Colonel Wadsworth by Henry Clay, from Colonel's own daughter. Clayrabia is fifteen hands and her dam fourteen and one-half hands high. Clayrabia was foaled July 14, 1881, and is much larger than her dam.

"Claybeale Grant is a chestnut, with stripe in the face and three white legs, the nigh one forward and two behind. She was by General Beale, already mentioned and described; she is also his first get. The dam of Claybeale Grant is Nell Andrews, who was also the dam of Islam by Linden, and Islam was her virgin foal. Claybeale is the last of three foals from Nell, and is the largest at same age of the three; and while all three were perfect and beautiful, this daughter of General Beals is the handsomest foal I have ever seen, except General Beals by Leopard, from Mary Sheppard.

"It has been a challenging question to me since the spring of 1880, why I bred to General Grant's Arabians?

"My main reason for breeding to General Grant's Arabs was the hope that something should grow into a national value from the Arabian blood. To give other reasons in detail necessarily involves reflections covering a lifetime, hence my writings will be tiresome to uninterested persons."

Mr. Huntington devotes several pages of his discussion to explanations concerning the various part-bred Arabian horses and the results secured in France, Russia and elsewhere, in the production of a national horse through the use of Arab sires. While this is all very interesting reading, since it has no great value to present-day Arabian horse owners and breeders, this portion of his book is omitted.

Mr. Huntington further states:

"That others valued Arabian blood as I did was evident from occasional importations of it; but in no case can I remember their use being credited. From 1840 to 1860 I knew of quite a number so imported, two standing at Boston, three in New Jersey, three in Maryland, two in Virginia, and four in Kentucky.

"From the first, Arabian stallions worked into Kentucky, where they were used upon race-horse mares. Latterly, Mokhladi, Massaud, and Sacklowie, imported by the late A. Keene Richards into Kentucky, did more or less business upon all kinds of dams, as well as thoroughbred running-breds. I am willing to believe the public did not know, in truth, the value of Arabian blood in the coach, road, and trotting-horse as well as race-horse.

"When, however, credit is given to Kentucky for superior blood in her brood mares over any other State, and that superiority is credited to her thorough running-horse blood, which in an earlier day was the only type of horses she bred, we are inclined to look for a more direct cause. In doing so, we find that for forty years their dams have been under the influence of Arabian blood; no less than five different Arabian stallions having been imported directly into Kentucky since 1850. While these horses were obtained expressly to reinforce their running-horse blood, when they found it more important to breed general-purpose horses (as coach, road, trotting-horses and workers), they had the all-important Arabian blood to help them, whether to strengthen running or colder-bred mares. Now, in so writing of Kentucky, I will cite one single instance — of which I have many — showing the direct and positive value of Arabian blood in the coach, and trotting-horse. In 1854, Mr. L. L. Dorsey, of Kentucky, bred a daughter of the imported Arabian

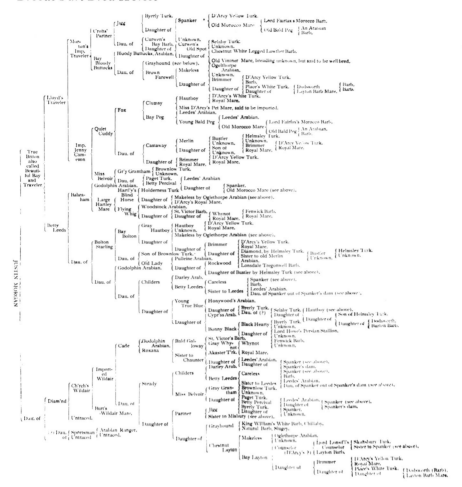

Tabulated pedigree of JUSTIN MORGAN showing him to be an in-bred Arabian. (Taken from Battel's Morgan Horse Registry.)

Zilcaadie to a little inbred Morgan horse called Vermont Morgan. The get and produce was called Golddust, from his golden color. This colt, foaled in 1855, was bred upon the principle of once out and thrice back to a primitive blood, for Justin Morgan was Arabian-bred.

"The horse Vermont Morgan was but fourteen and three-quarters hands high, and was inbred to Justin Morgan's blood. Now, when he is put to the daughter of imported Zilcaadie, one of the most beautiful stallion colts known in this country was the result; I mean L. L. Dorsey's stallion Golddust. He grew to be sixteen hands high, weighing very nearly thirteen hundred pounds, and for trotting speed was the peer of anything before bred in Kentucky. 'He was trotted many races, never being beaten; one of them was a match race for ten thousand dollars, which he won by over a distance.'

"As a getter, Golddust was the most positive sire for beauty, size, and wonderful trotting speed in his colts, calling to mind Andrew Jackson, similarly bred, also imported Messenger of similar breeding. It makes me nearly wild as I write, that I cannot induce men to put away prejudice and use reason. I do not wish the reader to obey my teachings, but would beg of every man interested in the breeding of horses to think deep, embracing every opportunity to enlighten himself. We have already too many writers who demand their readers to do as they say in print; I simply urge men to be better informed of themselves.

"Such a crop of colts as were the first get by Mr. Dorsey's Arabian-bred horse had no parallel in the breeding of beautiful coach, road, and

LINDEN TREE. An Arabian stallion presented to General Grant by the Sultan of Turkey.

trotting-horses, except in the get of imported Messenger, Andrew Jackson, and his son Henry Clay, all three being similarly bred to Arabian blood influence. Moreover, these sons and daughters of Dorsey's old Golddust had the same high nervous temperament possessed by the get of Andrew Jackson and Henry Clay, also credited to the get of imported Messenger.

"In the matter of Golddust, the war broke out, and his possibilities for Kentucky and the country at large were cut short. I remember a lot of horses and mares by Golddust, which Mr. Dorsey sent on to Long Island at the beginning of the war. They were in a large barn near John I. Sneidicker's place, near the old Union track. I examined them many times, and will say that to-day, such good horses are rare. After the war, attempts to establish Golddust were frustrated from two causes; first was owing to the multitude of coarse horses, more fashionable in the name, and second was the mistaken idea of improving the blood of Golddust through infusion of the blood of the rigid running-horse with

LEOPARD. An Arabian stallion presented to General Grant by the Sultan of Turkey.

its instinct. Had Mr. Dorsey selected inbred Morgan and high-type Clay mares for his horse he would by this time have created a 'national coach, road, and trotting-horse' without equal in the world. The same could have been accomplished with Messenger, or with Young Bashaw, or Andrew Jackson, or Henry Clay. The opportunities for a 'national horse' have presented themselves, but have not been embraced because of want of intelligent application to the object upon the part of gentlemen of means. General William T. Withers, of Kentucky, is now working towards such a base. I know him to be creating a superior maternal foundation, but whether he will introduce the right form of blood in the male, remains to be seen.

"Naturally, he will feel pride in establishing his breed through his Almont; and while Almont did possess largely of Arabian blood through Andrew Jackson and Pilot, and the maternal foundation will be solid through 'Clay' and Keene Richards's Arab mares, his results would be more uniform and every way more satisfactory, were he to make the king of his haras a direct descendant of a high-type Arabian stallion, through a Morgan, Jackson, or a Clay mare; but small mistakes by the individual have disappointed more than one Napoleonic attempt. The General remembers that by the male are the names given; and that rich mother-earth grows poor seed into prominence. Such seed, however, must be sustained by always rich mother-earth, for renewed vitality. God's laws are perfect; man cannot improve upon them. Atavism, or sporting back, is more apt to come through the blood influence of the dam than of the sire. I will soon speak particularly of that.

"But why did I breed to General Grant's Arabs, you ask?

"When I have asked a man why he bred a mustang, his reply was, For fun! Was there any sense in the act or in the reply?

"To this time I have been placing the argument so that reason within the reader would answer the question.

"When William H. Seward's Arabians arrived in 1860 (now twenty-five years ago), I had quite a little information upon blood and breeding of horses, — more, indeed, than some men ever will have; but as it is very unprofitable information, I trust all young men will not be so foolish as I have been. However, I was in the boat, so had to keep paddling and stopping the leaks at the same time; and here I am today, barely afloat: I know, however, there is a safe harbor for me at the end.

"We learn of great facts through deep problems, slowly. It takes time. Thorough investigations are very difficult.

"From 1820 to 1860 I believed I had made a careful inquiry and investigation into such Arabian stallions, with results, as had been imported to America to the date of arrival of the late Mr. Seward's horses; but the war was under way, stopping, for the time, all else.

"Later, as a dealer and still experimental breeder, the question of Secretary Seward's Arabian horses came up, and my search for them proved like most others of the kind: they had been thrown away. What was left to show for them was being credited to 'time-standard bred horses'; thus, the two best colts to date by one celebrated 'time-standard' bred horse, are from a granddaughter of the only son of one of Seward's Arabian horses, out of a granddaughter of Old Henry Clay; which facts are not known, so the time-standard bred horse gets all credit for the two mares got by him.

"Up to the time of the arrival of General Grant's Arabians I could find no record of the attempts by any man or men to create, with intent and purpose, any specialty from the Arabian horse, while my investigations warranted an effort, as my writings have shown.

"Russia and America demand coach, stage, and road-horses to a greater extent than any other nation; and they must be of a class adapted to general-purpose uses.

"Russia has created and established her national horse upon that base of trotting instinct, and I have shown she did it upon the same Arabian blood used by England and France for their separate, distinctive national horses.

" 'Haste is waste'. I was prepared for the arrival of General Grant's Arabs. I believed, as will any American, that they must be of the highest possible type. No empire or nation would insult herself by presenting to so great a man, also the one representative man of so great a nation as ours, an inferior gift from its representative animal life. General Grant's Arabs had to be the purest and best.

"The best results obtained by any crosses are not through abrupt, but by affinity crosses, with the instinct bending in the way you want. The Arab being plastic, reinforces a high-type of man's creation by its more vitalizing blood. To breed it to the race-horse, makes that blood hotter and stouter in its instinct established; and so with any other high forms of man's creation. Bread is not flour, nor is flour wheat; and yet except for the wheat there would be neither flour, bread, cake, nor pie. So in breeding; there must be the wheat, the seed; the life. In horses it is the Arabian seed, blood, and life from which man can create.

"I have implied that extreme physical conformations and developments, with rigid instincts as created by man, are very difficult to change.

"We wanted a national horse of a type which should conform itself to our greatest demands; which were stage, coach, road, and for track uses as trotters.

"We could not afford to mould over the running-horse to such purposes; indeed, time and money have proven it too uncertain.

"We had the trotting instinct already moulded to a type we wanted;

GENERAL BEALE. A half-Arabian stallion, a son of General Grant's Leopard.

what we needed was to build this type up to a degree of superiority; and the only way was to reinforce it with fresh, pure blood from the cause, — i.e., Arabian blood; this General Grant had been sent from abroad in his two Arabian stallions, and he offered it to his people.

"Upon their arrival the only blood we had adapted for good, prompt results, was that of Henry Clay. Its physical and instinctive organs would assimilate more readily than that of any other type of horses we had, because of itself purer in the primitive blood. It came nearer to Sir Thomas Morton's saying of three hundred years ago, 'Once out and thrice back to a primitive blood for best results'.

"When the General's horses arrived, I had two daughters of Old Henry Clay: both were got by him when he was owned in Monroe County, near Rochester, New York. One was a brood mare, being bred to a son of Henry Clay, her half-brother. I wanted virgin mares to send to General Grant's horses, if I could find them.

"I secured two young mares, coming four and five, in Michigan, in

HEGIRA. Half-Arabian stallion, the son of General Grant's Arab LINDEN TREE.

1880. They were own sisters, by Jack Sheppard by Henry Clay, out of his (Jack's) own daughter. The next best son of Henry Clay was Colonel Wadsworth, bred by the late William W. Wadsworth, who owned Henry Clay. This stallion, with one of his own daughters, went to Nashville, Tennessee. I went there, and, although the stallion was dead, found four of his daughters, aged at the time from two to seven (coming three to eight); the youngest being by him from his own daughter. I took this filly with the two best of the other three. The two Mr. Jewett had, but the little filly I put one side with the two Sheppard fillies and one daughter of Henry Clay. I next went to New York City and bought back a young mare I had sold there the fall before for seven hundred and fifty dollars, as a road mare, allowing fifteen hundred dollars for her. She was bred near Rochester, New York, and was by Red Bird by Henry Clay, out of an inbred Morgan mare. I now had five young, sound, healthy, virgin mares by Henry Clay, or by his sons, three being inbred, and all were choice; four being very fast natural trotters, and the fifth one would be were she not mixed at times in her gait.

"All this had been done in the fall, winter, and spring of 1879 and 1880, Grant's horses arriving in the summer of 1879.

"These mares I considered up to the English standard of blood and breeding."

As a latter-day comment on the great value of Mr. Huntington's breeding experiments, the following statement from the New York *Herald Tribune,* made by Baron Heftler, a Russian nobleman, and a breeder and owner of fine horses, is quoted:

"I have made a very important discovery since I came to America," said the baron, "and it is that of a family of Arabian horses from which the Darley Arabian came, and which was supposed to be extinct. The family is not extinct, for there are representatives within a few miles of this city [Oyster Bay]. The Arabian horse is the yeast by which all horse flesh is leavened. He is the basis of all horse flesh. He is the primitive horse, pure and not mongrelized. The European governments know this and have spent millions of dollars trying to procure them for the development of their native types. The English people were very fortunate in securing the Darley Arabian, the parent of the English thoroughbred.

"This one horse has been worth untold millions to them. Had they at the same time procured Arab mares of the same type, they would have been of inestimable value; but they could not do it. When it was too late, they attempted to procure them, and, after twenty years of effort in the Orient, purchased two or three stallions and mares at an enormous expense, which they were not fortunate enough to keep, owing to the enterprise of an enthusiastic American, who became possessor of them. This man spent a fortune in developing this family, and keeping the blood pure, and has practically sacrificed his life to this noble task.

"He has kept the fact rather secret that they were the family from which came the Darley Arabians. Recently, on account of his age, he sold his stock to younger men, who agreed to go on in the philanthropic work of keeping this species alive. They have several stallions and several mares each of which, I unhesitatingly state, is worth a king's ransom. You may better appreciate this when I state that in my country I have heard the expression of willingness to give 500,000 rubles for one or two Arabian mares of this family. I am in hopes that our government will take advantage of the fact that these mares are in existence, and will arrange for the purchase of some of the progeny."

At about the same time the following appeared in *The Rider and Driver:*

"SIX CLAY ARABIAN STALLIONS, AND TWO PURE ARABIAN STALLIONS AT PRIVATE SALE.

"The Huntington Stud owns the finest known specimens of Arabian horses in the civilized world. Its Arabian stallions and mares range from 15 to 15.3 hands. They are of the family from which the Darley Arabian came. All other Arabians are 14.2, and thereabouts, and are known as pony Arabs. All created types of thoroughbreds — the Orloff, the Percheron, the English and Kentucky thoroughbreds — are of Arabian basis.

"Their Clay Arabians are a cross between the pure Arab and Henry Clay daughters. All breeders of fine horses know that Henry Clay, the greatest horse of his time, was close to the Arabian blood, his great-grandsire being the imported Arabian Grand Bashaw. He was never beaten, and holds a record for endurance (his Arabian inheritance) of 76 miles in less than five hours, drawing a heavy two-seated surrey.

"Their venerable predecessor saved Henry Clay blood to the world by infusion of Arabian blood. He also obtained the Maneghi-Hedruj Arabians brought out of the desert by Major Upton, and propagated the family of Arabians which is destined to become the seed of the world.

"The Huntington Stud will give all its energies to the preservation of the Arabian and Clay blood selling its progeny yearly, offering this season six Clay-Arabian and two pure Arabian stallions at private sale. Stud service of both the pure Arabian and Clay-Arabians at $50, $75, and $100.

"The pair of horses sold to President McKinley for $7,000 were Clay Arabians, bred from this stock. Fourteen descendants of Abdul Hamid II, bred to good saddle and road-mares, sold by auction May 21, 1901, at the American Horse Exchange, averaged $1,439 each."

Baron Heftler, after his visit to the Huntington Stud at Long Island, took a three-month option, in the amount of $150,000 on ten head of pure-bred Arabian horses owned by that stud. He was attempting to have the Russian government purchase these horses for the establishment of a government stud to breed pure Arabian horses. Evidently this deal did not go through, and later on, some of these same horses were sold at auction.

A diligent search has been made concerning the breeders of Americo-Arabs, but it is not definitely known just how many individuals bred Americo-Arabs which were developed by Randolph Huntington. Evidently several persons probably owned and no doubt bred, in a small way, some of these horses. Since Randolph Huntington was engaged for twelve to fourteen years in breeding and developing this breed and the final dispersion of the stud founded by him did not occur until about 1906, it is a pleasure to note a report, in the June 8, 1901, issue of the Oyster Bay (N. Y.) *Pilot,* of the sale of several Americo-Arabs the foundation of which was secured from Randolph Huntington:

ANAZEH. No. 235. Sire—LEOPARD No. 233. Dam NAOMI No. 230. Bred by Randolph Huntington. (Courtesy of Thornton Chard.)

"After many years of trials and discussions in the horse papers, something practical and substantial has been shown by the advocates of the Arab blood. The sale in New York last week of a number of Americo-Arabs at an average price of over $1,800 per head demonstrates the fact that the Americo-Arab is already an established type. Although the sale was made by Theodore C. Patterson, Chestnut Hill, Pa., the whole credit is due to Mr. Randolph Huntington, Oyster Bay, as the founder of the type. The horses sold last Tuesday were mostly by Abdul Hamid

II, a son of Gen. Grant's Arabian Leopard, and out of Mary Sheppard, by Jack Sheppard, by Henry Clay; second dam Galusha mare, by Jack Sheppard. When the two stallions presented by the Sultan to Gen. Grant arrived in this country in 1879, Mr. Huntington was the only person to appreciate their value by breeding to them six of his best Clay mares, thus laying the foundation of a most desirable type of horses. More Arabian blood was infused into the type later by the importation of the pure bred Arab mares from England, Naomi and her daughter Nazil. It was mainly through influential friends in England and at great expense that Mr. Huntington succeeded in bringing these mares to this country, both of which proved great additions in establishing the Americo-Arab type.

"The gathering at the sale was unusually large, and much curiosity was evinced as to how the horses with Arabian blood would sell, and to say that a majority of the crowd was astonished at the sums bid is drawing it but mildly, and wonder was added to astonishment when it was learned that a majority of the offerings were withdrawn because the owner and consignor, Mr. Patterson of Erdenheim Farm, did not think the bids were high enough to justify him in letting his pets go. For instance, the 15-2-hand stallion Omar was bid up to $1,550 and the owner would not let him go. The little black pony bred gelding Blackbird, 13-3 hands, was run up to $700 and withdrawn. Several others were taken out after what most of the horsemen present considered extraordinarily high prices were bid for them. The 13-2-hand chestnut mare Gulnare was bid up to $875, and Mr. Grand turned to Mr. Patterson, saying: 'Let me sell her'. Mr. Patterson looked thoughtful for a moment, then nodded his head, and the mare was knocked down to M. Evarts, New York.

"The top price was realized on the brown mare Larissa, from a Clay mare which fell to Ed de Cernea for $3,500. He also bought Manila, a bay mare, sister to Larissa, for $2,050. Mr. De Cernea said that the mare would be prepared for the National horse show by the man for whom he bought them. All of the Americo-Arabs offered were by either Hamid II or the pony sire Kasim, known also as Abdul Hamid IV, both of which as stated above, were bred by Randolph Huntington as were their dams, of Oyster Bay. The sales were:

"Larissa, b. m. 1897, 15.2½ hands, by Abdul Hamid II — Lillian; Ed de Cernea, New York; $3,500.

"Manila, b. m. 1898, 15.3 hands, by Abdul Hamid — Lillian; Ed de Cernea, New York. $2,050.

"Love Not, br. m. 1897, 15.2 hands, by Abdul Hamid II — By Play; E. B. Hodge, Paoli, Pa.; $1,850.

"Ilderim, ch. h. 1898, 15.2 hands, by Abdul Hamid — By Play; Brush Brown, Newburg, N. Y.; $1,650.

"Phyllis, ch. m. 1897, 13.3½ hands, by Kasim — Maritje; T. Robinson, New York; $1,500.

"Gulnare, ch. m. 1898, 13.2 hands, by Kasim — Maritje; M. Evarts, New York; $875.

"Gray Friar, g. g. 1897, 13.3½ hands, by Kasim — Serita; T. Robinson, New York; $550.

"Strephon, ch. c., 13.3½ hands, by Kasim — Vera; T. Robinson, New York; $450."

From *The American Horse Breeder*:

"MR. HUNTINGTON'S TURN NOW.

"Those who have ridiculed Randolph Huntington's methods of breeding from Arabian stock received an eye-opener at the W. D. Grand sale in New York on the 21st inst. Six head of what Mr. Huntington calls Americo-Arabs brought $11,225 under the hammer, an average of $1,870.83 per head. Larissa, a four-year-old, 15.2½-hand mare, by Abdul Hamid II, son of the imported Arabian Leopard, owned at one time by General Grant, brought the top price, $3,500. She went to the bid of Ed. de Cernea, who also paid $2,050 for Manila, a 15.3-hand, three-year-old full sister of Larissa. It is announced that these mares will be put in shape for exhibition next Fall at the annual National Horse Show in Madison Square Garden. It is Mr. Huntington's turn to laugh now."

From the private papers of Randolph Huntington, which were supplied the author by Thornton Chard, the following letter from Homer Davenport is quoted, (under date of December 15, 1906, written at Morris Plains, New Jesrey) commenting on prices secured for some of the Huntington-bred horses at a recently held auction sale:

"My dear Mr. Huntington,

"I can assure you that it was with a great deal of regret, and real sadness, that I saw your horses sell in the Garden the other day, a stallion like Clay Kismet, bringing $120.00, Anazeh, $320.00, and one of his sons, I think, a four year old out of Nasley, bringing $35.00; Nahab $90.00.

"Sewell was out here and spent a Sunday with me, and since then has done no challenging.

"Your friend, Mr. Brush, called and stayed over night and the next day, and after I had bid him good-bye, and thinking that he was well on towards home, he came again, and said that he could not leave without again seeing the brown Maneghi Sbeyel stallion. Of course if he don't see you on his way North, he will write you. He thinks the Maneghi is possibly the greatest horse he has ever seen, and I quite agree with him.

"It was a treat to meet a real breeder like Mr. Brush, a man who really lives from the soil, not one who pollutes it.

"I have Mr. Gargiulo's picture, which he gave me while in Constantinople, to publish in my book; and I would like to publish the pictures of the Grant stallions, from the drawings in your book, or, better still, if you can loan me two pulled proofs; I would naturally give you credit; am also anxious to have a picture for the book of Kismet. Mr. Brush told me that you had some, and any of these pictures will be carefully taken care of, and returned, and published with courtesy from you.

"I have been fortunate enough to get hold of A. Keene Richard's catalog, with drawings of three of his horses made by the artist he took with him, Edward Troye. Keene Richards has never received justice, instead of his plant being a failure the very first colts that he had born in Kentucky, won everytime they were shown, against all competitors.

"Poor Sewell is hurting the Arab horse game though he don't know it.

"Do you know where I could buy a book on the Morgan horse?

"Yours very truly, Homer Davenport.'"

From another of the original Huntington papers secured from Thornton Chard a list is shown of eighteen horses of the Americo-Arab breed, sold on June 8, 1907, at public auction. The place is not given, nor is there any other information beyond the name of the horse, the buyer and the price at which it sold. One noticeable feature of this report is that the Hartman Stock Farm Company, of Columbus, Ohio, was the principal buyer of the better horses, and A. R. Jewell was also a heavy buyer. The prices of these horses ranged from a low of $55 to a high of $1,500. The entire report of this sale is quoted:

"Lot 1 — 'Clay Eclipse', W. R. Peters, $520.
"Lot 2 — 'Lady Washington' & filly, Hartman Stock Farm Co., Columbus, Ohio. Mr. Lawrence, Mgr. & Treas., $305.
"Lot 3 — 'Vakkar', A. R. Jewell, $175.
"Lot 4 — 'Shabaka', A. R. Jewell, $520.
"Lot 5 — 'Nagli', with colt by 'Khaled' (Sold in stall & not led out in very poor condition), Major Debervoise, $170.
"Lot 6 — 'Naomi 2nd', Hartman Stock Farm, $220.
"Lot 7 — 'Naglita', Hartman, $395.

143

"Lot 8 — 'Khaletta', Hartman, $520.

"Lot 9 — 'Naglina', Hartman, $500.

"Lot 10 — 'Narkeesa', Hartman, $530.

"Lot 11 — 'Ferida', Maj. Debervoise, $110.

"Lot 12 — 'Selena'.

"Lot 13 — 'Sodia'.

"Lot 14 — 'Arab Prince', A. R. Jewell, $380.

"Lot 15 — 'Gouniad', A. R. Jewell, $250.

"Lot 16 — 'Khaled', R. A. Sewell, $1,500.

"Lot 17 — Filly by 'Khaled', Maj. Debervoise, $55.

"Lot 18 — Filly by 'Khaled', R. V. Sewell, $230.

It is assumed, since one of these mares was listed as in too poor condition to be led out for sale and since others brought such very low prices, that these horses were probably in very poor condition due to a lack of care and feed. This stud had been going through very severe financial troubles for a considerable period, and therefore it is very likely that the above prices do not reflect the real value of the horses, since other sales of, and prices paid for, similarly bred horses at other times were very satisfactory.

Chapter II

Auction Catalogue Of The Huntington Collection Of Clay And Clay-Arab Horses

A T the American Institute Building in New York City on February 22 and 23, 1894, the Huntington collection of Clay and Clay-Arab horses, amounting to eighty-eight head in all, were sold at auction at receiver's sale. This collection represented nearly fifty years study, planning and breeding by Randolph Huntington, who was at that time a man of considerable years. Some time prior to this sale he and some of his friends organized a large corporation for the breeding and marketing of his Clay and Clay-Arab horses. This project appeared to be on the verge of considerable success, having sold a number of horses at extremely high figures to prominent buyers in several foreign countries, when the treasurer absconded with all the available cash. This left the corporation without sufficient funds to continue functioning and it was thrown into receivership and the horses sold.

145

AUCTION CATALOGUE OF

The Huntington Collection

OF

CLAY AND CLAY-ARAB HORSES,

TO BE SOLD BY ORDER OF

R. F. DOWNING, Receiver,

AT AUCTION

THURSDAY AND FRIDAY,

February 22 and 23, 1894,

Commencing each day at 10 o'Clock,

AT THE

AMERICAN INSTITUTE BUILDING,

THIRD AVENUE, BET. 63d AND 64th STREETS, NEW YORK.

ALL THE STOCK IS PLEDGED TO ABSOLUTE SALE.
No Postponement on Account of Weather.

SEND FOR CATALOGUES TO

PETER C. KELLOGG & CO.,

Auctioneers and Commission Agents in Improved Live Stock,

OFFICE : 107 JOHN STREET, NEW YORK.

NEW YORK:
JOHN POLHEMUS PRINTING CO., 121 Fulton St.
1894.

Title page from Randolph Huntington's personal catalog owned by the author. (Courtesy Thornton Chard.)

146

Anyone who has studied the life of Randolph Huntington and knows how valiently he fought for the Arabian inheritance of his horses for the greater part of his life will certainly understand and sympathize with the feelings he expresses in the preface he wrote for this catalog. Most of the material in this preface is quoted except that part that deals with a controversy about the pedigrees of certain Clay horses which he claims were faulty:

"The most difficult task I have ever undertaken with my pen, is writing this preface to my auction catalogue, because of the varied opinions of a public who may read it. No two horsemen have had like experiences, no two have studied alike, no two are gifted alike, and yet every one knows all about it — in his way. Proffered knowledge is offensive, and in horses and horse breeding it is antagonistic; hence the man who dare advance what he knows to be truths unknown to others as such, must have strong moral courage with actual knowledge.

"Within this catalogue are the names with abbreviated breedings of a plant of equines, the result of years of scientific study, observation, and research.

"The pedigrees are from my stock books and diaries, dating back long before a trotting register was thought of; and are correct (except in typographical errors) to my knowledge.

"The collection contains the purest and best of Clay blood in the country; and as pure Arab as can be found in any other. Its success financially and in the development of speed, has been proscribed by those circumstances which attend every enterprise not sufficiently backed by capital; and the fate of the ordinary inventor and discoverer has followed close the breeder of this plant; and yet, under the most trying and adverse conditions, with federal obstacles, a stud of horses is shown, the equal of the foundation stud for the English Thoroughbred, in the blood and breeding, and stronger and purer than was the Orloff stud when purchased from the Orloff estate by the Russian government.

"It is yet in its infancy. The colts and fillies offered in this sale, I had intended to become getters and producers, as stronger in the one blood than are the sires and dams. This preface is no place for a history of the plant. My object was to create and establish a truly American horse, of value from its blood qualities for export. To be so purified in one blood and truthful in its breeding, as to be sought for, rather than feared by the breeders of the Old World.

"There can be no national success in the breeding of horses beyond profitable home consumption, until such breedings shall be in demand by other highly civilized peoples for stock and brood purposes. Exporting now and then a few horses for gambling purposes, can never pay, or prove creditable.

"The breeding of horses is a scientific study, as practical in its demands as is the science of chemistry, of materia medica, or of surgery, in which students are not alike gifted; nor can one say he is more gifted than another. A trainer and driver may have wonderful skill in his profession, and the electric and magnetic influence of his hands upon the lines and mind of the horse, accomplish what few others can with the same animal; and yet, as a breeder, be entirely unfit; although a really first-class breeder is almost invariably a first-class driver, and able to detect speed, where an expert trainer and driver cannot, until he has tried and proved it.

"The breeder of these horses began in early boyhood, near sixty years ago, the breeding of chickens, doves, fancy pigeons, guinea pigs, rabbits, then game fowls and dogs; and was always in the stable with horses.

"Shoeing horses was of interest, and many was the dark evening I held a tallow candle for the smith to nail the shoes to genuine Messenger horses.

"For rapid progress in the study of blood influences in breeding, no animal life that I know of, is so good as the game fowl. It matures quickly and is exceedingly sensitive to a taint in the blood. A student in breeding must have a passion for it; begin young, and study close in little things of quick maturity. 'Like produces like', only when the blood is like.

"As a lad I was always looking for the best in blood; and my experiments were in feather to feather or blood to blood for best results. In crosses of pure blood, it is true I created temporarily pleasing results; but all crosses degenerated; ran out in time. Crosses must be sustained by crosses. They cannot be successfully interbred for any length of time. Pure breds of primitive blood can be, and have been interbred from the beginning. Does the North American deer degenerate from close breeding? or the lion?

"Has the leopard ever changed his spots through crossing? Are we crossing the thoroughbred Jersey cow through fear of degeneracy from close breeding?

"Such were my studies and questions between fifty and sixty years ago when we had lots of Messenger horses. Have we any of them today? No; what has become of them? They were crossed out.

"When, in maturer years, I devoted myself to horses and horse breeding, past experiences, with observations and knowledge, convinced me that best results were to be obtained only through close breeding of a pure blood. In seeking for a pure foundation blood, I accepted it as proven and established for ages in the Old World, to be such as was most closely allied to Arabian ancestry.

"Our famous horses, imported Messenger and Diomed, were England's pride, as her creation from Arab, and Arab-Barb blood. She boasted of them as Anglo-Arabs. Messenger, three times close bred to the Godolphin Arab-Barb, and Diomed from the pure bred Darley Arabian of the Maneghi-Hedruj family. Had we any such blood form, from the Arab or Barb of our own creation? Yes, in Henry Clay, even better than Messenger; equally pure and as strongly bred, carrying less cold blood than did imported Messenger.

"Knowing thoroughly well of Henry Clay as an individual, and of his true breeding, years ago I called him an Americo-Arab; an American creation from Arab, and Arab-Barb blood. The blood was fast becoming extinct. It was in good form, and its value (Arab inheritance) from first to last had been substantiated and emphasized by all reliable history.

"Acquired knowledge led me to selection from his best living sons and daughters, then to intensifying its blood through close breeding, to which I added the choicest bred grandsons and granddaughters, interbreeding all.

"General Grant's two horses, Leopard, the Arab, and Linden Tree, the Barb, arrived the summer of 1879; and that fall were placed on Gen'l E. F. Beale's farm at Washington. I improved the opportunity to still further augment the potency of my Clay family, by fresh infusion of its ancestral blood, through selecting six of my choicest virgin mares, one a daughter of Henry Clay; three were interbred granddaughters, and one was a granddaughter from a halfbred English mare, the sixth being strong in Messenger blood. This was the early spring of 1880; and I was fortunate in getting three horse colts with one filly. While growing these to become the major influence in my attempts, I hurried the close breedings of my Clays, for fillies to mate with my Americo-Arabs. In 1886, when the colts were old enough, and the Clay fillies sufficiently advanced, circumstances prevented me from breeding to any extent until the spring of 1891.

"My selection of sons and daughters of Henry Clay, were the mares Tächistà or Nell Pixley, a mare bred by Supervisor John L. Pixley, of Gates, Monroe Co., N. Y., stepfather of the celebrated Dr. John P. Munn of New York City. This mare, Nell Pixley, was born and so named in 1865, and was as good a mare as any man ever sat behind for one mile or a hundred. The other mare, Kate McPherson, was two years older and if possible a better mare. She was one year older than Mr. Charles Robinson's mare 'Daisy', the dam of Barkis. 'Daisy' when 4 years old, hitched to the pole with 'Brunett', could carry 'Brunett' into a dead run in any part of the mile; and my mare Kate McPherson was the better of the two. Both were from the same dam; my mare Kate, being by Henry Clay, and Mr. Robinson's mare 'Daisy', being by Colonel Wadsworth by Henry Clay. The dam of Mr. Robinson's mare (dam of Barkis) is recorded wrong in the Trotting Stud book, and of course the wrong breeding is entailed.

"An error in the pedigree of a horse or a mare when recorded in a stud book, does a world of damage. It does not stop in the individual, but multiplies rapidly to the injury of hundreds of breeders.

"But to go on with my selections from Henry Clay's sons and daughters, I will name in the male:

"Jack Shepard, Harrison Clay, Madison Clay, Ashland, Andy Johnson and his sons, Spink and Hepburn; Red Bird and his interbred son, Harvey W. (dam a daughter of Colonel Wadsworth, grandam the dam of his sire) ; Colonel Wadsworth, Black Henry; the Williams, or Fellows, or Lewis horse and Simmon's horse, every one of which were splendidly bred in the dams. Then for speed and trot, some of them trotted races in old fashioned heel and toe calked shoes, (hitched to high-wheeled, big ax thorough brace sulkies, weighing one hundred pounds and over) winning from 2:30 down to 2:22, when to win was the thing, and time not thought of, except to suppress, or keep back.

"All my dams and horses selected, were as close as possible to the one blood of Henry Clay; and my best results were from the closest possible breeding, following as I have said, nature's method in all wild animals. There can be no incestuous breedings in polygamous animal life. It has been continued for all time in the wild state, without degeneracy. In domestication, much crossing destroys life; shortens it, and generates new diseases.

"In horse-breeding, crossings lead to mistakes in pedigrees. One of the causes for the deplorable condition of the horse breeding industry in America today, is dependence upon mistaken or false registration. Our trotting stud books are full of false breedings, and as the majority of catalogues are made up from these books, the errors are multiplied; unfortunately these errors are associated with prominent old time horses and mares; and are multiplied in the offspring which are scattered with the false breedings to all parts of the country.

"In this catalogue it becomes a duty to myself and the public to correct one of them, a shameful error. Was it maliciously so? Charity questions — or probably not.

"The late Daniel S. Lathrop, of Albany, was a much loved personal friend of mine.

"He was a brother-in-law of Governor Stanford. Mr. Lathrop was in sympathy with my movements in Clay blood. In 1879 he urged me to add the horse Clay Pilot to my collection of Henry's sons and daughters, giving as a reason, the success Mr. L. J. Rose was having with it, but at that time unknown to eastern breeders.

"Mr. Rose also wrote to me 'that Clay Pilot was the greatest sire living; although he believed him dead'. I knew he was not; but I wrote Mr. Lathrop I did not want him because I would only have trouble regarding his pedigree; that he was recorded wrongly in the Stud Books, and that Mr. O. B. Gould, on whose farm the horse was born, and in which he had a half interest, could not get the error corrected, nor could Mr. Geo. C. Stevens; and I did not wish any more public controversy over false pedigrees; that I had none, and did not care to buy one to quarrel about. However, Mr. Lathrop kept at me to get that horse, so in the winter of 1882-3, through the kindness of my friends General Geo. E. Bryant and Hon. Clinton Babbit of Wisconsin, I secured him.

"The trotting stud book manufacturers knew, when I got Clay Pilot, and before I could make a move towards correcting his breeding as it was recorded, the entire land of horsemen were informed that the 'dam of Clay Pilot was a catch filly of unknown breeding'.

"Quickly followed the auction sales catalogues, and every time an animal was offered which traced to Clay Pilot, he was given as 'by Neave's Clay, dam, a "catch filly" ' Thousands of these catalogues were scattered over our country, also abroad, at the sales of W. L. J. Rose's horses, also Governor Stanford's and other California offerings. I endured it, for I believe in the old saying that 'truth though crushed to the earth would rise again.' The 'catch filly' business grew offensive; and having established it, the name of Clay Pilot was omitted in many pedigrees, only his son, 'The Moor' (without a father), being given to the world beating youngsters.

"Alexander Neave and Mr. O. B. Gould, who knew I had the horse, wrote me repeatedly, begging I would give the true age, and breeding of the dam of Clay Pilot; but no horse paper would accept it, and I certainly was not going to fool my time with pedigree manufacturers. The horse was not for public service; and if Stanford, Rose, Corbitt, Hamlin, and Wilson, of Kentucky, could boast of their fastest animals as descending from Clay Pilot with a 'catch filly' dam, I could stand it.

"By turning to the trotting stud book, we read 'Clay Pilot', bay horse, foaled in 1859, got by Neave's C. M. Clay, Jr., dam, by Pilot Jr., grandam, by Mambrino Chief (?).

"Now, every effort had been made to correct this mistaken pedigree; it could not be changed. The horse, Mambrino Chief, went into Kentucky the winter of 1854 and 1855. His stud service began season of

1855. A filly by him (Mambrino Chief) would be born in 1856, and when a yearling in 1857 must be bred to Pilot, Jr., and produce a filly when coming two, in 1858, which filly, while suckling its dam, must be bred to Neave's Clay, to produce Clay Pilot in 1859, as recorded in the trotting stud books. As ridiculous as this was, as well as purposely untruthful, both in the breeding of the dam and age of the horse (birth), it could not be corrected by the owners and breeders of the colt, in subsequent volumes; and there are hundreds of errors in ages and breedings of horses and mares equally bad, among the thousands of pedigrees recorded; nor can it be improved where prejudices are strong. One stud book for this entire land, recording mongrel bred horses, cannot be reliable. Is it any wonder that horse breeding in the United States should be in its present deplorable condition, and that the old world are afraid of our breedings and pedigrees? Gentlemen well informed and knowing the many errors, are insulted and slandered through the press, if they attempt public correction of falsely recorded breedings, and if he be a breeder, the value of his property is depreciated as far as possible by such press devoted to horses.

"The true breeding of the dams of Clay Pilot are given in this catalogue; and let me show the influence of Arab blood in Henry Clay and the dams of Clay Pilot. Clay and Pilot were both Arab and Barb bred horses, better in blood than the Orloff. Clay Pilot and Harry Clay were half brothers by Neave's Clay, the first, and best bred son of Cassius M. Clay by Henry Clay, the Americo-Arab. Strader's C. M. Clay, Jr. was an inferior bred half-brother to Neave's C. M. Clay, Jr., by C. M. Clay, because of the dam; and Harry Clay was inferior to Clay Pilot from same reason; and yet, all were close bred to Henry Clay.

"Harry Clay got the dam of Electioneer. Clay Pilot got The Moor (a small black horse). Minnehaha was a daughter of Nettie Clay, by Strader's Clay, the half-brother to Neave's Clay. In Minnehaha's paternal grandams, we find a daughter of the imported Arab, Stamboul, the direct blood cause for Clay.

"Now, Minnehaha, mated with The Moor, by Clay Pilot, produces Beautiful Bells, a mare inter-bred to the one same Clay horse, Cassius, by Henry, and reinforced by its blood cause, the Arab, from imported Stamboul. Beautiful Bells bred to Electioneer, whose dam was her cousin through Neave's Clay, produces Hinda Rose, the first three-year-old to beat 2;20, and the first yearling to trot in 2;36½, which filly was followed by eleven others so bred, among which were St. Bel, Chimes, Bell Boy, Palo Alto Belle, Bellflower and Bell Bird, to trot as a yearling in 2;26½. When, however, the mare was bred away from her intensified Clay-Arab blood to the horse Piedmont because of his record of 2;17¼, the product was a failure at trotting speed in the mare Rosemont (foal of 1883); but Rosemont bred back to the blood of her dam, in the dam of Electioneer, at once shows and proves that blood will tell when records fail, as the product 'Mont Rose', equals and even beats a trifle, her sister in blood, Hinda Rose.

"Now these facts are offensive to a great many; and were I to continue my illustrations upon the other side of the house of Electioneer, the entire country of horsemen would be in a rage at me. The phenomenal three year old filly, 'Fantasy', record of 2;08¾, is interbred to Arab blood through Clay; her sire being interbred to Neave's Clay, through Clay Pilot and Harry Clay, and her dam also of Clay blood. But I will restrain myself from going deeper and more plainly into this question by comparisons so distasteful to the uninformed and prejudiced public.

"As there are few men of today who ever saw Henry Clay, I will call special attention to my horse, Clay Truth, about to be given away (as his value in the stud is above a price). He is in build, substance, disposition, action, and in height, the duplicate of old Henry to which he is interbred. He has the same head, ears, and wonderful neck and crest of Henry Clay. The only difference is in the color and markings. Henry Clay was black, as was his sire. He had the off hind ankle white, and marked in the face with a crescent.

"Clay Truth (the American Hackney) is a chestnut, with narrow strip in the face, and the nigh hind ankle white, in place of the off one; but in every other way, he is the duplicate of old Henry Clay at the same age. His dam, Fan Stevens, had nine foals by the famous 'Bull Colt', Black's Hambletonian, by Rysdyk's Hambletonian, and the horse 'Greenfield', interbred to Rysdyk's Hambletonian; and as I owned four of the nine, I verified what I knew forty years before. Her last foal was Clay Truth, interbred to her Clay blood, and was worth more than one hundred like her previous nine.

"As few indeed have ever studied the true breeding of Henry Clay, I will introduce it in tabulated form. See next page.

"Flying Childers, King Herod, Eclipse, Trumpator, Diomed and Messenger were five of the greatest and best horses England ever bred; and each one was inter-bred to Arab, Barb and Turk blood, the Barb and Turk both being Arab bred horses.

"We of America accept the names of Childers, Herod, Eclipse, Trumpator, Diomed and Messenger as English Thoroughbreds; and to date have ridiculed their blood cause, the Arab and Arab-Barb, telling our young men to use a cross from the English Thoroughbred, if in their breedings for trotting horses, they would be successful.

"Such writers do not think to tell their readers that to cross the

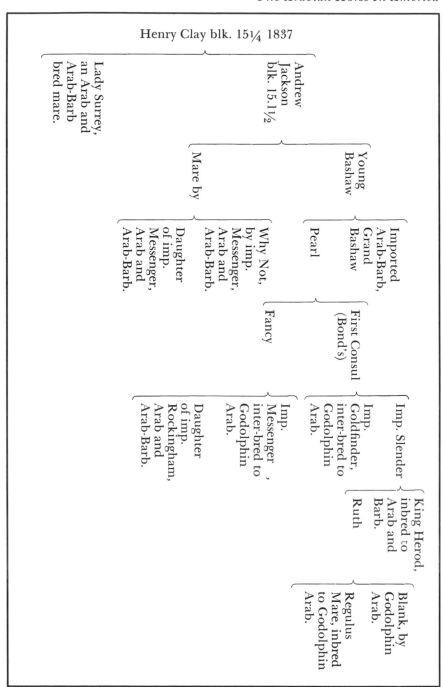

Henry Clay blk. 15¼ 1837

Andrew Jackson blk. 15.1½

Young Bashaw

Imported Arab-Barb, Grand Bashaw

Pearl

First Consul (Bond's)

Imp. Slender

Imp. Goldfinder, inter-bred to Godolphin Arab.

King Herod, inbred to Arab and Barb.

Ruth

Blank, by Godolphin Arab.

Regulus Mare, inbred to Godolphin Arab.

Mare by

Why Not, by imp. Messenger, Arab and Arab-Barb.

Daughter of imp. Messenger, Arab and Arab-Barb.

Fancy

Imp. Messenger, inter-bred to Godolphin Arab.

Daughter of imp. Rockingham, Arab and Arab-Barb.

Lady Surrey, an Arab and Arab-Barb bred mare.

English Thoroughbred out of his family is to produce a mongrel uncertainty. Nor do they tell them that the instinct to run has been cultivated for over a hundred years; but do tell them in another issue that if they would breed trotters, they must breed to trotters and not runners. What are the readers to do? Pure Arab and Arab-Barb blood is the direct cause for run, trot and pace; and is pliable under training to either of the three gaits, and just as that blood predominates in the animal, so will greater or less success be attained in breeding or training, although as colts 'they be tangle footed'.

"Andrew Jackson was a thoroughbred trotting-bred horse; and from four years of age could not be beaten at trot, nor was his son, Henry Clay, ever beaten.

"The same class of horse papers which advocates thoroughbred race horse blood for breeding trotters and coach horses, and with the same breath have informed their readers that 'Henry Clay' was a 'dunghill', and 'was soft', or 'a quitter', will do well to explain where it came from. No horseman that I know of today, would make a match for $2,500, mile heats, best three in five, against the fastest and best horse to be found, and then drive his horse 98 miles the day before the race over a public stage road to keep the engagement rather than pay forfeit; yet William W. Wadsworth did that with the game little horse, Henry Clay, whose Arab inheritance stood up to the task, and won the race with ease, in three straight, over a rough track, to a heavy, high-wheeled big axletree sulky in 2:35, and able to have beaten 2:30, if necessary, to win. This was in September, 1847, when to win the race and money was the object.

"Later, when Mr. Wadsworth's sister, 'Lib', whom he loved very much, and whom the rich and poor alike of the entire country idolized for her deeds of charity, lay at the point of death; a special physician at Rochester, 38 miles away, must be brought with all possible haste.

"The Wadsworth stables were full of thoroughbreds and half breds, broken to harness; but only one horse could be depended upon for speed and staying qualities, and that was the little giant, Henry Clay; so he was hitched to a wagon for two (called light in those days, but very heavy in these), with instructions to the driver not to stop longer than for the physician to get in. The horse made the distance, both ways, in less than two hours and a half each way, and the dear, good woman's life was saved, without the silghtest injury to Henry Clay.

"I have been urged the past ten years to publish a Clay Stud Book in connection with my Clay History, but declined from want of time. I now decide to do so, and secure copyright for such publication. All stallions and mares which are of Clay blood in the male, can be recorded with me for registration upon the same terms as charged for registry in stud books devoted to mixed bloods. Records not considered. Only purity of blood will grade the animal, and in all cases the breeder's name and address must be given. The finest and best coach horses we have ever had (and I was for years a dealer in them) were strong in Clay blood. Then for speed at trot, the fastest rates yet attained, rested upon the Arab and Barb blood of Henry Clay, Pilot and Morgan. The Morgan family, through the enterprise of Mr. Joseph Battell, has a Stud Registry, and certainly the Clay family is entitled to one. With such a book, purity of blood will be stimulated, and such as like to make crosses, will be able to know better what they are about than they now can by crossing mixed bloods. The registry of mongrel bred horses to be known only by number is worse in results than was the Louisiana Lottery, tending to poverty among the masses subjected to it. It also cultivates ignorance and deception in one of the most important industries of our land.

"In this plant of mine now being sacrificed, are colts and fillies purified in the blood of Clay, so that one interested, can with a horse colt, and two or three fillies, soon create a pure bred family of Clay horses; then in place of crossing out, introduce its blood cause, the Arab or Barb; but do not be deceived as to what it truly Arab and Barb. The Sultan of Turkey can issue all the firmans he pleases regarding export of Arab horses. It extends only to mongrels within his domains. Pure Arab horses are not found within his jurisdiction, except owned by some wealthy subject for his own uses.

"It is with difficulty the Sultan himself can obtain pure Arabs; and when it is announced through our daily press that the Arab horses shown at the Midway Plaisance were an exhibit by the Turkish Government, and that such government permitted attachment and sale by the sheriff, it is too ridiculous; but is believed by the masses, 'because in the papers'.

"Again and again I repeat it; the pure Arab is invaluable to any breeder of horses, and no good breeder in America can afford to be without it; but it is difficult and expensive to obtain. I have it as pure as the desert can produce; but it required years of practical study to know of it, then how to obtain. The Anezah tribes hate the Turk and keep as far from him as possible, as they do also the French.

"It would be a great pleasure to me if a syndicate of gentlemen would buy my plant as it stands, and continue its breedings. Annual sales from it in its purity of Clay blood, frequently reinforced with its Arab, and Arab blood, would soon give to America a National horse the equal if not superior to the national horse of Russia.

"There has never been a uniform high rate of speed attained either at running or trotting where the Arab blood did not predominate; nor did records attained, ever produce records, except the blood which permitted them under training, were united with the same blood in the female to produce the offspring. We have abundant evidences in our own country within the past fifteen years. Mr. C. J. Hamlin never succeeded in breeding speed from records or record bred horses until he interbred the blood of the Arab through Clay and Morgan. Nor did Mr. Jewett get speed from years of breeding to speed, until he interbred to the Arab blood of Clay.

"What did Mambrino Gift beget? I saw him make his record of 2:20 near twenty years ago and he was the first stallion to make such public record. He was flooded with brood mares because of his then wonderful record, but where are the multitudes of record breakers?

"It is the blood, gentlemen, and not the record that permits the record under careful, judicious and expensive training. A horse may possess blood enough to train to a high rate of speed, but not sufficient to impart to his offspring when through crossing it is still more diluted. In my Clay History and Clay Stud Book I can write with more freedom than in this catalogue, necessarily restricted in all ways, even to extended pedigrees.

"All buyers can obtain from me a full and extended pedigree of every animal."

Chapter 12

The Chicago World's Fair Of 1893 And Its Influence On The Arabian Breed In America

THE World's Columbian Exposition (more commonly known as the Chicago World's Fair) was held in 1893, and it had an important influence upon the Arabian horse in America.

Every country in the world was invited to participate in this exhibition and to erect a building where their products would be shown. Among the exhibits at the Fair was one from Turkey, which included forty-five Arabian horses.

World-famous owners and breeders of Arabian horses attended the Fair, including Randolph Huntington, J. A. P. Ramsdell of Newburgh, New York, Peter Bradley of Hingham, Mass., and Homer Davenport of Chicago.

Among the imported Arabs shown were the mare, Nejdme, No. 1, and the stallion, Obeyran, No. 2, both foundation animals in the Arabian

Stud Book. Several years later, two of the mares shown, Galfia, No. 255, and Pride, No. 321, and the stallion, Mannaky No. 294, were registered in the stud book. Offspring from these five animals are widely scattered throughout the United States and many breeding studs contain animals tracing to them as taproot foundation stock.

There is little doubt but that the formation of the Arabian Horse Club of America in 1908 had its greatest stimulus from the prominence given the Arabian horse at this World's Fair.

Because of financial difficulties, it became necessary in a short time for the Turkish company to sell the horses at a receiver's auction for the benefit of the creditors. The auction records show a definite discrepancy in number of animals on hand. Twenty-eight horses are recorded as sold; add to this the seven lost in a fire and we arrive at a total of only thirty-five horses, with ten unaccounted for if we are to believe the original claim to the effect that forty-five animals arrived in this country from Turkey. There appears to be no way to trace an explanation for the discrepancy.

There was considerable difference of opinion among various individuals about the Arabian horses exhibited and finally, in 1897, one of the leading horse papers in the United States, *The Horseman,* published at Chicago, called upon Mr. A. G. Asdikiah, a member of the Turkish Embassy in Chicago, to prepare a special report on this exhibition. His report was published in the June 15 and July 22 issues of 1897, and is quoted as follows:

"For the past two years several friends have asked me what I know about the Arab horses brought to this country during the Columbian exposition. For certain reasons, unnecessary to mention here, I have declined to say anything about the matter publicly, but in order to save time in answering private letters, I will give to the readers of *The Horseman* a brief history of the 'Hamidieh Hippodrome Company' a Midway attraction, and part of what I know about the horses.

"In the early spring of 1892 an employee of the Turkish ministry of agriculture, Suleyman Raji Effendi, a Syrian by birth, through the influence of Munir Pasha, then as now first chamberlain to the sultan, received a concession from the Turkish government to take a troop of Bedouin horsemen to Chicago. The request was at first refused, but the sultan was made to believe that the proposed enterprise was intended more as an exhibition of pure bred horses than as a show, and on this belief the concession was ordered granted under strict, I might say severe, conditions, some of which were:

"First — None but the purest bred pedigreed horses should be taken. Second — All the horses to be returned back to the desert. Third — The riders to be the best horsemen from the several friendly Bedouin tribes and from no other nationality. Fourth — Two cavalry officers to accompany the troop at the expense of the company, to supervise everything and see that the contract, which contained fifty-two such conditions as I have mentioned, was complied with.

"The granting of this concession made a great sensation in Constantinople, and in less than two days the money asked for — 25,000 Turkish liras ($112,000) — to carry on the enterprise was subscribed exclusively by Syrian capitalists in Constantinople, Beirut, Paris and Egypt. This was at a time when nothing was talked about but the great sargi (fair) in Chicago. Everything that was going to Chicago had such alluring prospects that the concessionaire, Raji Effendi, was offered for his share $15,000 spot cash, a free passage to Chicago and back, and all his personal expenses for six months, which offer he indignantly refused, but he agreed to take 2 per cent of the gross receipts of the show and furnish his own expenses, as the price of his concession. Let me say that this poor, deluded man's passage back to Turkey was partly defrayed by the Turkish commission.

"The Company was made up of men who might have been shrewd business men in dealing with the simple and confiding Bedouins of the desert, but who had no idea of American business methods, much less Chicago methods, and still less Chicago methods of World's Fair times. A large sum of money at their disposal, they had made a dazzling collection for a show, which might have been great in Beirut, but did not go in Chicago. Having chartered a Cunard steamer, they brought over with them 120 men, women and boys, (and a providential addition was made to the number on the way); 45 horses, 12 camels, donkeys, fat-tailed sheep, Oriental cracked wheat, soap (which they seldom used), oil, butter, cheese, flour, an immense quantity of barley, half a ton of horseshoes and, to cap the climax they had six large boxes containing 1,500,000 admission tickets to the show, printed in Beirut, the uniform price being one small American dollar a ticket — no reduced rates for minors, nor matinees, and no complimentaries.

"I was told several times that before leaving Beirut the stockholders had a hot all night session discussing the problem of printing these tickets. A member of the company, who owned a printing press, insisted that they should cut off 3,000,000 pieces, but after long discussion — and heaven only knows how these Syrians did discuss — the cooler heads carried the meeting and half of the number was agreed upon, with the proviso that the tickets be so printed as to be used more than once. To show the extreme foolishness of these people, I will state as an absolute fact that they even seriously thought of taking a printing press with them to save expense of cutting admission tickets. Of course these tickets were never used until late in November, 1893, when the directors ran away, leaving the desert-bred Bedouins to the mercy of Lake Michigan winds at Jackson Park. They burned these tickets at night to keep warm, and used to go early in the morning to Judge Ewing's court room and stretch themselves on the floor around the registers for their morning naps. Among the men were all the stockholders, each having one or more servants, according to the number of shares he held — riders, donkey boys, camel riders, ice cream lads (don't let me forget to say that they also brought several large tin cans filled with Syrian ice cream flavors), seven cooks, five horseshoers and over fifteen clerks and ticket sellers — to be brief, everybody who begged to be taken over was put on board. With this motley crowd of human beings and animals, and with their peculiar ideas of how a THREE MILLION DOLLAR SHOW should be run in Chicago, they left Beirut under the generalship of a man named Zalxal, with one Shakoor as his chief of staff.

"Early one bright May morning in the year of our Lord 1893 the neighborhood of Thirtieth Street and Michigan Avenue was shaken up as if by a terrible earthquake. The much heralded 'Humidieh Hippo-drome Co.' had at last arrived in Chicago, and before going to their resting place they had come to serenade the Turkish commissioners. After tramping over a poor newsboy, upsetting three milk wagons and driving hotel employees into hysterics, there they were with their pranc-ing steeds and flashing scimitars, men dressed in all the colors of the rainbow, directors sitting in open carriages with elegantly uniformed valets perched up with the drivers, donkeys braying, women screeching and the music the most deafening ever heard in any part of the globe. When 120 well-trained throats commenced yelling 'Long live the sultan', we thought the big Lakota Hotel, like the walls of Jericho, would fall down. Thus, the $3,000,000 Syrian show had landed in Chicago penniless.

"It is bad enough for strangers to fall in the hands of sharks in a strange land, but to fall in the claws of Chicago sharks is something terrible. The men had hardly settled and pitched their tents at the base-ball grounds, Thirty-fifth Street and Wentworth Avenue, and before the Turkish commissioners, who were supposed to look after their welfare and the two cavalry officers who were here to superintend their doings, knew anything, one Chicago shark had loaned them money at an ex-orbitant rate of interest and mortgaged all they had — horses, donkeys, tents, and wearing apparel; another had himself hired as manager of the show at an enormous salary, and with an iron-clad contract, and still another had made a contract to become the attorney of the corpora-tion at $600 a month salary. How these Chicagoans in the short space of thirty hours had worked themselves into the graces of these shrewd Syrian strangers and accomplished contracts, mortgages, etc., was more than we could understand. Thus from the very start they fell into the claws of sharks and were compeled to stay there until one by one the directors ran away, and those of the employees who were willing to return back to their desert homes were shipped away by the assistance of the Turkish commission and through the valuable intervention of Judge Ewing of the Cook County superior court — the man known to all the Bedouins as the 'righteous cadi' (judge).

"After staying at the baseball grounds for some time they were taken to the Garfield park race track. Here at the expense of over $400 of advertising and bill-posting they gave a performance and took in $16. Soon Chicago creditors were upon them like hungry vultures, and one bill-posting firm alone took possession of three stallions which were kept at a stable and served to mares with a small charge, for over two weeks. A fire, certainly of incendiary origin drove them back to Thirty-fifth Street again. In this fire they lost seven valuable horses, some of the camels and fifteen trunks full of clothing. The cause of this fire was certainly the result of the continual quarrels between the stockholders and the men who were left hungry and unprotected from the inclemencies of the weather. For two months we heard of nothing but fights and quarrels, lawsuits and bills, until the outfit was removed to the Midway Plaisance, where they gave their first performance on the Fourth of July. Such is the brief history of the 'Hamidieh Hippodrome Co.', the $3,000,000 Syrian show named after the sultan of Turkey.

"Now, as to the horses brought by this company, which it has pleased some to call 'scrub horses gathered in and around Damascus'. Maybe someone will question my authority in making these statements, and to those I will say that, as a member of the Turkish World's Fair commission, I came in daily contact with these men, fed them at the expense of the commission when they were hungry, helped those who were now and then driven out of the camp either by the directors or by their Chicago manager, went to the police courts when they were arrested for fighting — a frequent occurence; — thus, from the day they serenaded us on Michigan Avenue to the time the last miserable remnant was shipped away and the horses sold at auction, I was with these men either alone or with cavalry officers. I knew every man, woman and boy by name, and there was no question that they would not answer for me as to the origin and history of the horses. I have seen it stated in several papers, as I say, that the Arab horses brought to the World's Fair were a lot of scrubs gathered near Damascus. These sweeping denunciations are made by men who know absolutely nothing about the history and origin of the horses, who could not converse with the men, and who never saw any of the pedigrees, as I did.

"In justice to all concerned, I will say that some of the horses were among the purest bred Arabs that ever went out of the desert, and at least eleven of them had the customary written pedigrees, which I saw, read and took note of.

"When the troop landed in New York the U. S. Customs authorities levied a duty of $30 on each horse, the supposition being that the horses did not belong to any of the five families as stipulated in the McKinley tariff bill. After their arrival in Chicago I learned that eleven of the horses had written pedigrees and suggested to the commissioner-general to make an application to the secretary of the treasury and collect the $330, assuring him that this money would be refunded if the U. S. Treasury Department was informed of the fact. No matter what we tried to do for the members of the troop we always experienced some difficulty. Here were men accustomed to a different system of government and they could not be persuaded to forward the pedigrees to Washington without some security. The result of our advice and friendly suggestion was that it would be better for them to lose their just claim of $330 than send the documents to the government. They could not understand how the pedigrees could be returned to them after they had once reached the hands of government employees. Still they insisted that all the horses had pedigrees for fear that the commission would report to Constantinople that, contrary to their contract, they had brought over mongrel horses.

"The directors could borrow all the money they needed for their personal expenses and pleasures, while the commission had to provide for the people — especially for the women, children and the sick. Advice being of no avail, we threatened to sue them, having a copy of their contract in our possession, and secure these pedigrees. They promised to deliver them to me the next day. Went to Garfield Park to get the documents as agreed, and to my surprise could find none of the directors in the camp, but, knowing the Bedouin in whose care the papers were left, I demanded them. The poor old man, with tears in his eyes, begged me not to take them from him as the directors had told him that they would turn him out of the camp if he ever parted with his trust. In order not to embarrass the old man, I promised not to take them from him if he would show them to me. He produced a batch of ten pedigrees from his trunk, and I read every one of them by the assistance of one of the clerks who could speak Turkish, and wrote down as much of them as would enable me to prepare an application to be forwarded to Washington. When I had finished this work, I had this man Hadji

Hassan, of whom I shall speak later, show me the pedigreed horses. From this time on I knew which of the horses were pure breed Arabs. I never again saw these documents, the claim being made that they were destroyed in the fire together with thirty-four other pedigrees which I did not see, as they did not exist. However, against the accusation of the commission that they did not live up to their contract, these shrewd Syrians claimed that the documents were lost in the fire — an absolutely false claim, which we were powerless to contradict.

"To make themselves more secure they showed us a voluminous document signed by the governor of Bairut, who certified that the men had been faithful to the conditions of their contract, and that he was certain that these 'Faithful and honorable subjects of the Imperial Government will be at a great pecuniary sacrifice to themselves, an honor to the name of His Most August Majesty, the Sultan, before the civilized world'. Of course we knew how this certificate was procured — by bribery and trickery. The trick was this: It appears that at the start they brought from the desert to Bairut these eleven horses, some camels, donkeys, fat-tailed sheep and Syrian goats. Now, mind you, they were going to make a live stock exhibit. The pedigrees of the horses were submitted to the governor to convince the authorities that the troup would be organized in compliance with all the conditions of the concession. After securing the governor's signature they purchased such mongrel horses as would the best answer the purposes of a proposed show. Here is a copy of the catalogue by which the horses were sold at auction on January 4, 1894, at the Chicago Tattersalls.

"I prepared this descriptive list from a note book which I kept for the special purpose of writing down all I heard about the horses:

"Nedjme — *No. 1. Gray mare; 14¾ hands; foaled 1887; breed, Kehilan-Ajuz.

"Kiraby — *No. 2. Gray stallion; 14¾ hands; foaled 1885; breed, Saglawi-Sheyfi.

"Abbeian — No. 3. Gray stallion; 14¾ hands; foaled 1888; white nose; breed, Abeyan-Dahra.

"Sabuck — No. 4. Dark gray stallion; 15 hands; foaled 1888; breed, Treyfl.

"Dinyan — No. 5. Dapple gray stallion; 14.2½ hands; foaled 1887.

"Abbu Aley — No. 6. Dapple gray stallion; 14½ hands; foaled 1886.

"Obeyran — *No. 7. Iron gray stallion; 14½ hands; foaled 1889; breed, Seglawi-Obeyran.

"Gidran — *No. 8. Iron gray stallion; 14½ hands; foaled 1889; breed, Seglawi-Jedran.

"Zehna — No. 9. Gray mare; 14.2½ hands; foaled 1888; breed, Kehilan-Treyhi.

"Akhra — No. 10. Gray stallion; 14¾ hands; foaled 1887; breed, Kehilan-Akhras.

"Sirhal — No. 11. Light gray stallion; 15 hands; foaled 1886.

"Shamit — No. 12. Iron gray stallion; 15 hands; foaled 1887; breed, Hadban-El Furrd.

"Halool — *No. 13. Bay stallion; 15¼ hands; foaled 1886; breed, Kehilan-Ras El Fedawi.

"Miggour — No. 14. Bay stallion; 14¾ hands; foaled 1887; star.

"Simhan — No. 15. Bay stallion; 14¾ hands; foaled 1885; left hind foot white.

"Koukil — No. 16. Bay stallion; star and snip; left hind foot white; 14¾ hands; foaled 1889.

"Koubishan — No. 17. Light bay stallion; star and snip; 14¼ hands; foaled 1888; breed, Kebsyshan-El Omeyr.

"Haddad — No. 18. Bay stallion; star in forehead; right hind foot white; 15½ hands; foaled 1887.

"Kazoiv — No. 19. Bay stallion; black points; 15 hands; foaled 1887; breed, Kehilan-Mokhladi.

"Houraney — No. 20. Dark bay stallion; left fore and hind foot white; 15 hands; foaled 1887.

"Zarriffey — No. 21. Black mare; star; left hind foot white; 14½ hands; foaled 1888; breed, Kehilan; strain unknown.

"Abjal — No. 22. Black stallion; strip in face; left fore and hind foot white; white right hind coronet; 14½ hands; foaled 1885.

"Abbya — No. 23. Black mare; 15 hands; foaled 1885; breed, Kehilan, sub-strain unknown.

"Hassna — *No. 24. Dark bay mare; 14¾ hands; foaled 1889; breed, Managhi-Hedrij.

"Malouk — No. 25. Black stallion; star and snip; 14¾ hands; foaled 1888.

"Gallfea — *No. 26. Sorrel mare; one fore and both hind feet white; 14½ hands; foaled 1887; in foal to No. 2; breed Hamdari-Simri.

"Hannifey — No. 27. Chestnut stallion; 15¼ hands; foaled 1886; breed, Kehilan-Jasi.

"Manakey — *No. 28. Sorrel stallion; both hind feet white; 14¾ hands; foaled 1888; breed, Managhi-Slaji.

"The numbers having asterisks are those which had pedigrees. Three of the pedigreed horses — two stallions and a mare — were among those killed at the Garfield Park fire.

"I can say without hesitation, that the choicest of the lot in this sale went to Boston. They were purchased by one H. A. Souther, who was commissioned by a Boston gentleman to buy some of the horses at any price. Who these parties were I have been unable to find out to this day, neither do I know what became of the horses after they were taken east. By purchasing the stallions Nos. 7, 13, and 28 Mr. Souther, or his employer secured the plums of the lot, except the magnificent stallion No. 2, which the gentleman, for some reasons of his own, did not buy.

"The choicest and the best bred stallion in the lot was the horse Halool (Cat. No. 13). Halool was purchased from the Anazeh Bedouins by Hadji Hassan himself for 500 Turkish Liras ($2,250.) the second highest priced horse in the lot.

"As we will frequently mention Hadji Hassan, the readers will perhaps want to know who he was. He was a pure Anazeh Bedouin who did not know his birthplace, nor the date of his birth, only that at the age of 18 or 20, he joined a detachment of Arab irregulars and fought against the "Kafir" (Russia) in the Crimean war. He proudly exhibited eight scars made by Russian bullets during the war and the war of 1877. All his life Hadji Hassan had been a horse dealer among the Bedouins of the desert. He was at several times employed by the Turkish government to purchase cavalry horses. He was known from Aleppo to Egypt and Yemen as the best judge of Arab horses in the country. The Hippodrome Company hired him at the demand of the governor of Bairut at a high salary in order that the horses purchased should be of the purest blood. The company sent him among the Anazeh tribes and these eleven horses were all that Hadji Hassan bought. He not only had all the characteristics but all the prejudices of a true Bedouin. He would never eat outside of the camp for fear of touching pork, and nothing could persuade him to take a drink of any kind. His gorgeous costume and noble appearance made him a favorite with strangers visiting the camp, and he was continually invited out, but never ate nor drank anything. Halool was his favorite mount, and, in his estimation there was no breed like the sub-strain Ras-El-Fedawi of the Kehilan. The first choice of the stallions being out of the question, the old Bedouin and I discussed the second choice. His favorite for second place was Kiraby (Cat. No. 2), mine, Manakey (No. 28). Nothing he loved more than to talk horse, and I never went to the camp alone when he did not have some new proof to show that No. 2 was a better stallion than No. 28. The Sheyfi sub-strain of the Seglawi he considered far superior to the Alaji of the Managhi. As a pure bred Anazeh he had great respect to the Managhi breed, but he knew fro.n long experience that the only sub-strain of this breed that had any value was the Hedrij. He had no doubt as to the pure breeding of No. 28. He knew his breeder, the sires and dam, yet because the horse was a sorrel and had both hind feet white he was sure that the stallion had a flow of impure blood from some remote ancestor, while the stallion No. 2 had no mark or sign of such impurity. Therefore, complying with the judgment of my old Bedouin fried, I will say No. 2 was the second choice and No. 28 third.

"The fourth best stallion was Obeyran (Cat. No. 7) a half brother of No. 8, both inbred Seglawis and both purchased by Hadji Hassan from a reliable breeder, but why was one better than the other when both were of the same sizes and color and as much alike as two peas? Here are the arguments. The Seglawi-Jedran was the original and some magnificent horses belonged to this breed in olden times — horses that made history and romance in the desert. For centuries this blood has been sought by the breeders and the most valuable stallions have been bought by us at enormous prices, so that it is almost impossible to find a Seglawi-Jedran in the purity of its original blood. While the Obeyran substrain, although inferior to the Jedran and being of less value, was left in its original purity. As I said he bought both horses, he personally knew their breeder, he was sure the pedigrees were correct, yet he had some doubt in his mind as to the original purity of the Jedran.

"It would require more space than is allotted to me to give the detailed history of these horses as told by Hadji Hassan. If one of these Arabs should become a sire or ancestor of some speed in the future, then such history might be of some value.

"Among the mares the grey Nedjma took the palm. For a long time her pedigree was kept by Hadji Hassan and after the old man left Chicago it passed into the hands of one of the clerks, who refused to return it until his wages were paid. This document is still in existence, but not in the possession of the owner of the horse. Hundreds of times I saw this document and read it. She was 'a pure Kehilan of the purest' and belonged to the Ajuz substrain, yet she has been written up as a Seglawi, by what authority I do not know. For many months it was a puzzle to me why this magnificent pure bred mare was ever sold to go out of the desert. Was she stolen? Hadji Hassan said No! because he got her from her owner at 900 Turkish Liras ($4,200). Whenever I asked this question Hassan was as mute as a clam and repeatedly refused to give me a direct answer. 'If you people know anything about horses, watch and find out' was all he would say. I did watch day and evening, for over six months, but could see nothing wrong with her. She was as sound as a 'new-milled dollar' and had no blemish. When ridden by Hassan she was full of life and like a pure bred Arab, she was as docile and gentle as a lamb in her stall. About three weeks after the fair, while the men were still lingering at the grounds, I noticed that Nedjma was in use. I called my old friend and asked him if I was correct. He said: 'Yes — that mare has been in use for five years'. It was plain now. When three years old she had one colt, but she would never breed again. At the time of which I write she was eight years old. This is the reason why Nedjma was sold to be taken to this country. The first offer made for this mare was $3,500 by a wealthy lady. The directors refused to sell her, contrary to the commissioners' advice. In fact, the mare had attracted so much attention that the price put on her was $10,000. The second offer made late in October was $2,700 which was also turned down and finally I purchased the mare for $1,750 for a New York gentleman, paying $450 down, but before I could take possession she passed into the hands of the sheriff and I was out $450.00, as I could neither find the men to whom I paid the money nor could I get the mare. At the auction sale she was purchased for $1,200 by the receiver, who sold her afterwards for $800 to the same gentleman for whom I had bought her previously. I have heard very little of her since the mare went to New York. After knowing that the mare would not breed I still bought her for my friend because I believed that she could be bred if intelligent methods were used and the mare properly cared for. That she has had one or two foals since then shows that I was not mistaken in my judgment.

"One day during the World's Fair I had the honor to escort two gentlemen to the Bedouin camp. They were two of the best authorities on Arab horses in England and the United States — Rev. F. F. Vidal and Randolph Huntington. After a careful examination of all the horses I pointed out the little dark bay mare (Cat. No. 24) as my second choice among the females. She belonged to the Managhi-Hedrij breed and was as handsome an Arab brood mare as I ever saw. Like the rest of the pedigreed horses she was purchased from the Arazeh by Hadji Hassan. The third best mare was No. 26, which went to Boston, if I can remember right.

"As I said before, none of the owners of these horses are known to me except that of Nedjma, who, I understand, has changed hands lately. Therefore this information is unsolicited by anybody except the editor of *The Horseman*. My sole intention in giving part of what I learned about these Arabs to the public is to refute the sweeping statement, that these horses were scrubs of no breeding. Let is be known, in justice to all, that some of them were as magnificent and as purely bred Arab horses as ever were led out of the desert by any one or at any time."

The following advertisement appeared in a prominent Chicago paper in December 1893, announcing the sale of the Arabian horses that were exported for the purpose of exhibiting at the 1893 World's Fair at Chicago:

"By Tattersalls (of Chicago) Limited at their New Sale Repository, 16th and Dearborn Sts. Chicago, January 4th, 1894. Comprises 28 head.

"This offering comprises twenty-two stallions and six mares, which were on exhibition at the World's Fair, on the Midway Plaisance, constituting the 'Wild East', or 'Bedouin Encampment'. The exportation of this breed of horses is so zealeously guarded in the country from which they came, that a permit had to be obtained from the Turkish Government to even allow them to be brought to this country for exhibition. This encampment, however, was attached for debt, and these horses must now go under the hammer, at public auction, absolute sale, by order of the court, under the direction of Mr. Harry Byrne, receiver, and will afford the opportunity of a lifetime to secure specimens of this famous breed."

The *Breeders' Gazette,* of Chicago, in the 1890's was devoting considerable attention to the horse industry of the United States, and its report of the sale (January 10, 1894) is quoted as follows:

"Some interesting experiments in saddle horse and pony breeding will be undertaken by the use of the Arabian stallions brought to this country by the Bedouin encampment which was one of the Midway Plaisance attractions. It is alleged that a great lot of money was expended by Turkish capitalists in gathering this company of 'rough riders' from the Bedouin tribes and that for the first time in the history of the

Turkish Government the Sultan permitted the export of Arabian mares, holding the managers of the enterprise under heavy bonds for their return. We do not vouch for this statement. Preliminary performances at Constantinople are said to have been witnessed by great and enthusi-astic crowds, but the drawing power of the show in Chicago was so small that it passed into the hands of a receiver who disposed of the twenty-eight stallions and mares last week at Tattersall's, Chicago, at prices which are listed in our news columns. The interesting feature of the event is the fact that several of the stallions go to a Colorado ranch where they will be used on native mares in an attempt to breed a high class of saddle horses, and Mr. Bradley, of Bradley fertilizer fame, sends several stallions to his farm near Boston, where he will essay the produc-tion of polo ponies from Southern-bred mares. The result of the intro-duction of this much-vaunted Arabian blood will be watched with great interest.

"SALE OF ARABIAN HORSES.

"The imported Arabian horses used by the Bedouins for hippodrome purposes in Chicago during the World's Fair were sold by public auction at Tattersalls, Chicago, Jan. 4. A good crowd of bidders was in attend-ance and the prices realized were fairly satisfactory, considering the use to which the horses had been put. It is stated that for the first time the Sultan of Turkey issued a permit allowing the exportation of Arabian mares, holding the exporters under heavy bonds, however, for the return of the mares. The Bedouin show played in hard financial luck from the first and finally wound up in the hands of a receiver as the Wild East Show on Midway Plaisance. While exhibiting at Garfield Park early in the season before going to Midway several of the most valuable horses were destroyed by fire. The horses purchased by Mr. H. A. Souther go to the farm of Mr. Bradley, of Bradley fertilizer fame, near Boston, where the stallions will be used on Texas or Southern-bred mares with the view of producing a superior class of polo ponies. The stallions bid off by Mr. Wrenn will be taken to the big Colorado ranch of Messrs. Sam and Frank Dahl, John Condon and L. Schumm, with headquarters at Gypourn, where they will be used in the production of saddle horses from ranch mares. The average price for the twenty-eight head was $360. Details follow:

"Nedjma, gray mare, 14¾ hands, foaled 1887 — C. Kindorf, Chicago, $1,200.

"Kiraby, gray stallion, 14¾ hands, foaled 1885 — J. S. Mounts, Chicago, $400.

"Abbeian, gray stallion, 14¾ hands, foaled 1888 — C. Kindorf, $225.

"Sabuck, dark gray stallion, 15 hands, foaled 1888 — J. S. Mounts, $250.

"Dinvan, dapple gray stallion, 14.2½ hands, foaled 1887 — C. Kindorf, $275.

"Abbu Aley, dapple gray stallion, 14½ hands, foaled 1886 — P. J. Wrenn, Chicago, $225.

"Obeyran, iron gray stallion, 14.2½ hands, foaled 1889 — H. A. Souther, Boston, $325.

"Zebna, gray mare, 14.2½ hands, foaled 1888 — P. J. Wrenn, $250.

"Akhra, gray stallion, 14¾ hands, foaled 1887 — Same, $225.

"Sirhal, light gray stallion, 15 hands, foaled 1886 — H. A. Souther, $175.

"Shamit, iron gray stallion, 15¼ hands, foaled 1887 — P. J. Wrenn, $200.

"Halool, bay stallion, 15¼ hands, foaled 1886 — H. A. Souther, $450.

"Miggour, bay stallion, 14¾ hands, foaled 1887, star — C. Kindorf, $275.

"Simhan, bay stallion, 14¾ hands, left hind foot white, foaled 1885 — J. S. Mounts, $135.

"Koukil, bay stallion, star and snip, left hind foot white, 14¾ hands, foaled 1889 — C. S. Jones, Chicago, $275.

"Koubishan, light bay stallion, star and snip, 14¼ hands, foaled 1888 — Same, $275.

"Haddad, bay stallion, star in forehead, right hind foot white, 15½ hands, foaled 1887 — Same, $150.

"Kazoiv, bay stallion, black points, 15 hands, foaled 1887 — Same, $350.

"Houraney, dark bay stallion, left fore and hind foot white, 15 hands, foaled 1887 — Mr. Potter, Chicago, $385.

"Zariffey, black mare, star, left hind foot white, 14¼ hands, foaled 1888 — C. S. Jones, $195.

"Abjal, black stallion, strip in face, left fore and hind foot white, white right hind coronet, 14½ hands, foaled 1885 — Same, $190.

"Abbya, black mare, 15 hands, foaled 1885 — Souther, $200.

"Hassna, dark bay mare, 14¾ hands, foaled 1889 — Jones, $210.

"Malouk, black stallion, star and snip, 14¾ hands, foaled 1888 — Same, $225.

"Gallfea, sorrel mare, one fore and both hind feet white, 14¾ hands, foaled 1887, in foal, to No. 2 — Souther, $350.

"Hannifey, chestnut stallion, 15¼ hands, foaled 1886 — J. S. Mounts, $325.

"Manakey, sorrel stallion, both hind feet white, 14¾ hands, foaled 1888 — Souther, $550.

"Gray mare — Tobe Broderick, Chicago, $800."

These comments prove without any doubt the previous information given by Mr. A. G. Askidian, as well as information to be found in "My Quest of the Arabian Horse" by Homer Davenport, "The Arab Horse" by Spencer Borden, and "The Horse of the Desert" by W. R. Brown.

Following the 1893 Chicago World's Fair a considerable number of Arabian studs were established, principally in the eastern part of the United States. Such studs as the Hingham Stud at Hingham, Massachusetts, owned by Peter B. Bradley, consisted of a number of the horses sold at the Chicago receiver's sale as well as a large number of the horses imported from the Orient by Homer Davenport. Another stud in nearby Pennsylvania was owned by J. A. P. Ramsdell. Both became quite well known for the production of pure-bred Arabians, as did the stud of W. R. Brown which later became the largest of its kind in the United States. The latter contained principally horses secured from Spencer Borden, Hingham Stock Farm, and from English and Oriental importations. Arabian studs were later established by Albert W. Harris in Wisconsin and California, and by W. K. Kellogg in California. While it cannot be said positively that these studs were all the result of the pure-bred Arabian horses that were brought to the World's Fair, it stands to reason that had it not been for this sale of pure-bred horses to different sections of the country, it is unlikely that so many Arabian studs would have been established.

At still a later date other well-known Arabian studs were founded, such as Travelers' Rest of Gen. J. W. Dickinson, in Tennessee, the Arabian Stud Farm of Henry B. Babson, in Illinois, that of L. W. Van-Vleet in Colorado, and the well-known stud of Rodger A. Selby in Ohio.

Chapter 13

Pure-Bred Arabian Horses Imported Into The United States (1879-1948)

As recounted in previous chapters, the first pure-bred Arabian horses to arrive in the United States were two stallions, imported by Ulysses S. Grant; the next importation of any note was made by Randolph Huntington nine years later; and the first importation of any size was made by The Hamidieh Society for exhibition at the 1893 Chicago World's Fair. While more than forty horses were in this importation, only five were registered in the Arabian Stud Book as foundation animals.

The first importation of considerable size was made by Homer Davenport of Morris Plains, New Jersey, in 1906, followed by Spencer Borden in 1905 to 1910; and W. R. Brown in 1918 to 1923. Small importations were made by others from time to time.

In 1926 W. K. Kellogg, a wealthy manufacturer of breakfast foods, then living in Pomona, California, made a very sizable importation of Arabian horses from the Crabbet Stud of England. These horses greatly influenced the breed during the next twenty-five years since they carried some of the most popular blood lines available. In 1928, 1930 and 1932 Roger A. Selby of Portsmouth, Ohio, an owner of the Selby Shoe Company, also brought in Arabian horses from the Crabbet Arabian Stud. Mr. Selby's stud was greatly reduced in 1949, although a small number of breeding Arabs were maintained.

In 1930 and 1931 Albert W. Harris, a Chicago banker, imported four head of Arabian horses; in 1932 W. R. Brown imported another seven from Egypt; and in 1934, Joseph E. Draper of Claremont, California, imported five Arabian horses from Spain. J. M. Dickinson of Travelers' Rest Farm made an importation of eight head from the leading Arabian studs of Poland in 1937, and another in 1938. One of the horses in the group was the famous Polish Arabian racing stallion, Czubuthan, (1499 Arabian Stud Book) the sire of the largest number of registered Arabian horses of any stallion in the United States during the following ten years. Raffles sired the same number but it took him thirteen years.

The following lists importations from 1879 to 1940:

ARABIAN HORSES IMPORTED BY EX-PRESIDENT U. S. GRANT.

Year	Number	Sex	Name	Breeder
1879	233	S	Leopard	Sultan Abdul Hamid II
1879	234	S	Linden Tree	Sultan Abdul Hamid II

ARABIAN HORSES IMPORTED BY RANDOLPH HUNTINGTON

Year	Number	Sex	Name	Breeder
1888	230	M	Naomi	Rev. F. Vidal, England
1893	231	M	Nazli	Rev. F. Vidal, England
1893	232	S	Nimr	Rev. F. Vidal, England
1891	253	S	Kismet	Desert Bred
1893	244	S	Garaveen	Rev. F. Vidal, England

ARABIAN HORSES IMPORTED BY THE HAMIDIEH SOCIETY

Year	Number	Sex	Name	Breeder
1893	1	M	Nejdme	Hedje Mehmed, Damascus, Syria
1893	2	S	Obeyran	Desert Bred
1893	21	S	Gouneiad	Imperial Streletsky Stud, Russia
1893	294	S	Mannaky	Desert Bred
1893	321	M	Pride	Desert Bred
1893	255	M	Galfia	Desert Bred

ARABIAN HORSES IMPORTED BY HOMER DAVENPORT

Year	Number	Sex	Name	Breeder
1907	24	M	Markisa	Lady Anne Blunt, England
1906	25	S	Haleb	The Gomusa Tribe of the Sebaa Anazeh
1906	26	S	Houran	The Gomusa Tribe of the Sebaa Anazeh
1906	27	S	Muson	The Roala Tribe of the Sebaa Anazeh
1906	28	S	Hamrah	The Ibn Badan el Awagi Anazeh
1906	29	S	El Bulad	Hassan son of Mosisia of the Anazeh
1906	30	M	Wadduda	The Faddan Anazeh Tribe
1906	31	S	Gomusa	The Gomusa Tribe of the Sebaa Anazeh
1906	32	S	Azra	The Tribe of El Mogathra
1906	33	S	Deyr	The Anazeh Tribe
1906	34	S	Mowarda	The Anazeh Tribe
1906	35	S	Kusof	The Anazeh Tribe
1906	36	S	Euphrates	The Faddan Anazeh
1906	37	S	Antar	Hassan Tassen Pasha in Aleppo
1906	38	M	Reshan	The Anazeh Bedouins
1906	39	M	Abeyah	The Shammar Tribe
1906	40	M	Urfah	The Anazeh Bedouins
1906	41	M	Werdi	The Anazeh Bedouins
1906	42	M	Farha	The Anazeh Bedouins
1906	43	M	Hadba	The Shammar Tribe
1906	44	M	Jedah	The Shammar Tribe
1906	45	M	Haffia	The Shammar Bedouins
1906	46	M	Enzahi	The Shammar Bedouins
1906	47	S	Moharra	The Anazeh
1906	48	S	Nedjran	Desert Bred; Imp. to England by Capt Gainsford in 1902
1906	64	S	Masoud	The Anazeh Bedouins
1910	80	S	Berid	Lady Anne Blunt, England
1910	81	S	Jahil	Lady Anne Blunt, England
1910	82	S	Abu Zeyd	Hon. George Saville, England
1906	111	S	Abbeian	Desert Bred

ARABIAN HORSES IMPORTED BY SPENCER BORDEN

Year	Number	Sex	Name	Breeder
1906	162	M	Antika	Crabbet Arabian Stud, England
1911	165	M	Risalda	Crabbet Arabian Stud, England
1911	166	M	Rosa Rugosa	Crabbet Arabian Stud, England
1910	197	S	Hauran	Crabbet Arabian Stud, England
1906	202	S	Razzia	Crabbet Arabian Stud, England
1905	210	S	Imamsada	Hon. Miss Ethelred Dillon, England
1909	211	M	Ghazala	Ali Pasha Sherif, Egypt
1905	222	M	Nessa	Hon. Miss Ethelred Dillon, England
1905	224	M	Mahal	Hon. Miss Ethelred Dillon, England
1898	237	M	Shabaka	Lord Arthur Cecil, England
1906	245	M	Rosetta	Crabbet Arabian Stud, England
1905	246	M	Rose of Sharon	Crabbet Arabian Stud, England
1906	247	M	Rumeliya	Crabbet Arabian Stud, England
1905	248	S	Hail	Hon. Miss Ethelred Dillon, England
1898	250	M	Raksh	Hon. Miss Ethelred Dillon, England
1908	251	M	Butheyna	Crabbet Arabian Stud, England
1906	258	S	Rodan	Crabbet Arabian Stud, England
1909	261	M	Amra	Crabbet Arabian Stud, England
1908	282	S	Halim	Crabbet Arabian Stud, England
1911	284	M	Radha	Crabbet Arabian Stud, England

ARABIAN HORSES IMPORTED BY W. R. BROWN

Year	Number	Sex	Name	Breeder
1918	343	S	Berk	Crabbet Arabian Stud, England
1918	344	M	Baraza	Crabbet Arabian Stud, England
1918	345	M	Battla	Crabbet Arabian Stud, England
1918	346	M	Rijma	Crabbet Arabian Stud, England
1918	347	M	Ramla	Crabbet Arabian Stud, England
1918	348	M	Ramim	Crabbet Arabian Stud, England
1918	349	M	Rishrash	Crabbet Arabian Stud, England
1918	350	S	Rajafan	Crabbet Arabian Stud, England
1918	351	M	Rokhsa	Crabbet Arabian Stud, England
1918	352	M	Kasima	Crabbet Arabian Stud, England
1918	353	M	Kerbela	Crabbet Arabian Stud, England
1918	354	M	Nueyra	Crabbet Arabian Stud, England
1918	355	M	Numera	Crabbet Arabian Stud, England
1918	356	S	Nafia	Crabbet Arabian Stud, England
1918	357	M	Razna	Crabbet Arabian Stud, England

ARABIAN HORSES IMPORTED BY W. R. BROWN

Year	Number	Sex	Name	Breeder
1918	358	M	Simawa	Crabbet Arabian Stud, England
1918	359	M	Felestin	Crabbet Arabian Stud, England
1919	381	S	Rizvan	Crabbet Arabian Stud, England
1921	454	S	Bahka	In Pau, France
1921	455	M	Babel	In Pau, France
1921	456	M	Makrine	In Pau, France
1921	457	M	Balkis 2nd	In Pau, France
1921	458	M	Badine	In Pau, France
1922	485	M	Kola	In Pau, France
1923	509	M	Hamida	S. G. Hough, England
1923	510	M	Hama	S. G. Hough, England
1932	885	S	Zarife	Prince Mohamed Aly, Cairo, Egypt
1932	886	M	Roda	Prince Mohamed Aly, Cairo, Egypt
1932	887	M	H. H. Mohamed Ali's Hamama	Prince Mohamed Aly, Cairo, Egypt
1932	888	M	Aziza	Prince Mohamed Aly, Cairo, Egypt
1932	889	S	Nasr	Prince Mohamed Aly, Cairo, Egypt
1932	890	M	H. H. Mohamed Ali's Hamida	Prince Mohamed Aly, Cairo, Egypt
1932	891	S	Silver Yew	Prince Mohamed Aly, Cairo, Egypt

ARABIAN HORSES IMPORTED BY W. K. KELLOGG

Year	Number	Sex	Name	Breeder
1926	595	M	Ferdisia	Crabbet Arabian Stud, England
1926	596	M	Ferda	Crabbet Arabian Stud, England
1926	597	S	Raseyn	Crabbet Arabian Stud, England
1926	598	M	Rossana	Crabbet Arabian Stud, England
1926	599	S	Rimal	Crabbet Arabian Stud, England
1926	600	M	Raida	Crabbet Arabian Stud, England
1926	601	M	Rifla	Crabbet Arabian Stud, England
1926	602	M	Rasafa	Crabbet Arabian Stud, England
1926	603	M	Bahreyn	Crabbet Arabian Stud, England
1926	604	S	Nasik	Crabbet Arabian Stud, England
1926	605	M	Rifda	Crabbet Arabian Stud, England
1926	606	M	Rasima	Crabbet Arabian Stud, England
1926	607	S	Raswan	Crabbet Arabian Stud, England
1926	608	M	Bint	Crabbet Arabian Stud, England
1926	612	S	Razam	Crabbet Arabian Stud, England

ARABIAN HORSES IMPORTED BY W. K. KELLOGG

Year	Number	Sex	Name	Breeder
1926	613	S	Ferdin	Crabbet Arabian Stud, England
1927	615	M	Farasin	Crabbet Arabian Stud, England

ARABIAN HORSES IMPORTED BY ROGER A. SELBY

Year	Number	Sex	Name	Breeder
1930	790	S	Mirage	The Sebaa Arabs of the Anazeh Tribe
1928	808	S	Mirzam	Crabbet Arabian Stud, England
1930	809	M	Kiyama	Crabbet Arabian Stud, England
1930	810	M	Hilwe	Crabbet Arabian Stud, England
1928	811	M	Kareyma	Crabbet Arabian Stud, England
1930	812	M	Selmnab	Crabbet Arabian Stud, England
1928	813	M	Indaia	Crabbet Arabian Stud, England
1930	814	M	Raselma	Crabbet Arabian Stud, England
1928	815	M	Rifala	Crabbet Arabian Stud, England
1930	819	M	Jerama	Crabbet Arabian Stud, England
1930	855	M	Namilla	Crabbet Arabian Stud, England
1930	856	M	Rasmina	Crabbet Arabian Stud, England
1930	857	M	Rose of France	Crabbet Arabian Stud, England
1932	950	S	Rahal	Crabbet Arabian Stud, England
1932	951	S	Selmian	Crabbet Arabian Stud, England
1932	952	S	Raffles	Crabbet Arabian Stud, England
1932	953	S	Menzil	Crabbet Arabian Stud, England
1932	954	M	Rishafieh	Crabbet Arabian Stud, England
1933	973	M	Rimini	Crabbet Arabian Stud, England
1933	974	S	Nureddin	Crabbet Arabian Stud, England

ARABIAN HORSES IMPORTED BY ALBERT W. HARRIS

Year	Number	Sex	Name	Breeder
1924	517	S	Nuri Pasha	S. G. Hough, England
1924	518	M	Ana	Crabbet Arabian Stud, England
1931	851	M	Samirah	The King of Hejas and Nejd
1931	852	M	Tairah	The King of Hejas and Nejd
1931	853	M	Dahma	The King of Hejas and Nejd
1930	854	M	Nufoud	The King of Hejas and Nejd
1931	943	S	Sunshine	Mohamed Id El Rouaf, Consul of Hejaz and Nejd

ARABIAN HORSES IMPORTED BY JOSEPH E. DRAPER

Year	Number	Sex	Name	Breeder
1934	1215	M	Nakkla	Bred in Spain
1934	1216	S	Ras-el-Ayn	Bred in Spain
1934	1217	M	Menfis	Bred in Spain
1934	1218	M	Barakat	Bred in Spain
1934	1219	M	Meca	Bred in Spain

ARABIAN HORSES IMPORTED BY J. M. DICKINSON

Year	Number	Sex	Name	Breeder
1934	1028	M	Aire	Guilherme Echenique, Filho, Brazil, S. A.
1937	1292	M	Maamouna	Royal Agricultural Society, Cairo, Egypt
1937	1309	M	Przepiorka	The Polish "State Arab Stud" at Janow-Podlaski, Poland
1937	1310	M	Lassa	The Polish "State Arab Stud" at Janow-Podlaski, Poland
1937	1311	M	Liliana	By Estate of Jana Kleniewskiego, "Zagloba-Opole," Poland
1937	1312	M	Mattaria	At the "Behen," Stud of Counts Roman and Jozef Potocki, Warsaw, Poland
1937	1313	M	Niwka	The Polish "State Arab Stud" at Janow-Podlaski, Poland
1937	1314	M	Nora	The Polish "State Arab Stud" at Janow-Podlaski, Poland
1937	1391	M	Sielanka	Estate of Jana Klieniewskiego, "Zagloba-Opole," Poland (Imp. in utero)

IMPORTATIONS U. S. GOVERNMENT REMOUNT SERVICE FROM POLAND, HUNGARY, AND CZECHOSLOVAKIA FOLLOWING WORLD WAR II

Year	Number	Sex	Name	Breeder
1945	3932	S	Lotnik G	Poland
1945	3933	S	Witez II B	Poland
1945	3934	M	Chloe G	Poland
1945	3935	M	Wierna B	Poland

IMPORTATIONS U. S. GOVERNMENT REMOUNT SERVICE FROM POLAND, HUNGARY, AND CZECHOSLOVAKIA FOLLOWING WORLD WAR II

Year	Number	Sex	Name	Breeder
1945	3936	M	Tarnina G	Poland
1945	3937	M	Iwonka III Ch	Poland
1945	4001	M	231. Kuhaylan-Zaid-8 G	Hungary
1945	4002	M	243. Mersuch III-3 G	Hungary
1945	4003	M	Stola G	Czechoslovakia
1945	4004	M	Werra G	Czechoslovakia
1945	4005	S	Pilot G	Czechoslovakia
1945	4006	S	Wisok B	Czechoslovakia
1945	4007	M	Zalma B	Czechoslovakia
1945	4008	M	Wierka B	Czechoslovakia

ARABIAN HORSES IMPORTED TO CANADA BY MR. P. J. SMITH AND MRS. A. M. SMITH

Year	Number	Sex	Name	Breeder
1947	4227	S	Ranix B	Mrs. A. M. Smith, England
1947	4228	M	Rosheba G	Miss Mary Russell, England
1947	4229	M	Kurrah G	Thriplow Farms, England

George J. O'Brien of Los Angeles, California, was presented with an Arabian stallion and mare in 1947 by H. R. H. Amir Saud Ibn Abdul Aziz Al Saud, of Arabia and they were imported the same year.

Year	Number	Sex	Name	Breeder
1947	4231	S	Munifan	Arabia
1947	4232	M	Munifeh	Arabia

Smaller importations were:

ARABIAN HORSES IMPORTED BY MR. EUSTIS

Year	Number	Sex	Name	Breeder
1900	22	S	Ibn Mahruss	Lady Anne Blunt, England
1900	23	M	Bushra	Lady Anne Blunt, England

ARABIAN HORSES IMPORTED BY E. P. HATCH

Year	Number	Sex	Name	Breeder
1910	76	M	Lisa	Desert Bred

ARABIAN HORSES IMPORTED BY
TURKISH MINISTER AT WASHINGTON

Year	Number	Sex	Name	Breeder
1910	77	S	Jameel	Anazeh Bedouin Tribe

ARABIAN HORSES IMPORTED BY F. LOTHROP AMES

Year	Number	Sex	Name	Breeder
1905	160	M	Shibine	Crabbet Arabian Stud, England
1910	164	M	Narda II	Crabbet Arabian Stud, England
1909	238	S	Astraled	Crabbet Arabian Stud, England
1910	309	S	Crabbet	Crabbet Arabian Stud, England

ARABIAN HORSES IMPORTED BY JOHN H. LAPHAM

Year	Number	Sex	Name	Breeder
1917	206	M	Zobeide	Hon. Miss Ethelred Dillon, England

ARABIAN HORSES IMPORTED BY WILLIAM H. FORBES

Year	Number	Sex	Name	Breeder
1893	239	S	Bedr	Crabbet Arabian Stud, England
1893	240	M	Jamila	Crabbet Arabian Stud, England

ARABIAN HORSES IMPORTED BY J. A. P. RAMSDELL

Year	Number	Sex	Name	Breeder
1895	241	S	Shahwan	Ali Pacha Sherif, Egypt
1893	242	M	Rakushen	Hon. Miss Ethelred Dillon, England
1893	243	S	Ras Aloula	Hon. Miss Ethelred Dillon, England

ARABIAN HORSES IMPORTED BY AMEEN RIHANI

Year	Number	Sex	Name	Breeder
1928	687	S	Saoud	King Ibn Saoud's Stable, Ar-Riyadh, Nejd
1928	688	M	Noura	King Ibn Saoud's Stable, Ar-Riyadh, Nejd
1928	689	M	Muha	King Ibn Saoud's Stable, Ar-Riyadh, Nejd

ARABIAN HORSES IMPORTED BY K. A. BISTANY

Year	Number	Sex	Name	Breeder
1929	721	M	Saada	Najib Bey Souliman, Syria
1933	965	S	Al-Mashoor	Abdallah Azaar, Syria
1933	966	M	Alya	Chickrallad Abdallah, Syria

ARABIAN HORSES IMPORTED BY HERMAN W. FRANK

Year	Number	Sex	Name	Breeder
1929	738	M	Malouma	Mahmoud Matlak, Egypt
1929	739	S	King John	Desert Bred

ARABIAN HORSES IMPORTED BY HENRY HERBERMANN

Year	Number	Sex	Name	Breeder
1930	816	M	Exochorda	Royal Agricultural Society, Egypt
1930	817	S	Ibn Nafa	Royal Agricultural Society, Egypt

ARABIAN HORSES IMPORTED BY CHARLES R. CRANE

Year	Number	Sex	Name	Breeder
1931	876	M	La Tisa	Desert Bred
1931	877	M	Mahsudha	Desert Bred

ARABIAN HORSES IMPORTED BY HENRY B. BABSON

Year	Number	Sex	Name	Breeder
1932	892	M	Bint Bint Durra	Royal Agricultural Society, Egypt
1932	893	M	Bint Saada	Royal Agricultural Society, Egypt
1932	894	M	Bint Bint Saabah	Royal Agricultural Society, Egypt
1932	895	M	Maaroufa	Prince Mohamed Aly, Egypt
1932	896	S	Fadl	Prince Mohamed Aly, Egypt
1932	897	M	Bint Serra I	Prince Kamel el Dine, Egypt
1932	962	S	Metsur	Prince Kamel el Dine, Egypt

ARABIAN HORSES IMPORTED BY MISS FRANCES M. DODGE

Year	Number	Sex	Name	Breeder
1934	1063	S	Ibn Gamila	Royal Agricultural Society, Egypt

ARABIAN HORSES IMPORTED BY FREDERICK L. WEHR

Year	Number	Sex	Name	Breeder
1940	1875	M	Indian Dawn	Crabbet Arabian Stud, England
1940	1876	M	Crown of India	Crabbet Arabian Stud, England
1940	1877	S	Rosanthus	Crabbet Arabian Stud, England

The San Simeon Stables made a late importation — in 1948 — of desert-bred Arabians that should provide future breeding stock of much value for the Arabian breed as a whole in the United States. This was the first importation of any size made direct from desert countries for many years and because of the diminishing numbers of pure Arabian horses in this country the importation is of special interest. A short description of this transaction is taken from the February-March, 1948, issue of *The Horse Lover:*

"One of the greatest shipments of Arabian Horses ever to reach America from Arabia was completed recently by San Simeon Stables of the Hearst Ranch, San Simeon, California.

"Climaxing a five-and-one-half month search in the Middle Eastern countries of Arabia, Preston Dyer, manager of San Simeon with John Williamson as photographer and Doctor Pulling as veterinarian arrived in California with fourteen head of those priceless blue bloods of Arabia, the rare and beautiful horse of the desert.

Arabian mares and colts with a Palomino mare and colt in pasture at the P. K. Wrigley, Jr., ranch on Catalina Island.

Palomino stallion, SHARIK'S SUN, sired by SHARIK No. 1784 Arabian stallion.

"Did I say priceless? The lot is estimated to have cost an even 100 grand, or a fraction over $7,000 each, landed in their fertile seaside pastures of California.

"The trip in search of the equine aristocracy took them approximately 25,000 miles — to England, France, Italy, Tripoli, Egypt, Syria, Mesopotamia, Iraq, the Northern Arabian desert and Lebanon.

"The stallion, Arkahn, was a gift from the Foreign Minister of Lebanon, by name Henri Pharoun. This stallion ran on the race tracks of Arabia and Egypt (races once a week, on Sundays) during two racing seasons, participating every Sunday in the speed races. This remarkable bay stallion won every race over a two-year period, accounting for seventeen consecutive wins. He is a smooth-turned, medium-sized Arabian stallion, still as sound on his legs as a colt.

"Mr. Dyer secured the finest animals he could find. On one occasion while searching among the wandering tribes of Northern Arabia, he spied a beautiful mare of distinction among the great horse breeding tribes of Bedouins, noted for their production of fine horses for centuries. He negotiated and finally purchased the prize animal, and knowing of the great attachment of the Bedouin for his horse, Mr. Dyer hastened to depart before 'circumstances' or the Bedouin's change of mind would deprive him of this desert beauty.

"Alone, Preston Dyer mounted the mare and into Bazra, a small town, he rode, thence across the mountains a distance of 85 miles to the collecting point of the horses destined for America. The trip was made by Mr. Dyer alone, sleeping at night on the ground in a sleeping bag while the mare was hobbled near by. They both arrived safely at the shipping point and the mare is now a prize at San Simeon. Someday, if you are fortunate enough to visit this ranch and see their wonderful horses, Mr. Dyer may show you the Arabian steed which he rode all alone over the far reaches of the Arabian desert. The horses were shipped by boat from Arabia to France, a voyage lasting six days, thence twenty-one days across the Atlantic to New York, and from New York to San Luis Obispo by train, four days. Each horse was crated for the entire journey. No injuries or deaths occurred on the trip. The horses arrived with no noticeable swellings, puffs or leg trouble of any kind, a remarkable tribute to the toughness of fiber and soundness of the legs of the pure-blooded Arabian.

"Mr. Dyer was a man well qualified for such an undertaking, not only is he thoroughly versed in what constitutes the true blood horse, but his years of practical experience have taught him to be alert for performance, for conformation, for soundness and general over-all excellence expected by such a breeding program as is so rigorously followed by San Simeon Stables.

"In the opinion of many horsemen, Preston Dyer talks Morgan horses and knows Morgan horses with the best of them. The same might be said of the Thoroughbred, the Morab (Morgan-Arab cross), the Palomino and the Appaloosa, the breeding of which Mr. Dyer supervises along with their production of the pure-bred Arabian.

"It is planned to use the newly imported Arabian stallions on the older Arabian mares at San Simeon and in like turn for the present to use the older Arabian stallions on the newly imported Arabian mares and thus saturate the blood stock already well known with a new infusion of the blood so close-up to the desert.

"San Simeon Stables for many years have been prime producers of fine Arabian horses, having secured their seed stock originally from the world famous W. R. Brown stud of Berlin, New Hampshire, the W. K. Kellogg Arabian Horse Ranch at Pomona, California, and others.

"San Simeon is now in a position to assume national as well as world leadership in the breeding and preservation of the noble, ancient, and world-esteemed Arabian Horse, and horsemen everywhere will rejoice to know that in America there reposes a goodly supply of that 'eternal yeast', 'the Arabian Horse', not only a good horse in himself, but one whose blood has made other breeds great, and the original source of all superior light horse blood, according to the Encyclopedia Britannica. 'As the horseman of today looks about him, and among horses, and observes beauty, speed, grace, fire, good action, gentleness and fineness, yet toughness of fiber, he sees that eternal value of the Arabian desert horse, as it has so benefited and improved horse blood for thousands of years'. — From the writings of John Hervey — 'Salvator'.

"America and the World owe a debt of gratitude to the owners and management of San Simeon stables for their most worthy contribution to this end."

The list of importations follows:

Year	Number	Sex	Name	Country
1947	4205	S	Snounou G	Syria
1947	4207	S	Bourhane G	Syria
1947	4210	S	Mounwer Ch	Syria
1947	4212	S	Arkane B	Syria
1947	4216	S	Zamal G	Syria
1947	4217	S	Ghamil Ch	Syria
1947	4206	M	Najwa G	Syria
1947	4208	M	Layya G	Syria
1947	4209	M	Kouhailane G	Syria
1947	4211	M	Lebnaniah G	Syria
1947	4213	M	Mansourah G	Syria
1947	4214	M	Rajwa G	Syria
1947	4215	M	Bint Rajwa G	Syria
1947	4218	M	Nouwayra G	Syria

Chapter 14

Some Well-Known Importers Of Arabian Horses

I N previous chapters, details have been given concerning leading importers of Arabian horses. Actually, since 1730 there have been only a few who imported these horses in such numbers and with such attention to blood lines, as to have greatly influenced the production of the breed in this country.

Some of the individuals mentioned only in passing in other chapters, who have contributed in an outstanding way to the development of the Arabian horse in the United States, are described in the following pages.

HOMER DAVENPORT

The subject of this sketch was born in Oregon shortly after the Civil War, but spent most of his early life in San Francisco. He became a proficient cartoonist — devoting special attention to drawings of horses — early in his life and went on to become a world famous cartoonist in later years. Much of his working life was spent on leading newspapers in Chicago and New York. Mr. Davenport states in a book written by him that from earliest childhood he was interested in horses and that this interest came into being when he was four years old because of his admiration of a picture — on a horse liniment package — of a beautiful Arabian with head held high and magnificent carriage.

Mr. Davenport was working on the Chicago Herald in 1893, the year of the Chicago World's Fair and it was here that he got his first look at some typical natural Arabian horses when he came upon the previously mentioned Hamidieh Hippodrome Company, then appearing at the Fair, with its group of forty-odd pure Arabians. He states that he came upon this group of horses while walking down the street and was so carried away by their appearance that he followed them all over town and back to their headquarters, and thought of nothing else during the next few days.

In late 1895, Homer Davenport went to New York to work for one of the leading newspapers of that city, and at this time began investigations that eventually led to his importation, direct from the Middle East, of twenty-six head of exceptionally fine pure-bred Arabian horses which later became important as the foundation animals of many of the most prominent Arabian horse breeding stud farms.

CHARMAIN No. 860. A 17-year-old Arabian mare of Davenport breeding.

As soon as Mr. Davenport arrived in New York, he contacted Randolph Huntington (see previous chapters) and inquired concerning the whereabouts of the Arabian horses he had seen at the Chicago World's Fair. He was successful in tracing one of the best of the lot, a mare, then owned by Peter B. Bradley of Hingham, Mass. Davenport continued his search for several years and he eventually located several of them in the New England states.

All the while, Davenport continued to read and study every bit of information he could collect on the breed and developed an intense interest in actually seeing and studying the Arabian horse on his native grounds. In 1906, with the assistance of Peter B. Bradley and in the company of two other men, John H. Thompson, Jr., and C. A. Moore, Jr., he finally got to the Middle East where he selected and supervised the purchase of twenty-six stallions and mares from desert Arabians. A great many of these horses, after their arrival in this country, were sent to the Massachusetts breeding farm of Peter Bradley and the rest to Mr. Davenport's Desert Arabian Stud Farm at Morris Plains, New York.

Unfortunately, these desert-bred Arabians had not passed through England and been recorded in the General Stud Book, and Mr. Davenport had been ignorant of the importance of properly executed affadavits testifying to the purity of their breeding, so they were not eligible for registration in the American Stud Book. The direct result of this exclusion was the formation of a new stud book, called the Arabian Stud Book, by the owners and breeders of Arabians in the United States.

As a natural consequence, there was a great deal of conflicting opinion among leading horse breeders of the day regarding the authenticity of Mr. Davenport's importations. One of the most critical opponents of the whole undertaking was Spencer Borden, a leading breeder of the time, and for some years there was considerable ill feeling between the two men.

Although many of the leading studs of Arabian horses in this country contain animals that trace to foundation stock known as Davenport breeding, not all of the horses he imported were used for producing pure-breds. Some of them were bought for riding and others for producing part-bred Arabs.

A study of the Arabian Stud Books will show that the Davenport Desert Arabian Stud and Homer Davenport as an individual registered forty-three Arabian horses in the first volume of the Stud Book. Some of the principal stallions imported and registered in said volume were Haleb, Hamrah, El Bulad, Deyr, Euphrates, Muson, and Nedjran.

Among the mares registered probably the best known was the mare Wadduda, whose name appears in many Arabian pedigrees to this day.

Other prominent mares in the lot were Abeyah, Urfah, Haffia and Hadba. The principal reason that many of these horses did not find their way into the Arabian Stud Book was because the number of mares that were bred each year was very small and some of them, for one reason or another, did not produce or were probably not bred to Arab stallions.

The second volume of the Arabian Stud Book was not published until 1918. By that time the differences between Spencer Borden and Homer Davenport had been satisfactorily adjusted, and in Volume II we find that Interlachen Farms of Fall River, Massachusetts, owned by Spencer Borden (who had refused to register any of his Arabians in Volume I), registered twenty-five Arab horses that were on his farm and ten horses as foundation stock which he had owned but which were by that time dead.

JAMIL ABDULLAH AZAM No. 1258. An extreme classic type Arabian stallion of Davenport breeding.

While Peter B. Bradley, owner of Hingham Stock Farm, was one of the early breeders of Arabian horses in the United States, it is evident from the information available through the Stud Books and elsewhere that his interest in the Arab horse did not extend to the point where he spent a great deal of personal time and effort with this breed. He evidently was the owner of these horses which originally, in the 1908 Stud Book, were registered under the name of Davenport Desert Arab Stud of Hingham, Massachusetts. By the time the second volume of the Arabian Stud Book was published in 1918, the name of this breeding establishment had been changed from the Davenport Desert Arabian Stud to the Hingham Stock Farm under the ownership of Peter B. Bradley, and in this book the registrations were made under this designation. The following Arabian horses were registered: twenty-one stallions; five colts; thirty-five mares; seventeen fillies; eight geldings; and twenty-one dead.

It is evident from the above that in the consideration of the influence of individuals on the development of the Arabian breed in the United States the Davenport Desert Arab Stud and Hingham Stock Farm are practically one and the same. Davenport personally selected the horses imported while Peter B. Bradley financed the importation and the breeding operation of the stock farm which was founded upon these animals.

SPENCER BORDEN

Spencer Borden was evidently a very well-to-do Massachusetts citizen whose principal business was cloth bleacheries. He evidently had one qualification that set him apart from several other early importers and breeders of Arabian horses which was that he was a very widely experienced horseman in his own right.

Spencer Borden maintained his breeding establishment — Interlachen Farms — at Fall River, Massachusetts. It is quite evident from several references in clippings and other data that Mr. Borden was a great admirer of Randolph Huntington and his Arab horses and that his interest in the breed was kindled by the sight of Huntington's fine Arabs. His first importation, consisting of two mares, Shabaka (No. 237) and Raksh (No. 250), was made in 1898. These mares were registered in Volume II of the Arabian Stud Book as foundation mares in the year 1918. In this volume it will be found that Spencer Borden registered seven stallions, three colts, three fillies, ten mares, two geldings and ten foundation pure-bred Arabs that were dead.

Borden continued to import Arabian horses in small numbers until

1909. His earlier importations were principally from the stud of Miss Dillon, in England. Among the better known Arabs that have had considerable influence on the breed in the United States were the stallions Imazada (No. 210) and Rodan (No. 258), as well as the well-known mares, Shabaka (No. 237) Raksh (No. 250) and Rose of Sharon (No. 246).

Spencer Borden will go down in Arabian history as the breeder of two of the most widely known Arabian brood mares in the United States, i.e., Guemura (No. 277) and Gulnare (No. 278), both daughters of the famous Ghazala (No. 211) imported in 1909 by him. Had Mr. Borden not bred a single other animal he would have been remembered as having had a great influence upon the breed and its development in America.

In 1906, Mr. Borden wrote a very valuable book entitled, "The Arab Horse," in which there is to be found a lot of general information on the Arabian horse both in its native land, in England and in the United States. Most of his importations had been made before this book was published and students and breeders of the Arab horse will find much valuable information in the book. It was long out of print but was recently reprinted, and now, fortunately, is available.

In 1912 Mr. Borden, who had been a cavalryman, published privately a book entitled, "What Horse for the Cavalry," in which he sets forth in considerable detail the history and use of the Arab stallions in the production of remount or cavalry horses in leading European countries. These studies involved reports from Holland, Germany, France, Austria and Hungary. It is a valuable book for breeders and students of the Arabian horse but unfortunately it has been out of print for nearly forty years and it is very difficult to locate copies. The book is very well illustrated, mostly with part-bred Arabs suitable for producing cavalry or war horses.

The following is from a letter received in October 1949 from a grand-daughter of Spencer Borden, Blanche Borden Frenning:

"I am sure that no book about the Arabian Horse in America would be complete without mention of all Grandfather did for Arab horses in this country. As his oldest grandchild, living at Interlachen with him until I was married, I grew up on Arabs and remember with youthful enthusiasm most of his famous horses and the excitement of Arabian importations.

"Grandfather was an extremely colorful personality, doing fantastic things until he died in 1921. In fact, I believe that he rode to Nishnil-Novgorod in Russia in his early 20's, and had ridden from the Pacific coast to the Missouri River in his teens. He was born in 1849.

"When his interest switched to pure-bred Guernsey cattle, he sold most of his Arabs to Mr. W. R. Brown — reserving, without broadcasting, what he considered the two best mares. One of these he gave to me and one to my cousin. (We were both unmarried and able to support horses in those days.) Unfortunately, mine ate a piece of baling wire and died a year later. My cousin, however, showed hers in Madison Square Garden for many years; always taking prizes to the dismay of the large breeders, and re-proving his judgments of quality."

The influence that Spencer Borden had on the development of the Arabian horse cannot be passed over without another mention of the last importation (1909) he made to the United States, the famous brood mare, Ghazala, bred by Ali Pacha Sherif of Cairo, Egypt, and registered in the General Stud Book in England, here in the American Stud Book (that is, the Jockey Club) and also in the Arabian Stud Book. She produced while owned by Mr. Borden the two unusually good brood mares Guemura, foaled in 1912 and sired by Segario, and Gulnare, foaled in 1914 and sired by Rodan. Guemura produced a total of seventeen foals, and died at twenty-six. Among the offspring of this

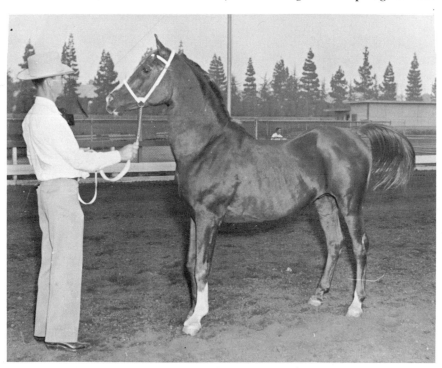

GULASTRA A.H.C. No. 521.

famous daughter of Ghazala was Ghazi (No. 560), who was for many years, until his death, one of the senior stallions at Hearst's San Simeon Ranch of California. Another son, Gharis (No. 623) was one of the prominent stallions used by J. E. Draper, also of California. In addition to these two very popular Arabian sires Guemura produced some other well-known stallions as well as some exceptional brood mares. Mares that are daughters and granddaughters of Guemura are widely sought by Arab breeders throughout the United States.

Gulnare, among her offspring, produced the famous stallion, Gulastra, (No. 521), which was sired by Astraled (No. 238). Gulastra became one of the prominent Arabian sires of the breed in this country.

WILLIAM R. BROWN

William R. Brown founded Maynesboro Arabian Stud at Berlin, New Hampshire, in 1912. His Arabian stud was formed at a time when it was possible to get several exceptionally fine Arabian breeding horses that had already been imported or bred by other individuals. Some of the most widely known and most valuable breeding animals at the Maynesboro Stud were secured from such importers and breeders as Homer Davenport, Spencer Borden, Mr. J. A. P. Ramsdell and other prominent breeders.

In 1918 Mr. Brown started importing Arabian horses on his own account, and from this date until 1923 he must be given credit for importing some of the most notable Arabian horses, with the widest influence of any such horses ever owned in the United States to that time. For several years Mr. Brown continued to breed Arabians at his farm and in 1919 a catalogue of his stud shows that he was the owner of eighty-eight pure-bred registered Arabian horses and had his principal stud at Berlin, New Hampshire, with another large-sized stud at Decorah, Iowa, and a smaller one at Cody, Wyoming.

In 1932 he imported seven valuable Arabian horses direct from Egypt. Prior to this time most of his importations had been made from Crabbet Stud, in England. The records will show that most of this last importation was sold to J. M. Dickinson, of Travelers' Rest Stud, Nashville, Tennessee. Other earlier importations were seventeen pure-bred Arabians from Crabbet Arabian Stud in 1918, and another horse from the same stud in 1919; in 1921 five Arabian horses from France; in 1922 an additional horse from France; and in 1923 two horses from S. G. Hough, of England.

Mr. Brown was a tireless worker for the promotion of the Arabian

---

MAYNESBORO ARABIAN STUD

BERLIN, NEW HAMPSHIRE, U. S. A.

(FOUNDED 1912)

THOROUGHBRED

ARABIAN SADDLE HORSES

REG. AMERICAN STUD BOOK   REG. ARABIAN STUD BOOK

AT STUD   ## FOR SALE

RIDING   BEAUTY
    DRIVING   GENTLENESS
        CAVALRY   ENDURANCE

CATALOGUED BY STRAINS AND FAMILIES

SEASON   :   :   :   :   1922

Maynesboro Arabian Stallion Catalog for 1922.

horse and the demonstration of this breed as a satisfactory cavalry mount. For several years endurance rides of 300 miles each were held in the New England states based on what were considered cavalry requirements, and Brown finally won the permanent cup given by the United States Army after three of his Arabs had won at least one of such rides. Arabian horses were in the minority in these contests but in practically every instance they gave a fine account on their weight-carrying ability and endurance.

These rides were all conducted under the sponsorship of several important horse organizations, and the general regulations were practically the same. In order to explain the object and general purpose of them, the following portions of a booklet entitled, "Conditions of the 1922 Endurance Ride" are quoted:

"These Endurance Rides, approved by the War Department, the Chief of the Army Remount Service, the Chief of the Bureau of Animal Industry of the Department of Agriculture, and the Sponsors, are designed to stimulate interest in the breeding, care, and use of good saddle horses of a general utility type, possessed of stamina and hardiness, and at the same time having the necessary quality to render them suitable for use in the mounted service of the United States. These Endurance Rides are planned for the horse and not the rider, and while it is fully appreciated that it is quite impossible wholly to eliminate the human factor from the equation, yet every effort has been brought to

Left to right: TESCHIDA No. 1991. Gray mare and colt DU CARAM.
KARIFA No. 2863 Ch/G mare and filly.

bear to minimize the effect of that factor, and still maintain the public interest. Entries are solicited equally from the military service and civilian life.

"The total distance to be covered will be approximately 300 miles. The contestants will ride 60 miles per day for each of the five successive days, regardless of weather. The distance for any given day may be slightly more or less than 60 miles, according as stabling accommodations may be available. All contestants shall follow the prescribed route. All contestants shall stop at the same place at midday and at night. The Ride shall be laid over a course designated by a committee appointed by the Board of Sponsors. The turnings of the course will be plainly marked for direction by arrows, and every mile will be indicated by a number from 1 to 60 for each day. The colors of these arrows and numerals are to be selected by the Route Committee."

ALBERT W. HARRIS

Albert W. Harris, a well-known Chicago bank and trust company owner for many years past, was a very important breeder of Arabian horses for many years. Mr. Harris secured his first pure-bred Arab from the Homer Davenport importation of 1908. Several years prior to this time he had been breeding what are commonly known as Indian ponies on his farm near Lake Geneva, Wisconsin.

There is no doubt that Mr. Harris was an excellent judge of horseflesh since he had been a student of horses from his early days in Minnesota and an expert in horsemanship for many years afterward. He was a particular enthusiast of the endurance race mentioned in previous pages.

Mr. Harris first became acquainted with the Indian or Cayuse pony, also called a mustang, during his boyhood years in Minnesota. He became fond of the breed and convinced of the excellence of its ancestry, and in time experimented with the breeding of an Indian mare to a thoroughbred Arabian stallion, for the first such cross-breeding in the Midwest.

After he took up residence in Chicago, Mr. Harris commissioned a friend named McClain to procure for him a number of Indian mustangs from the nearby Indian territory. The first shipment included seventeen mares and one black stallion. For several years the mares were bred to the original stallion, and the filly offspring were bred to stallion offspring of the same sire. The horses were in constant use by the Harris family

Group of Arabian mares and colt. Left to right: KIFFAH No. 1333, PERA No. 1107, CARIOCA No. 2009, Champion NABIKA No. 653, BEN DYAB No. 2861.

KAMIL A.H.C. No. 1912. Stallion and group of fillies.

and friends at their farm near Lake Geneva, Wisconsin, and they turned out to be, although small, not only tough and hard-working animals, but also very satisfactory for driving and riding.

In 1941, Mr. Harris prepared an excellent book entitled "The Blood of the Arab, the World's Greatest War Horse," which was privately printed by the Arabian Horse Club of America. This book deals in considerable detail with the Indian mustang and recounts Harris' experiences in breeding them, as well as their general usefulness for war and other purposes. The book is of great value to students of the horse.

I am old enough to have had a limited experience with and to have observed, in a small way, the mustang or Indian pony so ably described in Mr. Harris' book. In my youth and for some years afterward, during the early part of the 1900's, it was common for horse dealers in Western states to ship mustangs into the section of Ohio where I lived and sell them for buggy and riding purposes. At the time, the ponies would sell at prices ranging anywhere from twenty-five or thirty dollars up to fifty dollars each, except for the occasional very fine animal which might bring a slightly higher price. They were very small, rarely weighing as much as 900 pounds when in first-class condition and generally not more than 850. They rarely exceeded fourteen hands, but they did have very beautiful heads and often good tail carriage, evidences of their considerable quantity of Arabian blood. The first buggy horse I ever owned was

EZ ZUHRA A.H.C. No. 3585.

a gray Western mustang called Dan. Dan was a very tough, good using horse and for many years one of the most satisfactory buggy ponies in the area, though he lacked the usual style of the breed.

In 1908, Albert W. Harris purchased his first pure-bred Arabian horse, Nejdran, Jr., a Homer Davenport importation, and as a result developed a friendship with Davenport. Harris purchased other Arab horses from time to time and finally, in 1926 made a small importation of horses on his own account. He is listed as an Arabian horse owner in Volume I of the Arabian Stud Book, as Vice President and a Director of the Arabian Horse Club in 1927-1937 and as President and a governing member in 1944.

Mr. Harris' interest in the Arabian horse continued to grow with the breed in the United States, or perhaps faster than the breed generally did, at least during the first twenty-five or thirty years after the Stud Book was founded. Several years after he had established the Kemah Breeding Farm in Wisconsin, Mr. Harris started an Arabian breeding farm in California, at a time when there were only a few Arabs in the entire United States. This farm was abandoned in about 1945 or 1946 and at that time Arabs had increased in California and other western states to a point where it was likely that seventy-five per cent of the pure-bred registered Arabs in the United States were owned west of the Rocky Mountains.

Mr. Harris owned for a considerable number of years in the neighborhood of forty to fifty Arabs as well as several part-bred Arabs, generally Anglo-Arabs. Norman W. Harris, his son, produced and kept most of the Anglo-Arabs on his farm.

The Arabian breed was fortunate in having such a friend as Albert W. Harris because for many years, from 1908 when the Arabian registry was formed, until about 1940 he was highly instrumental in keeping alive interest in the Arabian horse. Until around 1940 there were somewhat less than 2,000 Arabs registered in the Arabian Horse Club Stud Book, and the registration of these horses was largely looked after, though indirectly, by Mr. Harris. The registrar changed several times from 1908 to about the 1940's, at which time the registry office was moved to Chicago where it has remained for a number of years under the guidance of a full-time secretary. It is my personal opinion that Mr. Harris served as the financial angel and is one of the strongest exponents and one of the staunchest friends that the Arabian horse in the United States ever had.

For many years he has been known among the Arabian fraternity as the producer of strong, well-doing Arabian horses. Mr. Harris, together with several of the other early owners and breeders of Arabian horses was engaged in this business of producing Arabian horses principally for his own pleasure and at no time did he have to make any sacrifices or concessions that might conflict with his own ideas about the production of this breed of horses. Many breeders of Arabian horses throughout the United States as well as in several foreign countries have purchased their initial breeding stock from Mr. Harris. Whenever the Harris Arabs were placed in competition with other Arabs or with other horses, they usually gave a very good account of themselves. In addition to endurance rides and some showing, the Harris Arabs have been trained as running horses, as well as in dressage.

Mr. Harris retired in 1949 from any activity as an official of the Arabian Horse Club, but it is quite evident that the horses he bred and distributed over more than twenty-five years will continue to add to the reputation of this man who is, by all odds, the dean of Arabian horse breeders in the United States.

CARL R. RASWAN

Carl R. Raswan, of New Mexico, has had more first-hand experience than any other individual in America with the Arabian horse in his native land, having spent many years with Bedouin tribes. It was largely

William Wrigley on SABA'H No. 1320 leading band of mares and colts.

due to him that the famous Kellogg Stud was established in California. Mr. Raswan supervised the assembling of the breeding stock when this stud was founded and served in an advisory capacity for some time. Breeders and students of the Arabian breed cannot and would not attempt to overlook the importance and value of the Kellogg Stud in popularizing the Arabian horse in America.

Several years after the founding of the Kellogg Stud, Mr. Raswan spent considerable time at the V.V. Lazy Ranch at Boulder, Colorado, where he advised Mr. VanVleet in the breeding operations and the development of what has become the best known Arabian breeding farm in the United States.

Carl R. Raswan is the author of two very popular books "Drinkers of the Wind," and "Black Tents of Arabia." These books are known to, and enjoyed by, nearly all Arabian horse breeders and lovers in the United States. Mr. Raswan has been engaged for some years in the preparation of a very exhaustive book on families of the Arabian breed.

ROGER A. SELBY

Roger A. Selby, a well-known shoe manufacturer, of Portsmouth, Ohio, a lover of fine horses, and a student of their breeding for some twenty-odd years, became one of the most widely known and probably one of the most successful breeders of classic Arabian horses in the world. At various times, he also owned some excellent specimens of the American Saddle breed.

In an illustrated catalogue put out by him under the name of The Selby Stud in 1937 he included the following comments:

"The finest pure-blooded foundation stock of Arabian Horses has been imported over a period of time. With these selected horses as a nucleus, this truly remarkable breed of animals, deservedly famous in history and story, is being preserved and propagated in its greatest purity.

"These highly distinctive animals are fully worthwhile for themselves alone. But with pure breeding in their native land now decadent, and only a few hundred of the pure specimens remaining scattered about the world, it must be largely through the application of a spirit of sportsmanship that this unusual breed, the ultimate result of centuries of refinement, can be preserved and increased undiluted by alien blood.

"The Arab is the true source of all the best horse blood. Once gone that source can never again be created. A concerted effort will be well worthwhile on the part of those who love horses to conserve the finest living specimens of this preeminent breed."

His first importation of Arabian horses was in 1928 from the Crabbet Stud, in England. This importation consisted of eight head of Arabian horses, among them the fine gray mare, Kareyma (No. 811); the gray mare Rifala (No. 815); Indaia (No. 813) bay mare, and the bay mare Hilwe (No. 810). These were all extremely high-grade and it is doubtful whether any other Arabian stud in the last twenty-five years in the United States has ever owned a pair of finer Arabian mares as to type, conformation and breeding than Rifala and Kareyma. The stallion imported for use with these mares was a chestnut, Mirzam (No. 808).

This importation was sufficient foundation for the rapid development of a good-sized breeding stud. Because several of these mares were mated more than once with American Saddlebred stallions this stud did not grow too rapidly for the first four or five years in total number of pure-bred Arabs.

In 1930 Mr. Selby was fortunate in securing from the Crabbet Stud one of the most widely known Arabian stallions, Mirage (No. 790). Mirage was born in the Middle East and was selected when a colt for the private stud of King Faisal of Iraq. Later on he came into the possession of the Crabbet Stud and in 1930 Roger A. Selby was able to get possession of him. Mirage and Rifala were the only Arabian stallion and mare that had won championships in both England and America at

MIRAGE No. 790. Champion Arabian stallion.

the time up to 1937. I do not at this time recall any other Arabs in the United States that had won championships in both countries.

In addition to Mirage in 1930 Mr. Selby imported the chestnut mare, Rasmina (No. 856), and the gray mare, Rose of France (No. 857). Rose of France was a granddaughter on both sides of the famous Skowronek, the stallion for which the Crabbet Stud refused a $225,000 offer from the Russian government. She was one of the very high-grade mares imported by Mr. Selby for his breeding stud.

Mr. Selby made another importation in 1932 from the Crabbet Stud consisting of four stallions and one mare. The best known stallions in this importation were Raffles (No. 952) a gray, and Rahal (No. 950) a chestnut. Raffles was an inbred son of Skowronek and one of the smallest Arabian stallions seen in the United States, standing well under fourteen hands. He sired the third largest number of pure-bred Arabs, although his first colt was not born until he was twelve years old. The explanation for this late use of Raffles in the stud is that he was such a highly prized private mount that he was not put to breeding until he was eleven years

RAFFLES No. 952. Arabian stallion at trot.

old. This, of course, cut his breeding career by at least six years. When his first colts began to arrive and showed such high quality, and good conformation, he was very heavily used until he was more than twenty-five years old.

The Selby Stud has enjoyed a unique position among breeders of the high-grade classic, or antique, type of Arabian horse for many years. Much of this reputation has been earned through the offspring of the famous champion Mirage, who died after only a few years in the stud, during which time he sired only a small number of colts, and Raffles. It is doubtful whether any other Arabian breeding farm at any place or at any time ever owned four more beautiful, classic Arabian horses than the two gray mares, Rifala and Kareyma and the gray or white stallions, Mirage and Raffles. Thousands of horse lovers and hundreds of owners and breeders will carry forever in their minds their impressions of these horses. I never had the privilege of seeing Mirage in life, but from his pictures and from the study and observation of his offspring it is impossible to reach any other conclusion except that he probably was one of the greatest specimens of the Arabian breed that ever existed.

I saw the other three and I cannot find words to properly describe them. I recall vividly visiting the Selby Stud in company with another Arabian owner and breeder and going to one of the small pastures in which the three mares stood. They were greatly alike in type and conformation except that Rose of France was approximately one hand, or four inches bigger than the other two mares. On the day of our visit they were being pestered almost beyond endurance by small gnat flies which gathered on their backs. As we walked through the pasture lot approaching them, they started toward us in much the same way as one might expect a person to approach. When Kareyma reached my friend she walked up beside him, not waiting to be petted or greeted in any way, and

RAFFLES No. 952 at 23 years of age beside the Ohio River.

practically asked him to brush from her back the gnats that were tormenting her. As soon as he performed this task for her, she stepped forward sufficiently to turn around and come back and present her other side for the same service. This unique act so impressed me that I am sure I will never forget it as long as I remember anything.

Arabian horses bred at the Selby Stud were used as foundation animals by many leading studs not only in the United States but in several foreign countries. These foundation animals have been unusually successful in the show ring and there are very few horse shows of any size in this country that do not contain representatives of Selby blood lines. Those Arabian horses combining the blood lines of both Raffles and Mirage have been particularly successful in the show ring. Labor conditions and other factors have made it difficult to carry on proper breeding operations so the Selby Stud was greatly reduced in 1949.

Left to right: RASRAFF No. 2365, RAFARAH, No. 2624, RAFFNA, No. 3779. These 3 won the get of sire for RAFFLES.

Chapter 15

The Founding Of The Arabian Horse Club Of America

A RABIAN breeders in the United States organized and incorporated the Arabian Horse Club of America in 1908. It is evident from available stud books that the first such book was printed in 1909 by the Mail and Express Job Printing Company, of New York City. The revised edition, same year, is considered Volume I. The original stud book registered the names of eleven owners of horses and seventy-one animals. For some mysterious reason the registrations in the original book bore the notice "Class A." Evidently the originators of the Club had in mind some different types of registrations or the foundation animals would not have been so registered. The last animal registered in the original book was Mekka, bred and owned by the Davenport Desert Arabian Stud. The revised edition contained the names and addresses of twelve owners of Arabian horses and four additional horses. Number seventy-four El Jafil (the speedy), is the next to the last horse registered in this volume, but the last horse registered Ghanim, was given the number seventy-nine. No explanation is given for the gap in numbers.

207

The officers shown in Volume I were: President, James A. Lawrence, Pataskala, Ohio; First Vice President, Peter B. Bradley, Boston, Mass.; Second Vice President, Herman Hoopes, Philadelphia, Penna.; Secretary and Treasurer, Henry K. Bush-Brown, Newburgh, N. Y. The Directors were: J. A. P. Ramsdell, Newburgh, N. Y.; Homer Davenport, Goshen, N. Y.; Charles Arthur Moore, Jr., of N. Y.; Michael T. Horner of Baltimore, Md.; and C. E. Perkins of Burlington, Iowa.

The owners listed in the book were: Homer Davenport; the Davenport Desert Arab Stud, Hingham, Mass., and Goshen, N. Y.; Eleanor Gates, Alma, Calif.; Albert W. Harris, Chicago, Ill.; Hartman Stock Farm, Columbus, Ohio; N. J. Hess, N. Y.; R. Stuyvesant Pierrepont; C. E. Perkins, Burlington, Iowa; Robert V. Sewell, Oyster Bay, N. Y.; Hon. Clifford Sifton, Ottowa, Canada; J. A. P. Ramsdell, Newburgh, N. Y.; and Gilbert Twigg.

The Arab horses registered in this volume were described briefly as to color, breeding, and breeder and owner.

Some portions of the Constitution and By-Laws of the Arabian Horse Club are reproduced in the following paragraphs. Ordinary corporate details are omitted.

"1. The name of the corporation is 'The Arabian Horse Club of America.'

"2. The objects for which it is formed are investigating, ascertaining and keeping a record of the pedigree of Arabian horses, and of instituting and maintaining, owning and controlling and publishing a Stud Book or Registry of Arabian horses in the United States of America and Canada, and the promoting, patronizing and holding exhibitions of such horses; the purchasing, leasing, owning, mortgaging, or otherwise disposing of real estate, buildings and personal property.

"It is not proposed to exercise the power and right of holding or conducting trotting or running or steeplechase race meetings, or to hold, maintain or conduct trotting or running or steeplechase races at such meetings, or to exercise the particular powers conferred by Section 3 of said Chapter 570 of the Laws of 1895 and amendments thereto.

"3. The capital stock of this corporation shall be five hundred ($500.00) dollars, and shall be known as the Common Capital Stock of said corporation.

"4. The number of shares of which the capital stock shall consist shall be one hundred (100) shares of the par value of five ($5.00) dollars each.

"5. The location of the principal business office of said corporation shall be in the Borough of Manhattan, City, County and State of New York.

"6. The duration of the corporate existence of said corporation shall be fifty (50) years.

"7. The number of directors of said corporation, who shall manage the affairs thereof, shall be five (5), each of whom shall be a stockholder having at least five (5) shares of the capital stock of said corporation...."

In 1913, the members of the Arabian Horse Club issued a third revision of the stud book entitled The Arabian National Stud Book, Volume I. At this time, evidently, the Club had in mind the registration of part-bred Arabs in addition to pure-breds. The following were the officers: President, Peter B. Bradley, Boston, Mass; First Vice-President, F. L. Ames, Boston, Mass; Second Vice-President, C. E. Perkins, Burlington, Iowa; Secretary and Treasurer, Henry K. Bush-Brown, Washington, D. C. The Directors were: James A. Lawrence, Charles Arthur Moore, Jr., Michael T. Horner, and Richard Walton Tully.

Under the heading, "Arabian National Stud Book Rules for Registration," the Club lists regulations covering the new policy of permitting the registration of horses that were half-Arab and half-Thoroughbred, Trotter, Kentucky Saddle, Morgan or Clay, as follows:

"Section I — Horses may be registered in the Stud Book of the Arabian Horse Club of America under the following rules:

"Rule I. Any horse bred in Arabia which is accompanied by an Arabic certificate bearing the seal of a tribal Sheikh as to its purity of blood, and which horse is unquestionably of Kuhl or Kehilan strain; Provided, that the word of such Sheikh as to the breeding of the animal be vouched for by a Consul or other representative of the United States Government.

"Rule II. Any horse of pure Arab blood furnished with certificate of registration in the General Stud Book of England, the Australian Stud Book or Le Studbook Francais, Registre des Chevaux de Pur-Sang.

"Rule III. Any Arab horse whose sire and dam are registered in the Stud Book of the Arabian Horse Club of America or in the American Stud Book.

"Rule IV. The offspring of horses registered in any of the Stud Books mentioned in Rules I, II, and III.

"Registration numbers shall be consecutive as to Section I.

"Section II — Rule V. Any imported Barb or other Arab horse not bred in Arabia which is accompanied by authentic proof of their purity of blood.

"Rule VI. One * to be prefixed to the class number of produce of Arab horses having five top crosses of pure Arab Blood. That is, the American Thoroughbred having only $3\frac{1}{8}$ per cent of the mare with which these records begin.

"Rule VII. Americo-Arab. For the registration of the produce of stallions registered in Section I, II of the Arabian Stud Book, when bred to mares of established breeding in the following groups: Thoroughbred, American Trotter, Morgan, Kentucky Saddle, and inbred Henry Clay family, recognizing the above well known stud books. The registration numbers to be consecutive as Section II, and to be prefixed by the following letters to denote the separate families:

"Family 'A.' Thoroughbreds — Part I. The produce of Registered Thoroughbreds of proved genetic potency.

"Part 2. Produce of Thoroughbreds and Arabs registered in the Arabian Stud Book Section I or II, Family 'A.' Recognizing Weatherby's General Stud Book, The Australian Stud Book, Le Studbook de Francais de Pur-Sang. The American Thoroughbred Stud Book.

"Family 'B.' Trotters — Part 1. The produce of Registered Trotters of proved genetic potency.

"Part 2. Produce of Registered Trotters and Arabs. Recognizing American Trotting Register, Arabian Stud Book.

"Family 'C.' Kentucky Saddle Horses — Part 1. The produce of Registered Kentucky Saddle Horses.

"Part 2. The produce of Kentucky Saddle type and Registered Arabs in Section I and II. Recognizing the Kentucky Stud Book and the Arabian Stud Book.

"Family 'D.' Morgans — Part 1. The produce of Registered Morgans of proved genetic potency.

"Part 2. The produce of Registered Morgans and Arabs.

"Family 'E.' Clays — Part 1. The produce of Clay mares having fifty percent or more of the blood of Henry Clay or fifty per cent or more of Arab blood from recent approved breeding of kindred type.

"Part 2. The produce of Clay mares registered in Part I and Arab sires registered in Sections I and II of the Arabian Stud Book.

"For horses to be registered in Part 1, of Families A., B., C., D., they must show by the photograph that they possess some of the essential qualities of the original Arab and of strains of breeding that reproduce themselves.

"Mere speed records and registration in existing stud books do not in themselves qualify for registration, but demonstrated ability to produce qualities of excellence and uniformity in their offspring will be considered as qualification.

"Registration numbers shall be consecutive as to Section II.

"APPLICATIONS FOR REGISTRATIONS — Each application shall be made in duplicate, and such application shall be accompanied by a 4 x 5 photograph of horse showing its markings.

"Application shall bear three spaces for names, which shall be designated as first, second and third choice; applicant will supply therein such first, second and third choice of names he desires, which shall be subject to the acceptance or rejection of registrar, as a means to avoid duplication of names.

"Owners of stallions registered in this Stud Book shall mail a certificate of any and all services within thirty days following the date of such service to the registrar.

"Members of this Club are prohibited from exhibiting breeding animals which are registered in this Stud Book, in any class or show which has not been arranged and approved, and where judges of such classes have not been approved or named by the Executive Committee of this Company.

"In all cases of sales of animals registered in this Stud Book, the party who has made such sale will be required to forward a transfer certificate made out on blanks furnished by this Company to the registrar. A record of such transfer will be made free of charge on the Stud Books, providing such transfer certificate is sent to the registrar within thirty days from time of sale. After which time $1.00 per transfer will be charged.

"Resolved, That pursuant to Section 3 of Article IV of the By-Laws of this Company, a committee to be known as the Advisory Board be, and the same hereby is, appointed to act in conjunction with the Board of Directors of this Company on such matters and business as may be deemed advisable.

"Resolved, That pursuant to the provisions of Section 3 of Article IV of the By-Laws of this Company, a class of membership to be known as Honorary Members be and the same hereby is established, the persons elected to such Honorary Membership to be designated or appointed by the Advisory Board of the Company.

"Thereupon, the names of Mr. Randolph Huntington and Mr. Joseph Battell were proposed as Honorary Members of the Company, and upon motion duly made and seconded, those persons were made and constituted Honorary Members of this Company.

"It was further, upon motion duly made and seconded, unanimously

"Resolved, That any person, upon a vote of a majority of the Board of Directors of this Company, may be made a member of the Club, upon payment of a membership fee of ten dollars ($10.00); membership in the Club to entitle a member to all of the privileges and rights of the Club, except the right to vote upon any matter affecting the organization of the Company and the right to any dividends or participation in financial returns to the Company.

"Sec. 1. The following schedule of fees has been adopted by this Board:

Fee for registration of horses belonging to non-members $5.00
Fee for registration of horses belonging to members 3.00
Fee for registration of foals under six months belonging to
    non-members ....• 3.00
Fee for registration of foals under six months belonging to
    members 2.00
"Sec. 2.
Fee for registration of mature horses shall be $3.00
Fee for registration of foals under one year .... 2.00."

This book was quite well illustrated with pictures of the leading Arabian horses of that period. The book itself was published in two sections and contained a total of eighty-eight pages. 127 Arabians were registered in it.

This volume lists a total of twenty-seven owners as compared to a total of twelve in the revised edition of the original Stud Book. They were:

Armstrong Bedouin Stud, Holmdel, N. J.; H. J. Brown, Portland, Maine; H. K. Bush-Brown, Washington, D. C.; Harry Chandler; Ralph E. Forbes, Boston, Mass.; Meldrum Gray, Columbus, Ohio; Albert W. Harris, Chicago, Ill.; C. P. Hatch, Port Washington, N. Y.; Hartman Stock Farm, Columbus, Ohio; Dr. J. N. Henderson, Berkeley, Calif.; N. J. Hess, New York City; Hingham Stock Farm, Hingham, Mass.; Herman Hoopes, Philadelphia, Pa.; Michael T. Horner, Baltimore, Md.; R. M. Jereissati, Atlantic City, N. J.; James A. Lawrence, San Francisco, Calif.; Chas. E. Perkins, Burlington, Iowa; R. Stuyvesant Pierrepont, Brooklyn, N. Y.; J. A. P. Ramsdell, Newburgh, N. Y.; Hon. Clifford Sifton, Ottawa, Canada; Henry W. Shoemaker, New York City; A. G. Spaulding, New York City; S. C. Thomson, San Francisco, Calif.; Richard Walton Tully, Arcadia, Calif.; Gilbert Twigg, Markham, Va.; Lieut. Henry Watson, Fort Riley, Kansas; and Albert N. White, Greenfield, N. H.

In Section two under the title "Amerio-Arabs," a total of fifteen owners of part-bred Arabs are listed, several of whom were also owners of pure-bred Arabs registered in Section one.

Under Section two, sixty-eight animals were registered and they were described in much the same way as the Arabian horses in Section one. A study of the list of owners shows that even at that early date these owners were scattered over the entire United States.

In 1918 the Stud Book was again published, and while no number is given to this book it was actually Volume II of the series. The officers of the Arabian Horse Club at this time were: President, W. R. Brown, Maynesboro Farm, Berlin, N. H.; Vice President, Chas. E. Perkins, Burlington, Iowa; Secretary and Treasurer, H. K. Bush-Brown, Washington, D. C.; Registrar, Miss Ethel Boyd Bowers, N. Y., N. Y. The Directors were: W. R. Brown, Maynesboro Farm, Berlin, N. H.; Chas. E. Perkins, Burlington, Iowa; H. K. Bush-Brown, Washington, D. C.; Anita M. Baldwin, Los Angeles, Calif.; Peter B. Bradley, Boston, Mass.; Hamilton Carharrt, Rock Hill, S. C.; Warren Delano, New York, N. Y.; Howard Stout Neilson, Althea Farm, Darien, Conn.; and Richard Walton Tully, N. Y., N. Y.

A summary of the owners and registration in this volume is as follows:

Owners of Arabian horses	57
Stallions registered	79
Colts registered	29
Mares registered	113
Fillies registered	44
Geldings registered	16
Number in Stud Book that are dead	81
Living Arabians	281
Total registered to that date	362

In this edition of the Stud Book a short history of the Arabian horse is presented by H. K. Bush-Brown, while seven pages on the Standard Conformation and Type, were compiled by W. R. Brown. For the first time, registrations of mares were accompanied by an account of their produce and of stallions with their get. The registration of half-bred Arabs was dropped, although the Club agreed to keep a record of these half-breeds as best it could. In the final pages of this volume "The Principal Strains of Arabian Thoroughbred Stock" was compiled by W. R. Brown, and a list of the principal reference books of value to the Arabian breeder concludes the book, which is well illustrated with pictures of the leading Arabs of that period in the United States.

In 1927 the Arabian Horse Club of America issued Volume III of the Arabian Stud Book. The officers at that time were: President, W. Robinson Brown, Maynesboro Arabian Stud, Berlin, N. H.; Vice President, Albert W. Harris, Kemah Arabian Stud, Chicago, Ill.; Secretary and Treasurer, H. S. Gregory, New York, N. Y. The Directors were: W. R. Brown, Berlin, N. H.; W. K. Kellogg, Pomona, Calif.; A. W. Harris, Chicago, Ill.; C. W. Jewett, Indianapolis, Ind.; and Martin A. Towle, Boston, Mass.

In this volume some of the rules of registration were changed. The following is quoted from "Rules of Registration":

"Rule 5 — No horse will be registered in the Stud Book of the Arabian Horse Club of America by any name which is a duplicate in any manner of a name already registered; nor will numerical nor alphabetical affixes or suffixes of any name appearing in the Stud Book be allowed hereafter; nor the suffix 'Sr.,' or 'Jr.,' . . .

"It being well known that the Arabian horse has been a large factor as a cross in establishing many of the most useful type of horses, and in order to encourage the creating of new types, the following rules have been adopted:

"Rule 1 — There shall be kept on file, for any breeder, at the office of the registrar, a book of office records if such breeder will fill out suitable registry blanks furnished by the Club at a charge of one dollar for registration, of stallions, mares, colts and fillies, the produce of crossing registered Arabian stallions or mares; with Americo-Arab stallions or mares registered in Section II of the first edition of the Stud Book; and their get; or, with stallions or mares of other established breeds; or with the product of colts or fillies so got; or with the product of any combination of the above.

"Rule 2 — For the use of breeders, designating names will be allotted to denote the predominant cross, and if, in the course of time, a sufficient number of individuals have been recorded, perpetuating in form, action, disposition, quality and powers of prepotency, a new similar and distinct type or family of sound and useful horses, upon sufficient investigation, the directors of the Club will assist in the introduction of such new type to the public and aid or assist such breeders in the establishment of a new Club and book of record for the same, if desired.

"Rule 3 — The following names have been allotted:

"Anglo-Arab — English Thoroughbreds Registered in any General Stud Book, with Arabians.

"Americo-Arab — All former Registrations in Section II of Americo-Arabs or their get being largely a Clay Trotting Stock Cross, with Arabians.

"Norse-Arab — Pure-bred Norse Ponies, with Arabians."

A study of this Volume III will show an increase in initiation, membership and registration fees which were practically the same as those adopted and published in the National Arabian Stud Book. A total of thirty-three associated members of the Arabian Horse Club are listed. An index of the horses registered together with their numbers occupies pages thirty-six to forty-three. A total of ninety owners of Arabian horses is listed. This book is well illustrated and contains a total of 639 registered horses. The last name that appears is Yasmini, a bay mare, (No. 639) foaled May 8, 1927.

The Founding Of The Arabian
Horse Club Of America

In 1937 the Arabian Horse Club of America issued Volume IV of the Arabian Stud Book. The officers were: President, W. R. Brown, Berlin, N. H.; Vice President, Albert W. Harris, Chicago, Ill.; and Secretary-Treasurer, H. S. Gregory, Berlin, N. H. The Directors were: W. R. Brown, Berlin, N. H.; Albert W. Harris, Chicago, Ill.; W. K. Kellogg, Pomona, Calif.; J. M. Dickinson, Nashville, Tenn.; and R. A. Selby, Portsmouth, Ohio.

This volume contained several short descriptive articles, one by Albert W. Harris, one by Jacob M. Dickinson, and another by Roger A. Selby. An article of considerable importance entitled "Endurance of Arabians," was taken from "The Horse of the Desert," by W. R. Brown. A summary of the Arabian horse population of the United States indicated that 236 owners owned 469 mares and 319 stallions and fifty-six geldings, and that owners in foreign countries numbered twenty-two, who owned twenty-seven mares, twenty-six stallions and one gelding. Several pages are included that show the importations of Arabian horses that appear in the Stud Book. This list gives the year imported, the registration number, sex, name of the horse, name of the importer and the breeder. Also the families of the various horses registered were given. A total of 1,391 horses were registered in this volume, the last one being Sielanka, a bay mare bred in Poland and imported by J. M. Dickinson, of Travelers' Rest Arabian Stud, Nashville, Tennessee. An index from page 177 to 188 with four pages of names of reference books on the Arabian horse completes the book. The illustrations are indexed.

Volume V of the Arabian Stud Book was published in late 1944 and the last registration was number 2,924, a bay mare, Zalihah, foaled July 14, 1944. Volume V contains all of the Arabian horses previously registered in the other Stud Books, in other words, starting with number one, the gray mare, Nejdme, foaled in 1881, and exhibited at the 1893 Chicago World's Fair, after which she was put to breeding.

This volume introduced some innovations in the publication of a purebred registry book, giving only the animal's name, registration number, sex and color, date foaled, sire and dam, and breeder or importer, or both. Previous volumes had given the family or strain name of the Arabian horses, but this feature was dropped in Volume V. Many breeders have complained about this and would much prefer to have the original description and strain or breed families inserted in the book. Volume V also dropped the notation showing that many of these registered animals were already dead.

Probably the greatest change was the inclusion of an index or key to the progeny of the Arabian horses registered in the Stud Book. The number of the Arab is given in bold-face type and this corresponds to the registration number of the animal. The numbers following the bold-face

THE ARABIAN HORSE JOURNAL
1943

PUBLISHED BY

THE ARABIAN HORSE CLUB OF AMERICA

OFFICE OF THE SECRETARY, BARRINGTON, ILLINOIS

Booklet published by the Arabian Horse Club of America for its members.

type are in italic or light-face type and these represent the registered progeny of the particular animal under whose number they are found. The book also contains a complete index of horses by name and number. It is very well illustrated.

The officers of the Arabian Horse Club of America at the time Volume V was published were: President, Albert W. Harris; Vice President, Henry B. Babson; and Secretary-Treasurer, Frank Watt. The Directors were Henry B. Babson, Chicago, Illinois; J. M. Dickinson, Franklin, Tennessee; Albert W. Harris, Chicago, Illinois; Roger A. Selby, Portsmouth, Ohio; and L. W. Van Vleet, Denver, Colorado. The governing members were: Henry B. Babson, Chicago, Illinois; Colonel Frank L. Carr, Washington, D. C.; J. M. Dickinson, Franklin, Tennessee; Daniel C. Gainey, Owatonna, Minnesota; Albert W. Harris, Chicago, Illinois; Roger A. Selby, Portsmouth, Ohio; Fred E. Vanderhoof, Woodlake, California; L. W. Van Vleet, Denver, Colorado; and C. A. West, Pittsburgh, Pennsylvania.

Volume V contains a very fine article entitled, "The Arab Horse," by Albert W. Harris, a reprint from the July-August 1944 issue of *The Horse.*

Because the growth of the Arabian breed in the United States had been developing very rapidly for three or four years before Volume V was published, a much larger number of new registrations appear as compared with previous volumes. There were approximately 325 associate members of the Arabian Horse Club at the time of publication.

Following the publication of this volume Supplements I and II were published. When Volume VI was published in 1949 it did not include the 2,924 Arabs registered in Volume V but the registrations extended from 2,925 to and including 5,157, a chestnut mare registered as Baba.

Volume VI of the Arabian Stud Book followed the same pattern as Volume V. Henry B. Babson was President instead of Albert W. Harris.

The book contained a list of approximately 650 associate members which is practically twice the number belonging to the Arabian Horse Club when the previous volume was published. During the five years between volumes, more than 2,000 new Arabs were registered or sixty per cent as many animals as were registered from the beginning of the Arabian Stud Book in 1908 up to 1944.

At the annual meeting in December 1949 the Directors of the Arabian Horse Club of America changed the name to the Arabian Horse Registry for the reason that they concluded that the Arabian breed was getting to be of such size that a separate organization or group was needed to promote the best interests of the breed. Since the original Club had been organized solely as a registry it was thought best to designate it as such.

After this action the following notice was sent to the associate members:

"HIGHLIGHTS OF ARABIAN HORSE CLUB REGISTRY MEET-ING, December 1, 1949

"1. Governing members, directors and officers for 1950:

    *Henry Babson, President, Chicago, Illinois

    *L. W. Van Vleet, Denver, Colorado

    *D. C. Gainey, Vice President, Owatonna, Minnesota

    *Donald Jones, Porterville, California

    *Chester A. West, Pittsburgh, Pennsylvania

    Walter Ross, Kansas City, Missouri

    Robert B. Field, Leavenworth, Washington

    Norman Harris, Chicago, Illinois

    Leland E. Mekeel, Whittier, California

(*indicates Directors)

"2. Approved Treasurer's report and voted to send operating statement to all Associate Members.

"3. Provided for Membership Relations Committee.

"4. Voted to print copy of Constitution and By-Laws so as to make them available to Associate Members upon request.

"5. There was considerable discussion about the enthusiasm and good work being done by various State and Area associations, most of which have come into being during the past few years. The Board asked the Membership Relations Committee to give assurance of good will to all of these groups, and to indicate a willingness to give aid should they decide to move forward with their expressed hope for a National Arabian Show and Trail Ride Organization.

"6. The Directors voted that hereafter there shall be printed on the back of Associate Membership application blanks the following:

"The Arabian Horse Club Registry of America is a non-profit organization created to maintain a registry of pure-blood Arabian horses under extremely rigid rules.

"It is administered by ten Governing Members who annually elect a Board of Directors from among their own number. Vacancies among the Governing Members are filled by the Directors from a list of competent and substantial owners of Arabian horses.

"Each Governing Member is required to pay annual dues of $50.00, attend the annual meetings, and along with the Directors pay all of his own expenses incidental to the meetings.

"Horses eligible for registration are:

"1. Horses whose dam and sire are registered in the Arabian Horse

Club Registry of America's Stud Book, or the Arabian Horse Society of England's Stud Book.

"2. Imported horses with satisfactory papers may be approved for registration by the Directors after inspection shows that the horse is a credit to the breed.

"The present advantages of being an Associate Member are:

"1. They can register their foals for half price.

"2. They receive a Stud Book free as published.

"3. They receive free a supplement of horses registered as new supplements are published.

"4. The Secretary will be glad to furnish them with ownership information regarding horses at any time.

"While Associate Members have no vote in the management of the Registry, constructive suggestions are always welcome and assured of the attention of the Board of Directors.

"7. The registration fee for imported horses was raised to $100.00 if registered during the calendar year imported; after that $300.00.

"8. From the Secretary's Report: At the beginning of the last fiscal year there were 645 Associate Members. During the year we received 112 new Associate Members and 8 reinstatements. We lost from death and resignations 77 — leaving us a new membership of 688.

"We have registered approximately 5,500 horses and there are probably 4,500 living horses. Recorded owners number 1,300.

"There has been a noticeable increase in the number of owners in the Eastern States this year.

"Volume VI of the Stud Book was distributed the first of August. This was sent without cost to all Associate Members.

"Note: We have just received the good news that the American Horse Shows Association has altered its rules so as to accept registered Arabians and thus our horses are officially eligible for their shows."

In 1944 the Arabian Horse Club of America published a twelve-page illustrated book entitled, "Arabian Horses." The purpose of this book was to briefly state the specifications of a typical and desirable Arabian horse in non-technical language that horse lovers or Arab fanciers could understand. Five pages in this book have to do with the general conformation, type and specifications from which an individual would be able to select and judge a typical pure-bred Arabian horse. Some additional information is given as to the origin of the Arabian horse, his qualities, and the uses to which he is usually put. All of this material is in condensed form but is very valuable and helpful. A short mention is made of the Arabian horses in the United States together with some comments on breeding and registration. Four pages of this book are devoted to illustrations of some typical and well-known Arabian horses in this country.

This small booklet has been and will, no doubt, continue to be available to anyone interested in the Arabian horse, from the Arabian Horse Club of America at a price of $1.00 per copy.

One of the most valuable pieces of literature put out by the Arabian Horse Club Registry is a small booklet of sixty-four pages published in late 1950, by Albert W. Harris.

Mr. Harris speaks with great authority in giving the history of the Registry. For many years he was practically the Arabian Horse Club. This booklet is introduced by the governing members of the Registry and others, and it contains Nejdme I, which mare was and is the No. 1 Arab registered in the Arabian Stud Book.

This history deals briefly with the early owners and importers of Arabian horses and early members of the club. The officers of the registry association are given for several of the more important years covered by this history and various comments about Arabian horse activities are to be found within its pages. Some mention is also made of some individual horses and their records.

While many Arabian horse students and owners have access to a complete file of the Arabian Stud Books to date, there are many items of personal interest in this book that are not available in the other Stud Books. These are of particular value and interest to present-day Arabian horse owners and breeders because practically every one of them knows or has met either Mr. Harris or some of the other officers of the Registry association. This book will be of great value in the years to come because it has compiled and assembled between its covers many items of interest that tend to become lost or misplaced as time goes on. It has been distributed to the members of the Arabian Horse Club Registry of America and may be purchased from the association for $3.00.

Chapter 16

Comments On The Influence Of The Arabian Horse On The Thoroughbred

I N 1935, Charles Harrison Redmon, a graduate student at the University of Kentucky, made a detailed study of the influence of the Arabian horse on the development and future of the Thoroughbred horse, which he used as part of his thesis. Many more thorough studies have been made, yet there were certain facts brought out in this one that are of more than usual interest, which is the reason for their inclusion in this chapter.

Of principal value is the information Mr. Redmon gives on the experiences of Dr. George A. Feris with Arabian horses, and his use of them during the war with Mexico. It is of more than usual interest to note that Dr. Feris was personally acquainted with Mr. A. Keene Richards, the Thoroughbred breeder at Georgetown, Kentucky, and that Dr. Feris consulted with him at a meeting in New Orleans prior to Mr. Richards' visit to Arab countries to import Arabian horses in the 1850's.

Information such as Mr. Redmon has secured and used in his thesis is usually very difficult to come by and is of real interest to Arabian breeders. The thesis is quoted as follows:

"President Thomas Jefferson imported Arabs — mares and stallions. So did several old-time Southern turfmen. But the most notable Arabs to reach us since the Civil War were the two gray stallions which were presented by the Sultan to General Grant in the course of his tour around the world. They were very fine animals of unknown pedigree, standing each fourteen hands and three inches. Both lived a great age, leaving behind them, in the West and in the East, a worthy progeny. Thus, there is one blood source ready to hand. Another comes through the mares and stallions sent by the Sultan to the Columbian Exposition. He understood that they were to be sent back, but they have stayed with us — in virtue of a foreclosure sale. Mr. Peter B. Bradley, of Hingham, Massachusetts, got the most of them, and from them has bred pure Arabs, besides crossbreds, with trotters, hackneys, thoroughbreds and mustangs. The only pure Arab to win a prize at the New York Horse Show is of his breeding. A colt by Abeyan out of a trotting mare, also won first prize in the yearling class, at the New York State Fair in 1904. It is Mr. Bradley's opinion that his halfbreeds are better for general purposes than the fullbloods, also that the trotting cross gives the best results, in spite of the failures elsewhere of the Arab cross to increase the speed of the trotter.

"In the grey mare Nedjme, Mr. J. A. P. Ramsdell, of Newburgh, got the best animal that came to Chicago — possibly the best ever brought to America. Her pedigree, afterward stolen by a Syrian in hope of reward, showed her breeding to be flawless. In addition, Mr. Ramsdell has imported from England the white stallion Shahwan, bred by Ali Pacha in Cairo, and pronounced by Sir Wilfrid Blunt to be as fine a horse as ever came out of the desert, and Garaveen, an English Arab, by the unbeaten racer Kismet, out of a fine Arab mare. From such stock it is not surprising that Mr. Ramsdell had bred horses worthy of their pedigree.

"The first record we have of the Arab in America was the importation of the stallion Ranger, about 1765, to New London, Conn. In 1838, J. D. Elliott imported a number of both sexes. The late A. Keene Richards brought them to Georgetown, Kentucky, in 1856. His plant was making the most rapid strides toward success, when it was destroyed by the Civil War. The blood of his horses, however, is found in the present Kentucky saddle horses, six and seven generations back, and there is little doubt that much of the beauty of that splendid animal today is traceable to the horses that A. Keene Richards imported. The next importation was the two stallions given to General U. S. Grant, by the Sultan of Turkey. These were of unknown families, but they sired many beautiful and useful horses.

"A number of Arabian horses were brought to the World's Columbian Exposition at Chicago, in 1893. The Sultan was induced to permit these horses to come to America for the exhibit, and through mortgages they were eventually held. Nine were burned to death in their stalls at the Exposition by the Syrians that brought them, as the outcome of a wrangle. From these horses, however, came the best results of any Arab horses brought to America. Most of them were bought by Mr. Peter B. Bradley, of Hingham, Massachusetts, who crossed them on some of our best breeds, besides breeding them in their purity. With a pure horse of his breeding, Mr. Hess, of New York City, won the only blue ribbon ever won over our own types of saddle horses, with an Arab in open competition. Mr. Bradley also bred a trotter, two removes from Arab blood, that trotted to a record of 2:30 in the sixth heat of his first race. He produced the finest types of polo ponies and accomplished much with the Arab blood.

"Although never bred to as great an extent in America as in England, many good Arabian horses have been brought over and their influence is very noticeable especially in the old Morgans. They have also been used at different times to improve almost every type — draft-horses, roadsters, etc.

"The famous gray charger ridden by General Washington in the Revolution, was a son of Ranger, a desert-bred Arab that was imported to New London, Conn., about 1765. In 1837 Commodore Elliott brought in a number of mares and stallions, but although recorded in Bruce's American Stud Book, their disposition is not noted. Keene Richards also made some notable importations in 1854, but unfortunately practically all were lost in the Civil War.

"Altogether, in the century between 1760 and 1860, forty-two Arab horses and twelve mares are known to have been imported to the United States, including those presented to General Grant by the Sultan of Turkey. Most of the best pure Arabs in the country are related to these.

"Of late years the greater number of Arabs have come from England instead of direct, though a few breeders have gone to Arabia for them.

"George A. Feris, M.D. (1810-1891) during the war between the United States and Mexico rode a horse by *Medoc* — (Medoc, foaled 1829; by *Eclipse*. Died by accident at Col. Buford's, Kentucky, 1839. Bruce. A.S.B.) 1st dam Imported *Amarath* (Amurath) (Amurath at one year of age was imported to New York in 1833 from Tripoli. He was brought from Nubia to Tripoli in 1832. Bruce. A.S.B.) (Barb) 2nd dam by Imported Stamboul (Arabian). (Stamboul, Ch. h. of the Ugedi tribe was selected from Sultan Mahomoud's stables in Constantinople and presented to U. S. Minister Rhind. The horse was sold (about 1831) for the benefit of the U. S. for $575. Bruce. A.S.B.)

"Medoc was killed by a lance thrust at the battle of Buena Vista.

"General Grant's *Leopard* and *Linden Tree* arrived in America in 1879.

"Secretary William H. Seward had had presented to him in 1860, two Arabian horses; (*Maanake Hedrogi;* red horse 7-8 years old, from Beyroot 1860, *Siklany Gidran;* 2 years, 2 months old, from Syria, 1860. Bruce. A.S.B.). After a search of eight years Randolph Huntington traced these two horses through the efforts of Hon. John E. Van Etten of Kingston, New York, to find that there was just one descendant there, a mare bred by the late Judge Westbrook; also that a man in Ohio named Meyers had a granddaughter of one of the Seward horses; 'and she proved the blood'.

"Huntington tried for several years to get exact information from Kentucky about the A. Keene Richards Arabians, which were, by far, the most important importations of eastern blood, both for quality and quantity, that had ever been made to the United States. These horses were imported 1853-56. The Richards Arabian blood was lost during the Civil War. This war occurred too soon after the importation for a settled plan of breeding to test out the benefits of these horses in the right way.

"Some descendants of the Richards' horses were still alive in 1888 and their blood had done good service in Kentucky, Texas, Mexico, and Canada.

"Randolph Huntington, had at Rochester, New York, a number of colts and fillies, the result of breeding his selected Clay mares — strong in the Arabian blood — to Gen. Grant's Arabian horse Leopard and Barb horse Linden Tree.

"Colonel G——, who is Huntington's neighbor, was, all through the Civil War, stationed in Louisiana. Huntington's Arabs stood at his farm on our Lake — (to take care) of his mares and mine, also one or two others.

"Colonel G——'s colored groom said to Mr. Huntington one day, 'Massa Huntington, your Arab stallions make me feel as though I was down in my old home in Texas'. This statement and further questioning led to the locating of Dr. George A. Feris, in Richmond, Texas. Huntington learned from Dr. George A. Feris by his own statement 'that no man in Kentucky or elsewhere at the North knows what I do about A. Keene Richards' importations'.

Comments On The Influence Of The
Arabian Horse On The Thoroughbred

"Dr. George A. Feris arranged an interview between A. K. Richards and himself at New Orleans to discuss importation of Arabian blood in 1855, (as nearly as Thornton Chard could find out) during race week of the old Mettaire (Metairie) Club. Thornton Chard says that this was the germ of the Richards' importation and that there must have been a lapse of several years between Dr. Feris' resolve to encourage Arabian importations and Mr. Richards' expedition, which was his second. T.C.

"Present at the meeting were, Richards, Buford and Viley of Kentucky, Bingaman and Minor of Mississippi, Wells, Kerner and Lecompte of Louisiana.

"The expedition to Arabia was composed of A. Keene Richards and Morris Keene of Kentucky and the great horse portrait painter Troye (Edward Troye) of England (also of France and America) — of their journey and adventures we will not speak now but will deal with the successful results: After an absence of 14 months they returned (1853-56) with the following prizes viz: by Geo. A. Feris.

" ' (1st) *Hamdan* (Dr. Feris owned him. R. H.) Gray colt 2 years old — from Nesjd, of the pure "Koheyl" [Kuhaylan] race — purchased from the Sheik of the Rouibah tribe of Bedouins, in whose family the stock had been kept pure for more than 300 years. [Foaled in 1854 and imported by Richards in 1856. Stood the season of '59 — at stable of Dr. Feris, Richmond, Texas. R.H. The finest that could be found in the tribe. Bruce. A.S.B.]

" ' (2nd) *Massoud*. Chestnut horse — fifteen hands high, purchased of the Anayza [Anazah] tribe of Arabians. [Foaled in 1844. Imported by Richards in 1853. R.H. The import date indicates that Massoud was the result of Richards' first expedition. T.C.]

" ' (3rd) *Mokhladdi*. Gray horse fourteen and one-half hands high, bought of the Zarabine tribe of Bedouins in Arabia Petra [Petraea]. [Foaled in 1844. Imported by Richards in 1853. R.H. The import date, 1853, indicates that Mokhladi was the result of Richards' first expedition. T.C.]

" ' (4th) *Sacklowie*. Bay horse — fifteen hands high — bred by the Anayza (Anazah) Bedouins. This horse was selected by Mr. Troye, the great painter, on account of his resemblance to the English racer of the present times. [Dr. Feris is referring to the 1850's when the English Thoroughbred was still thought of as the Anglo-Arab, although this title was officially discontinued after about 1830 T.C. Sacklowie was foaled in 1851. Imported by Richards in 1856. Died in 1860. R.H. The choice of the animal painter, E. Troye, over all the stallions he saw in the East. Bruce. A.S.B.]

" ' (5th) *Fysaul*. Chestnut horse fourteen and three-fourths hands high and of the "Koheyl" [Kuhaylan] and "Saclowie" [Saglawi] race and bought in the Desert from the Bedouin chief who bred him. [Foaled in 1852. Bought and imported by Richards in 1856. R.H. An Arab stallion from *Nesjd*. Bruce. A.S.B.]

" ' (6th) *Luli*. Gray mare of pure "Koheyl" [Kuhaylan] race bred by the Anayza [Anazah] tribe of Arabians. [This mare was imported in foal to Ahzee Pasha's chestnut Arab *Bagdad*. This colt foal was lost. Later she produced gr. f. *Mahah* by *Fysaul*; ch. f. by imp. Thoroughbred *Mickey Free*; gr. f. *Hopsie* by *Mickey Free*; gr. f. *Kaffeah* by *Fysaul*. Bruce. A.S.B.]

" ' (7th) *Sadah* [Dr. Feris took. R.H.] Gray mare — bred by Anayza [Anazah] tribe of Bedouins. She was my favorite of the entire importation. [Imported 1853. Bruce A.S.B. The import date indicates that *Sadah* was the result of Richards' first expedition. T.C.]

" ' 7th (8th) *Zurufa* [*Zareefa*]. [Imported in 1856. Bruce. A.S.B. *Zareefa's* produce: b. c. *Bazar* by *Fysaul*; b. f. *Benica* by *Fysaul*; gr. c. hy imp. Thoroughbred *Mickey Free*. Bruce. A.S.B.] Gray mare — a Barb from the desert of Zahara.

" 'This comprises the list of our importations. [Results of Richards' two expeditions, which Dr. Feris lumps together giving the impression that all the horses were imported after the New Orleans meeting. But Mr. Richards had already made his first expedition and importation as will appear later. T.C.]'

"The following is the produce of the pure stallions and mares (postmarked Richmond, Texas. December 3, 1887). George A. Feris.

" 'The produce of my favorite mare *Sadah* [Imported] was [pure Arab R.H.]

" ' (1st) (Dr. Feris) *Abdel Kadir* [pure Arab R.H.] Gray horse by Imported Arabian *Mokhladdi*.

" ' (2nd) [Dr. Feris R.H.]. *Boherr*. Foaled at sea [on the Atlantic] and got in Arabia by a favorite stallion of the Wahube [Wahabi] tribe of Arabs and she [*Sadah*] had many other foals but they did not belong to me. [Produce of *Sadah*: gr. c. *Boherr*; gr. f. *Zahah* by *Mokhladdi*; gr. c. *Abd-el-kadir* by Mokhladdi; ch. c. *Yusef* by *Massoud*; gr. c. by Thoroughbred *Knight of St. George*; gr. f. *Haik* by *Fysaul*; gr. f. by Thoroughbred *Mickey Free*; . . . by Thoroughbred *Mickey Free*. Bruce. A.S.B.]

" '*Abdel Kadir* was my choice of all the stallions and I owned him and *Hamdan, Boherr*, and *Bazar* who was by Imported *Fysaul* and out of the Imported Barb mare *Zurufa* [Zareefa], born in Kentucky and brought to Texas.

" '*Abd-el-Kadir* — known as the "Feris Arabian" is the horse who made his mark in Texas by his produce. He was "par excellence" the grand gentleman of his race.

'The colts of this horse were sold at enormous prices to Mexican stockman.

" '*Druse* [Dreuse] — gray colt for $1,600.00, he was out of *Hagar, (Hagar* by *Hamdan)*. Two others, one out of "Betsy Hardin," [Hardin by *Sultan* (Son of Am. *Eclipse,*] the other out of *Rehab* (*Rehab* by *Hamdan*) were sold together for $3,600.00.

" 'The gray colt *Sheik* [*Sheik* out of *Rehab*] two years old brought $3,000.00 [These horses were sold on their blood, though not for the purpose of racing. T.C.]'

"Although never bred to as great an extent in America as in England, many good Arabian horses have been brought over, and their influence is very noticeable, especially in the old Morgans. They have also been used at various times to improve almost every type — draft-horses, roadsters, etc. Of late years the greater number of Arabs have come from England instead of direct, though a few breeders have gone direct to Arabia for them.

"The first record we have of the Arab in America was the importation of the stallion Ranger, (some say that it was not known whether he was an Arabian, that possibly he was a Barb) in 1765 to New London, Conn. In 1838, J. D. Elliott imported a number of both sexes. The late A. Keene Richards brought them to Georgetown, Kentucky, in 1856. The Civil War put an end to his breeding operations.

"The next importation was that of the two stallions given to General U. S. Grant by the Sultan of Turkey. A number of Arabian horses were brought to the World's Columbian Exposition at Chicago in 1893. The horses sold to Americans were mostly bought by Mr. Peter B. Bradley of Hingham, Mass. It is said that J. A. P. Ramsdell, of Newburgh, U.S.A., got the best animal that came to Chicago — possibly the best ever brought to America. In addition, Mr. Ramsdell has imported from England the white stallion *Shawhan*, pronounced by Sir Wilfred Blunt to be as fine a horse as ever came out of the desert."

In order to not interrupt the flow of Mr. Redmon's thesis, his footnotes concerning source material are listed separately, as follows:

"Homer Davenport. 'Arab Horse'. *Cyclopedia of American Agriculture.* (Edited by L. H. Bailey.) The Macmillan Company, 1912, p. 447.

"A. C. Gaylor. 'History of Horses'. *Country Life.* 15:505, March, 1909. (Doubleday, Page & Co., New York.)

"Thornton Chard. 'Keene Richards' Arabian Importations'. *The Horse.* Vol. 15, No. 6, November-December, 1934. pp. 12-18."

In 1943 *The Blood Horse,* of Lexington, Kentucky, the leading publication devoted to the Thoroughbred horse, his breeding and racing, published a small booklet of twenty-eight pages, by J. A. Estes and Joe

H. Palmer, entitled, "An Introduction to the Thoroughbred Horse." *The Blood Horse* stated that many inquiries like the following were sent to the American Thoroughbred Breeders Association as well as to *The Blood Horse*:

"What is a Thoroughbred? Where did he come from? How does he differ from other horses? What care does he need? What should an ideal type look like? What do you mean by family numbers? How do you judge a pedigree? Where can I find some books about Thoroughbreds? All of these have been asked repeatedly, and more, the prize of all being a blunt demand, 'Please tell me everything about the Thoroughbred'.

"It has been impossible, practically, to reply adequately to these inquiries, because even the best-intentioned editor cannot compile and compose the answer to any one of these questions and get much else done during the same week. And yet we have felt that reasonable knowledge of the Thoroughbred ought to be available for the asking, and that any one who would make the acquaintance of this fine, fast, sensitive race should be helped within the limit of our capacity.

"The present brochure is an attempt at a general answer to the inquiries we have received, and even at the answering of some questions before they are asked. In it we have had the able assistance of Humphrey S. Finney, editor of *The Maryland Horse*, who contributed the section on care and uses and furnished many of the illustrations.

"And now we are prepared to answer, strictly from an English point of view, the first question, 'What is a Thoroughbred?' It is a horse which traces back in all branches, without flaw, to animals registered in the General Stud Book.

"It may have in its veins the blood of Arab, Barb, Turk, galloway, Scotch pony, cart horse, draft breed, Highland Dun, and heaven knows what else, though it will always be predominantly Arabian, Barb, or Turk. But it is descended from horses which, in the main, proved themselves on the race course, and whose descendants have proved themselves on the same testing ground, for approximately 250 years. Originally no more than the intention of being a race horse was needed to obtain entry, but the General Stud Book is now a closed circle; no blood not already in it can be admitted.

"To put it another way, the Thoroughbred is a horse descended, in all lines, from ancestors which were bred and trained for racing for approximately 250 years, and which were selected as breeding stock primarily by their performance.

"Perhaps a rather summary distinction among the three Eastern breeds which made up the great bulk of the ancestry of the Thoroughbred is in order. The Arab came from Arabia, of course, from a breed which was cultivated by the Bedouins for centuries. A pleasant myth is that Mohammed shut all the horses he could get into an enclosure without water for a few days, then released them in sight of a stream. As the horses thundered away to water, he had a trumpeter blow a battle call. Most of the herd went sensibly on, a few turned obediently back, and from these few the great Arabian strains were bred. The story is valuable only to indicate how long the Arab has been bred and for how many centuries the necessities of war have shaped his destiny. Physically the Arabian horse, mostly bay, stood about 14½ hands high at the withers, weighed from 800 to 1,000 pounds, had hard, dense bone, and a short back, and the general ability to carry weight for long distances under adverse conditions.

"The Barb got his name from Barbary (North Africa), whence he was brought into Spain by the Moors. A bit coarser than the Arab, he was of about the same size, and was also known for his speed and endurance. The Turk, a mixture of Arab, Persian, and other Asiatic breeds, was somewhat larger, standing from 15 to 16 hands high, and was more like the modern Thoroughbred in size and general appearance than the others. He came from Turkey, of course. Fundamentally, of course, these were all variations of light horses, springing from common ancestors.

"But not all of the early importations came with their proper credentials. The Lister or Stradling Turk, which was brought to England in the time of James I, was a part of the spoils of Buda. The Belgrade Turk was taken when Prince Eugene beat the Turks at Belgrade under the reign of Queen Anne. A good many others were the prizes of war, and they got their designation from the country whence they came. That is, a horse bought in Constantinople, or taken from the Turks, was pretty sure to be called a Turk, regardless of his actual ancestry, and an Arab brought from Spain or Barbary was likely to be considered a Barb. The difference among the three breeds, though they held in general, were not always enough to identify individuals beyond question.

"Of the many Eastern stallions introduced into England it is necessary to notice only a few, though it should be remembered that the others, too, had their part in making up the breed. However, only three have male lines extant today. The earliest of these is the Byerly Turk, mentioned by Cheny as 'Capt. Byerly's charging horse' in the Irish wars. There is a story that he also was captured from the Turks, but little else is known of him. He seems to have been foaled about 1679, and to have been in the stud as late as 1698.

"The Godolphin Arabian was foaled about 1724. He stood about 15 hands high, or an inch less, and several stories are told of him. According to one he was a present to Louis XIV of France by the Emperor of Morocco. Another is that he was stolen and taken to Paris. He got to England, at all events, and eventually came to the stud of the Earl of Godolphin. There is some argument that he was a Barb and not an Arabian, but since this is chiefly based on surviving paintings, it seems idle.

"The Darley Arabian has a slightly more certain origin. He was bought in Aleppo by Thomas Darley and sent to his father in England, arriving in 1704, at the age of four. He stood about 15 hands high. There are records in the stud book which show him to have had foals as late as 1735, but these are probably in error.

"One other might be mentioned. At about the time of Queen Anne, a grey stallion called Alcock's Arabian was brought to England, and he seems to be responsible for the color of virtually all of the gray Thoroughbreds now living. It should be familiar to the student that a grey horse must have at least one grey parent, and if the greys are followed through a pedigree, they will, with the scantiest of expections, go to the Alcock Arabian, though some of them will also trace, also in an unbroken sequence of greys, to the Brownlow Turk.

"The other three left more sizeable legacies to the Turf. Every Thoroughbred in the world today traces in male line to the Darley Arabian, the Godolphin Arabian, or the Byerly Turk. (Male line: son to sire to grandsire, etc.) In modern pedigrees, however, male lines are traced only to three descendants of these horses. The Darley Arabian is the great-great-grandsire of Eclipse (1764); the Byerly Turk is the great-great-grandsire of Herod (1758); and the Godolphin Arabian is the grandsire of Matchem (1748). No other branches of the original male lines exist, and modern horsemen trace pedigrees only to Herod, Matchem or Eclipse, in male lines.

"As the sires of the Thoroughbred race were few, so were their dams. Bruce Lowe, who probably did more work on female lines than anyone else, and to less purpose, estimated that there were fewer than 100 original mares in the stud book. Of these, only about 40 of the tap-root mares have persisted in male-female line. There are other foundation mares in America, Australia, and elsewhere, which may descend from these but whose pedigrees cannot be traced exactly, but this aspect of the subject will be discussed elsewhere.

"Most of the tap-root mares are unnamed, and are designated by the name of the sire or their owner, as Burton's Barb mare, Bustler mare, A Royal Mare, Mare by T. Gascoigne's Foreign Horse, Sister to Old Merlin, etc., in the original records. Prior has pointed out that only three, Queen Anne's Moonah Barb mare (imported in utero), the dam of Dodsworth, and a mare owned by Lord Arlington, have provable

Eastern origins. It should be mentioned that the 'Layton Barb mare' does not indicate the mare was a Barb, but that she was sired by a Barb.

"The foundation of the Thoroughbred, in the main, consisted in breeding imported stallions to native mares, and in breeding the daughters of such matings either to other imported stallions, or to such sons and male-line descendants of imported stallions as had shown conspicuous merit, with the result that in the course of a few generations the native blood had been obscured by the imported. The rage for imported stallions died out about a century after it began, probably because the horses which were being bred in England, particularly for racing and on a basis of performance, became more successful than miscellaneous and unraced stock which was brought in. From about 1750 forward, not a great deal of Arabian or other Eastern blood was imported, and the progress of English breeding consisted in mating the most successful mares to the most successful sires That is, inferior stock was discarded, the best retained.

"In the subsequent 200 years, the race horse has grown a good deal physically, and the descendants of the original Arabs and Barbs are now considerably taller than their ancestors; taking the average of the breed, the Thoroughbred's height is probably almost 16 hands, or five feet, four inches, measured at the withers. In 1873 Admiral Rous declared: 'The stature of Thoroughbred stock has increased since the year 1700 an inch every 25 years, and whereas the average size of horses then was 13 hands 3 inches, the average is now 15 hands 2 inches, and they can carry twice as much weight as 100 years ago.' (These figures are probably not strictly accurate.) The modern Thoroughbred has grown in speed also, and can run away and hide from the modern Arabian. Within the last year the bar has been raised against Arabian horses, and these can no longer be admitted to the American Stud Book. In a few brief words, the modern Thoroughbred is the result of selective breeding, over two centuries, for speed and stamina, as these are tested on the race course, and he has improved materially over the stock upon which his race was built.

"The history of the American Thoroughbred parallels that of the English rather exactly except for dates. It must be remembered that the settlers in Virginia, Maryland, and the Carolinas, where racing appeared first, were Englishmen, and were acquainted with English horses and racing practices. Since early newspapers are almost the only source of the records, it is not known exactly when races were first run. In New York, where horses were brought as early as 1625, but apparently with no respect to bloodlines (they were probably from Flanders), there was racing on Long Island at least as far back as 1665. Early records show races in the Carolinas in 1734, in Virginia in 1739, in Maryland in 1745. Presumably these were very informal affairs.

"But Governor Ogle introduced racing, 'between pedigreed horses, in the English style', at Annapolis in 1745, and this date may be said to mark, approximately, the beginning of Thoroughbred breeding and racing in North America. By tradition, the first Thoroughbred importation was the stallion Bully Rock, or Bulle Rock, in 1730, but as he was 21 years old when he arrived and as there were of course few opportunities for him to be mated with mares of racing heritage, his connection with later pedigrees is almost nil. The records show a few other importations before 1745, and in 1747 Governor Ogle brought over Spark and the celebrated mare Queen Mab at the same time. Traveller (Morton's) arrived in 1748, established an enduring reputation. In 1750 Col. Benjamin Tasker imported the famous mare Selima, which proved herself an outstanding racer, one of the most distinguished and lasting sources of excellence in American pedigrees, and the basis of innumerable arguments as to her ancestry (arguments now settled at last, but not in keeping with the American Stud Book). Governor Sharpe, also of Maryland, brought over Othello in 1755, and Janus and Fearnought came a few years later. The foundations of the American Thoroughbred were now laid.

"The Revolution interrupted the growth of Thoroughbred breeding, but as soon as it was over the stream of importations was reestablished, and by this time the stallions and mares being brought from England found many American-bred mates which had been tested on the race courses. Racing and the Thoroughbred gained rapidly in the postwar years, and there were many famous horses in the years from 1790 forward. As civilization moved westward across the Appalachians the Thoroughbred went with it, and it was not many years before Tennessee and Kentucky were breeding horses worthy of competition with the best along the Atlantic side of the mountains."

Chapter 17

Pomona Ranch

No history of the Arabian horse in America would be worth while if it did not give considerable prominence to the Pomona Ranch of W. K. Kellogg, where the Arabian horse has probably made greater history than at any other Arabian breeding farm in America. In a small booklet published July 1, 1937, the founder and owner of this ranch gives a general description of its purposes and aims and a short history.

Since the publication of this book the Kellogg Ranch has had a very checkered career. During World War II the University of California, with the consent of W. K. Kellogg, presented this ranch with its horses and equipment to the Remount Division of the War Department. The understanding was that this Arab breeding farm was to be used for the production of sires for cavalry or war horses. Shortly after World War II ended, the Remount was disbanded and many horses of the finest blood lines from this famous breeding stud were, unfortunately, sold at auction or otherwise disposed of. This action aroused resentment throughout the United States, and especially in California. Much pressure was brought to bear on Remount officials and on the War Department in an effort to get them to change their plans for the dissolution and abandonment of this famous group of breeding Arabs. After a consider-

POMONA ASTRAL. Arabian mare. A.H.C. No. 2987. Bay.

able period during which time many of the most famous animals had been disposed of, definite arrangements were made for the transfer of this property to other educational institutions in California. A definite program was then set up to carry on this ranch as an educational and breeding institution along the same general lines as originally followed by Mr. W. K. Kellogg.

First called the W. K. Kellogg Arabian Horse Ranch, after it was presented to the University of California and an endowment of $600,000 was set aside to conduct certain research work there, the name was changed to The W. K. Kellogg Institute of Animal Husbandry. Its avowed purpose was the breeding of high-grade Arab horses. Over the years, several hundred thousand persons have witnessed exhibitions at the farm, with resultant increases in favorable attention to the Arabian horse.

The following material is taken from the booklet, "The Romance of the Pomona Ranch":

"THE STORY OF A RANCH

"Behind the W. K. Kellogg Institute of Animal Husbandry at Pomona, California, behind the hundreds of acres of wonderfully cultivated land, behind the rolling fields of grain, the glistening orchards, the sun-bathed gardens — and most of all, back of the wonderful stables that have made the ranch one of the most interesting showplaces in southern California — there is quite a human story.

"It begins years ago and with a small Michigan boy who was living at that time in Battle Creek.

"And there was a horse — a gentle, broad-backed animal that was the boy's first and favorite pet. An Arabian, this horse was said to be.

"The small boy back in Michigan and his companions spent many a happy hour playing with their horse. They rode him bareback, climbed up his tail and slid down again many times in the course of an afternoon's play. And no doubt the gentle old horse enjoyed it all.

"And then tragedy came — heart-breaking tragedy, at least in the eyes of the boy who claimed the old horse as his special own. It was decided to sell 'Old Spot.'

"Then and there the boy declared that some day he would have horses — and that they would all be Arabians!

"That boy was W. K. Kellogg. . . .

"During one excursion he happened to visit the Arabian horse stud near Indio, California, established by the late Chauncey D. Clarke. That trip was the spark that fired the ambition of many years. That very day all Mr. Kellogg's boyhood dreams crystallized.

"In just a few short months he had purchased the Clarke stud outright and had begun his now famous Arabian ranch at Pomona. He had entered at last upon the realization of his ideals. To raise Arabian horses! To provide and preserve for American stables that noblest of all horse blood — the Arabian!

"It is interesting to delve into the background behind the horse that ranks so high in the affections of Mr. Kellogg. The famous Arabian!

"Its early history is shrouded in the veil of antiquity. For many centuries horses have been raised on the Arabian desert, and long ago their fame spread into Asia and Europe, thence throughout the world.

"Most of the evidence points to their having come originally from the Libyan tribes of northern Africa. And that by long and careful breeding the superior type of Arabian horses has been maintained for more than 3,500 years.

"The pure, desert-bred Arabian has always been noted for courage, intelligence and endurance. Accustomed to subsisting on scant water and forage, subjected to the burning heat of the desert, he is capable, nevertheless, of carrying heavy loads for great distances. Powerful and swift — raised almost as a member of the family by the desert tribes, he is invariably gentle, affectionate and tractable.

"For these many qualities the Arabian has been prized by every horse-loving age, and Arabian blood has been sought by breeders all over the world. But it has never been very easy to obtain. For one thing, the desert owners are true lovers of horses. They are seldom willing to part with their beloved stock. Especially is this true of mares, against the selling of which there is also a religious aversion.

"However, importations have been made from time to time to various parts of the world. England has perhaps benefited most by introducing Arabian blood into her stables.

"The record of the Arabian entitles him to the enviable title of 'Sire of nearly all fine horses.' For more than a hundred and twenty-seven years, every winner of the famous English Derby descended from an Arabian. Nearly 87 per cent of the winners descended from one great stallion — Darley Arabian, imported in 1706. Others from Alcock Arabian, and Godolphin Arabian. Famous Eclipse was a direct descendant of the Darley Arabian, as was Blaze, the foundation of the Hackney breed, and Imported Messenger, the great foundation American trotter sire. Diomed, the first winner of the Classic English Derby, was brought to Virginia and became the sire of many of our greatest racers.

"Another great Arabian which has left a highly prized line is Kismet. Kismet came out of the desert into India where he instantly won wide fame for speed and endurance. Later he was taken to England where he defeated all the best horses of his day. Finally he was brought to America; but the sea voyage brought on pneumonia, and this great stallion died within an hour after landing.

"Arabian blood, through the Thoroughbred, was the foundation of the present Morgan breed and played an important part in the foundation of the Kentucky saddle-horse. In Great Britan the Arabian horse has been bred for definite qualities through generation after generation and represents the peak in the development of the present-day Arabian.

"In America, the Arabian horse is just now coming into his own. The W. K. Kellogg Institute at Pomona contains the most outstanding collection that has ever been brought to this country.

"A good portion of the Institute herd has come from the Crabbet stud in England. This famous English stud was founded by Lady Anne Blunt, mother of the present owner.

"Lady Blunt lived for more than thirty years in the desert where she established a stable of the choicest animals collected from the leading

Bedouin breeders — later bringing them to England.

"At the Kellogg Institute are many outstanding names. For instance, there is Rossana, a gray mare sired by Champion Skowronek. She was Mr. Kellogg's favorite mount.

"And Rifla, whose brother was champion of England, and whose mother is full sister of the famous Arabian mare, Ramla, that won the first American endurance ride held under the auspices of the United States Army.

"It is a happy fact that the 'Arabian' that caught the fancy of Mr. Kellogg so many years ago was doubtless a member of the fine and noble strain that has contributed so much to the development of horses through the ages — and that will probably contribute most in the years to come.

"No one knows the wonderful qualities of the true Arabian better than the desert owners themselves who live by and with their horses.

"There was that famous old Algerian chieftain, Abd-el-Kader, a true son of the desert in his love of fine horse-flesh. These are his words:

" 'If in the course of your life you alight upon a horse of noble origin, with large, lively eyes, wide apart, and black, broad nostrils, close together; whose neck, shoulders, haunches, and buttocks are long, while his forehead, loins, flank, and limbs are broad; with the back, the shin-bones, the pasterns and the dock short; the whole accompanied by soft skin, fine, flexible hair, powerful respiratory organs, and good feet, with heels well off the ground — hasten to secure him if you can induce the owner to sell him, and return thanks to Allah morning and night for having sent thee a blessing'.

"And there is the last horse that Rudolph Valentino ever rode — Jadaan. This fine stallion was featured in the filming of the picture, 'The Son of the Sheik.' Many others have also been featured in motion pictures.

"THE PURPOSE BEHIND THE RANCH

"A great ranch, equipped with every modern convenience. White, spotless, fire-proof stables grouped around their quadrangle of emerald turf. Uniformed grooms and attendants. Acre after acre of fertile grain fields. Pastures, lush and green. And eighty-odd proud horses — the least of them a beautiful example of blood and breeding! . . . These, you will say, are quite a big realization of just a boyhood dream — and they are.

"Mr. Kellogg has realized his boyish ambitions perhaps more fully than ever he imagined during his most fanciful days. But the end has by no means come. Perhaps we might say the dream has broadened and widened into a great and shining ideal. And while the work in California is still a labor of love — it has behind it the lofty aim of public service. A clear and practical purpose: To provide and preserve a fertile source of blood and quality primarily for the stables of America.

"Thus, at the W. K. Kellogg Institute are being propagated the finest horses of the Arab strains that can be bred. Already the stables include over eighty animals and embrace some of the best blood of the entire Arabian world. The most modern methods of breeding are being carried on at Pomona. Size, height and saddle conformation are being developed with painstaking skill. Endurance and stamina are being preserved. Gentleness and docility.

"It is intended to make the W. K. Kellogg Institute a permanent source of high-type stallions and mares — breeding stock which will perpetuate the Arabian horse in America, and which at the same time will be used to improve the rank and file of our saddle horses that we may have better mounts for our cavalry, for pleasure riding and for polo.

"While this Institute is a comparatively new enterprise, Arabian horses have already been distributed to the states of New York, Oklahoma, Arizona, Michigan, Minnesota, Tennessee, Texas, Washington, Illinois, Montana, Oregon, Pennsylvania, New Mexico, Wisconsin, New Jersey, Connecticut, Nebraska, Utah, Iowa, Ohio, as well as many points in California. Exports of pure-bred Arabs have been made to Hawaii, Mexico, England, Canada, Santo Domingo, Central America and South America.

"The manager of the stud is Mr. H. H. Reese, who graduated in 1908 from Purdue University, where he specialized in horse husbandry. Mr. Reese was connected for some time with the United States Department of Agriculture at Washington, and with the United States Experiment Station at Beltsville, Maryland. He was later in charge of the horse-breeding work conducted by the government in Virginia and West Virginia. Still later he was made superintendent of the United States Morgan Horse Farm at Middlebury, Vermont.

"Already the Kellogg Institute is coming to be recognized as one of the outstanding Arabian studs of the world. The entire stable is registered with the American-Arabian Horse Club — and the names of many of the horses are entered both in the thoroughbred stud books of England and America.

"Few of us would be likely to choose horses — even Arabian horses — as the stuff dreams are made of. Yet, that's just what they are at Pomona. And out on the ranch and around the stables, it isn't hard to look at Arabian Rossana, Mr. Kellogg's favorite mount, and conjure up the picture of a small boy back in Battle Creek, playing in the sunshine of many years ago with his first true love . . . 'Old Spot.'

FERSARA No. 4104. Champion and grand champion 3-year-old Arabian mare.

"PRACTICAL FEATURES OF THE ARABIAN

"It is perhaps true, that many of the best friends of the Arabian have been, unwittingly, his worst enemies. They have covered him with romantic glamour and sentimental tradition. They have been inclined to place him on a pedestal reserved only for the aristocrat of aristocrats.

"Many of his wonderful, practical features have been overlooked in the 'aloofness' with which he has been regarded. These conditions have helped prevent the Arabian from winning the practical place he merits in the American horse fraternity.

"It is also unfortunate that only a few horsemen differentiate between the various breeds and types of horses which have been developed in Arabia and the Barbary States in North Africa. This has resulted in not only confusing the closely allied, but distinctive, breeds of Arabians and Barbs, but also their grades (from Kurdish and perhaps other ponies).

"Most of the horses brought from these sections, regardless of the purity of their lineage, have been called Arabians. Perhaps, it is safe to say that, with a few exceptions, these horses have been almost everything else but Arabians of the purest blood. Many of them have been mediocre individuals and have brought disrepute upon the class of horses that were such potent factors in the foundation of the thoroughbred and Hackney of England, the Percheron and Demisang of France, the Orloff of Russia, and the Morgan and American Saddle Horse of the United States.

"The real horseman, who is seeking the truth in horse history, will appreciate that the prepotency of the blood that was strong enough to make an impression upon the heterogeneous stock of two hundred years ago, and to make it possible for horse breeders of succeeding generations to evolve the various breeds — the best of their kind the world has ever seen — is still worthy of consideration in the solution of present-day horse breeding problems. The blood streams of the true modern Arabians are unpolluted, and have been kept pure during the hundreds of years that have intervened since Godolphin Arabian, Darley Arabian, Markham Arabian, Leede's Arabian, and others of their class.

"Historical research has definitely established that of all the horse tribes that are descended from the Libyan, the Arab has always been the most outstanding. It is also a well-known fact that the best of the Arabians are represented by five great families — the Keheilan, the Seglawi, the Abeyan, the Hamdani and the Hadban. While these families are interbred quite generally, the family names are still more or less adhered to by the Arabian horse fraternity.

"At the W. K. Kellogg Institute, the stallions now in service, as well as most of the mares selected for the permanent foundation of the stud, have blood lines that are as pure today as they were when the Sheiks first sent their finest specimens to improve the horse stocks of Great Britain.

"In our work-a-day world, horse breeding has been highly specialized. There is a particular kind, or type, of horse for nearly every purpose. The so-called general purpose horse of a decade or two ago is now a misfit. In consequence, the leading types of horses are those adapted to the turf, the hunting field, the show-ring, the bridle paths and for draft uses.

"The Arabian is pre-eminently a saddle-horse; the oldest real saddle-horse breed of today. For untold horse generations, he has been bred for work under a particular type of saddle, for the chase and war. In this field of effort, the high-class Arabian yields to no other horse in temperament and disposition. He is neither phlegmatic, nor is he so fiery tempered that only a skilful, fearless horseman can manage him.

"The Arabian is a horse you can chum with, a real trustworthy pal, one that adapts himself to the moods and whims of his riders — be he the business man seeking relaxation in the open, the youth who loves to feel the cold air tingle on the cheek, or perchance, milady, out for her constitutional in the park or city bridle path. The Arabian, on account of his close association with man for more than three thousand years, is most reliable; equipped with an exceptional amount of brains, which makes him the saddle horse par excellence.

"The Arabians excel most breeds in their refined, highly finished, distinctive type. As a breed, they are beautifully fronted, with a grand outlook — an exceptional head, with large expressive eyes, nicely arched neck, good sloping shoulders and front pasterns. They have a short coupled back and a turn of rib and depth of flank which are indicative of their great endurance; and leave little to be desired. In the typical representatives of the breed, the tail setting is such that it is unnecessary to resort to 'artificial tail setting,' to which so many object, to get a perfect tail carriage.

"Arabian horses are very free from leg unsoundnesses. Curby hocks and ringbones are seldom found. The eye ailment, periodic ophthalmia (moon blindness), is practically never, if ever, found in pure Arabian horses, and this is true also of the respiratory defects known as heaves and thick wind (roaring). While some strains of Arabian horses are rather small, other strains such as the Nureddin line are over 15.2 hands high. Arabians bred in America, if properly fed, also have more size than their ancestors, and it is a well known fact that the Arabian cross to other strains almost invariably results in larger stock. The Arab crossed with small Indian ponies produces horses larger than either the sire or the dam. The measure for Arabian horses however, should not be the measuring stick or the scales, as they have more endurance and weight carrying ability than horses considerably taller and heavier.

"At Pomona, two great objectives are being attained. The first — to preserve the purest Arabian blood for a contribution to the improvement of the light horse stock of America; second, to improve the incomparable Arabian himself."

Chapter 18

Arabian Horse Importation From Poland

ALTHOUGH Poland has long been recognized as an important breeding center for the Arabian horse, it was not until early 1937 that the first importation of note was made — by J. M. Dickinson, owner of the famous Nashville, Tennessee, Travelers' Rest Arabian Stud.

Tex Ewell, in the September-October, 1937, issue of *The Western Horseman,* gives a short description of this importation and describes the principal animals under the general title, "The Arab Horse":

"The first shipment from Poland, as far as is known, of pure-bred Arabians, has been received by Mr. J. M. Dickinson, of Travelers' Rest Arabian Stud in Nashville, Tenn. Six fine mares, each with a great history in back of her. They are of such high class quality and breeding that they are not for sale at any price, but are going to be used by Mr. Dickinson only as brood mares.

"In 1934, Mr. Dickinson sold 'Antez', his famous great racing stallion and outstanding sire, to the Arab Horse Breeding Society in Poland, and it was through their high regard for Antez, and the cooperation of

Count Alexander Dzieduszycki, president of the Arab Horse Breeding Society, that Mr. Dickinson was able to have these mares imported. They were purchased from various studs in Poland, and represent the best blood from the Country.

"Lassa, a seven-year-old chestnut mare, was foaled at the State Stud at Janow. Her sire, Koheilan I, was imported to Poland at the age of two, from the Hungarian State Stud at Babolna. He distinguished himself as chief sire in the State Stud of Poland for several years before being re-purchased by the Hungarian State Stud management. Among his colts are numbered the Derby winners of 1931, 1932, and 1934. Zulejma, Lassa's dam, traces back to the celebrated Sahara, imported in 1845 by Count Julius Dzieduszycki.

"Liliana, a seven-year-old grey mare, was sired by Linkoln, whose sire is an imported Arab Arslan whose blood can be traced in the pedigrees of some of the best produce of the stud at which he stood. Liliana's dam, Czapla, bred in the Janow State Stud, traces to the desert bred mares Gazella and Sahara imported in 1845 by Count Dzieduszycki. Czapla's sire Bakszysz, has left a number of valuable descendants, the most distinguished of them being Flisak, Derby winner in 1928, and Fetysz, sold and exported to Germany as leading sire for the German State Stud at Trakehen. Liliana is due to have a colt in August by Antez.

"Mattaria, an eleven-year-old grey mare, was purchased from Count Roman Potacki. This mare has given the Count four fillies, of which the two younger ones are by Antez. Mattaria's dam, Koncha, was foaled in 1918 in the celebrated stud of Count Potocki at Antoniny. She belonged to the small part of stud material which some faithful servants were able to save from destruction by hiding it in the forests during the bolshevik riots. Mattaria's sire, Kafifan, was imported to Poland from Prince Mohammed Ali's stud at Manial, Egypt. For many years before his death he was among the leading sires of money winners of Poland.

"Niwka, a five-year-old, dark grey mare, foaled in the State Stud at Janow. Dziwa, Niwka's dam, traces back through both her parents to the famous desert bred Arab mares Gazella and Sahara. Her son, Ofir, Niwka's half brother, is the most promising young sire of the Janow State Stud. Niwka was trained for racing and took part in the efficiency tests established by the Polish Government.

"Nora, a five-year-old chestnut mare, was also foaled in the State Stud at Janow. Nora's sire, Hardy, was raced for two years and during that time he was never defeated. Among other races, he won the Derby in 1930. After having passed the efficiency tests he was leading stallion at the State Stud in Janow. He is the sire of the Derby favorite for 1937. Nora herself was trained for racing.

"Przepiorka, a three-year-old chestnut mare, was foaled in the State Stud. Her sire, Almanzor, is a descendant of the famous mare Mlecha, imported from Arabia by Count J. Dzieduszycki in 1845. She is the youngest mare in the importation, but is already large for an Arab.

"Mr. Dickinson of Travelers' Rest has been breeding Arabs derived from the Maynesboro Arabian Stud that belonged to Mr. W. R. Brown, and the Interlachen Stud that belonged to Colonel Spencer Borden. These horses traced largely to stock bred at the Crabbett Arabian Stud, His Highness Prince Mohammed Ali in Egypt, the Stud of Mr. Guilherme Echenique in Brazil, South America, and France.

"The Arabian horse is enjoying more popularity and appreciation, and creating more interest and enthusiasm than ever before. They are enjoyed for their versatility and usefulness, their performance under saddle at three gaits or five, as hunters or jumpers, and in harness.

"The merits of an Arab horse lie in all-around usefulness and flexibility under saddle, and in exceptional soundness, healthiness, hardiness, and gentle but high spirit."

Chapter 19

Arabian Horse Breeding Cataloues
As A Source Of Information

STUDENTS of the Arabian horse in America could not possibly get a clear idea of the breed without a study of some of the more important stud catalogues that have been issued on this breed in times past. I have in my library several of these catalogues which contain certain information not available elsewhere. One of the most valuable books of this type has been published by the Travelers' Rest Farm, originally established in 1792 in Tennessee. This farm, many years after its original formation, passed to the ownership of General J. M. Dickinson, of Franklin, Tennessee, one of the heirs of the original founder, and he kept the name when he established an Arabian stud in Davidson County in 1930. Travelers' Rest stud was removed to Williamson County near Franklin, Tennessee, in 1937. In 1946 it was transferred to Santa Barbara, California, where it became known as Travelers' Rest Ranch. Two years later the stud was moved back to Tennessee and it was dispersed in 1949 by Mr. Dickinson, the owner.

The first Travelers' Rest catalogue in my file was copyrighted in 1941, but this is evidently not the first one printed since it is listed as a revised edition. The last and final edition I have was copyrighted in 1947.

The 1941 catalogue lists and describes all of the horses that had been owned and bred up to that time at Travelers' Rest, in 173 pages. The forepart of the catalogue deals at considerable length with general information on the Arabian horse, from a wide variety of sources. A general description of the Travelers' Rest Arabian Stud from the original foundation down to the time the breeding of Arabian horses was begun is given in some detail. A history and description of the principal Arabian blood lines owned and used by the stud is given considerable prominence.

This catalogue shows that many of the principal breeding animals in the Travelers' Rest stud were purchased from several well-known Arabian studs, such as Interlachen Farms, Kellogg's Arabian Farm, Kemah Farm, Maynesboro Arabian Stud, and the Selby Arabian Stud, as well as from Crabbet Stud, in England, from the leading stud farms in Poland and a few from various other sources. A detailed description is given of all the breeding animals in the stud, and along with a description of the mares is a list of produce. Some well-known Arabian mares listed are: Aire, Aziza, Fath, H. H. Mohamed Ali's Hamama, H. H. Mohamed Ali's Hamida and others of similar breeding and type whose names will be found in the pedigrees of the most prominent Arabs found in the United States at this time. Probably the most valuable feature of this well illustrated catalogue are the pedigree charts and index of all the horses that have been owned and bred at Travelers' Rest. These charts show extended pedigrees of all principal lines and important contributing lines, making it possible to determine the breeding and lines from which the animal came and the related animals in the corresponding generations.

Travelers' Rest catalogue contains a valuable department entitled, "Index of Horses." It covers many pages, lists the horses that have been bred or owned at the stud, gives their sex, color, the family to which they belong, their sire and his male chart and the dam and the female chart, the date foaled, the breeder of the animal, and finally information about what disposition was made of the animal.

The revised edition of the catalogue was published in 1947. This follows the same general form as previous catalogues but also contains descriptions of many new breeding animals then to be found in the stud. The following is a list of celebrated American-bred Arabs used at Travelers' Rest:

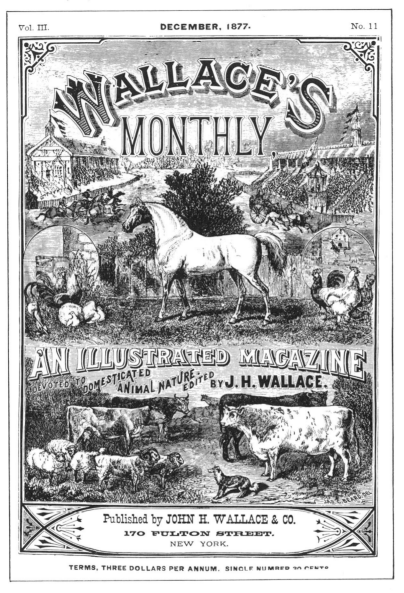

Vol. III.　　DECEMBER, 1877.　　No. 11

WALLACE'S MONTHLY,

AN ILLUSTRATED MAGAZINE
DEVOTED TO DOMESTICATED ANIMAL NATURE. EDITED BY J. H. WALLACE.

Published by JOHN H. WALLACE & CO.
170 FULTON STREET.
NEW YORK.

TERMS, THREE DOLLARS PER ANNUM. SINGLE NUMBER 30 CENTS.

Wallace's Monthly, the leading horse paper in the United States from 1875 to 1893, published much information on the Arabian horse.

"Antez, bred by F. E. Lewis II. Successful show ring winner and joint holder of ½ mile world's record for Arabs.

"Bazleyd, bred at W. R. Brown's Maynesboro Arabian Stud. Nat'l Ch. Arabian stallion and sire of prizewinners.

"Gharifet, bred at W. R. Brown's Maynesboro Arabian Stud. Champion mare and producer of prizewinners.

"Guemura, bred at Col. Spencer Borden's Interlachen Stud. Producer of 17 foals of great quality.

"Gulastra, bred at W. R. Brown's Maynesboro Arabian Stud. A horse of great quality noted for the refinement of his get.

"Gulnare, bred at Col. Spencer Borden's Interlachen Stud. Her descendants have accounted for trail ride and show-ring prizes in England and the U. S. including two national championships.

"Hira, bred at A. W. Harris' Kemah Horse Farm. Produced winner of a chicagoland trail ride.

"Kolastra, bred at W. R. Brown's Maynesboro Arabian Stud. First prize Arab, and highest scoring stallion of an Ohio trail ride.

"Ramghaza, bred in Texas by Col. Parke Houston. Producer of foals of highest quality, including Artatama that won first prize in Mexico City.

"Ronek, bred at W. K. Kellogg Ranch. A national prizewinner and subsequently Champion Arab stallion Illinois State Fair."

Some of the notable foals produced by Travelers' Rest Arabian Farm by the time the 1947 catalog was published were:

"Ahrany sired Tony, half-Arab winner of Vermont Trail Ride.

"Alyf has won stallion and harness classes in California.

"Artatama won first prize in open competition in Mexico, D. F.

"Bandos has won in a breeding class in California.

"Bataan became noted at the Pomona Quartermaster Depot (Kellogg Ranch).

"Chepe-Noyon has become a well-known stallion in Idaho.

"Falouma has won in a breeding class in California.

"Fayadan was National Champion Arabian weanling.

"Gara has won in several breeding classes in England.

"Gayza has won in breeding classes in the United States and England.

"Genghis Kahn won many open jumping classes in New Jersey.

"Gutne won breeding class prize in National Arabian Show.

"Hallany Mistanny has won prizes in California.

"Ibn Manial has become one of the most celebrated stallions in Brazil.

"Jagai was National Champion Arabian colt.

The Western Horseman has published much information on the Arabian horse.

"Jedran won in 'saddle-bred' competition as well as Arabian classes.

"Jellaby has won prizes in breeding classes in England.

"Ju-Dhar was a prize-winning colt in National Arabian Show.

"Kann has won prizes in breeding classes in California.

"Khyber was a prize-winning colt in National Arabian Show.

"Lwow has won in stock horse competition in Nebraska.

"Mahri has become a well-known stallion in Colorado.

"Nafud was a prizewinner in 'saddle-bred' competition in Tennessee.

"Ptolemy has been a prizewinner in Montana.

"Rafik became a well-known stallion in New York.

"Tirs has won in open saddle horse competition in Ohio.

"Tamerlane (Ang.-Ar.) won jumping championship Chicago International."

In Travelers' Rest 1947 catalog is found a list of the Arabian horses imported for this stud:

"Aeniza, bred by Prince Witold Czartoryski, Pelkinie. A producing broodmare in Poland that raced with moderate success.

"Babolna, bred by Wanda, Ploska, Sokolowo, Poland. Donated to U.S.R.S. with foal at side.

"Ba-Ida, bred by Prince Witold Czartoryski, Pelkinie. A producing broodmare in Poland, had raced with outstanding success, produced Bataan, the well-known 'black' stallion of the U.S.R.S.

"Czubuthan, bred by Prince Witold Czartoryski, Pelkinie. The most celebrated distance Arab racer of his day, and second ranking money winner in Poland.

"Derazne, bred at Count Potocki's Derazne stud in Poland, foaled at Travelers' Rest.

"Gileem, bred by Capt. the Hon. Geo. Savile, and a prize-winning mare at London, England.

"Janow, bred at Polish State Stud, Janow-Podlaski, foaled at Travelers' Rest.

"Kadira, bred by C. W. Hough, and a prize-winning filly at London, England.

"Kasmira, bred by Prince Witold Czartoryski, Pelkinie, and foaled at Travelers' Rest.

"Lassa, bred at Polish State Stud, Janow-Podlaski, producer of a winner in Poland and champion Arab mare of Illinois State Fair.

"Latif, bred by Tadeusz Gniazdowski, Osiek, Poland, foaled at Travelers' Rest.

"Liliana, bred by Estate of Jana Kleniewski, Zagloba-Opole, and a producing broodmare in Poland.

"Maamouna, bred by Royal Agricultural Society of Egypt.

Arabian Horse Breeding Catalogues
As A Source Of Information

ARABIAN HORSE NEWS

25 cents a copy

October-November, 1948

Featuring Arabian Horses—Their Owners and Breeders

ARABIAN MARE AND TWIN FILLY FOALS

PARETA, 1020, with her twin fillies sired by Ybarra, 1095, who were
foaled April 25, 1948, at the Pettigrew Arabian Stud, Muncie, Ind.

Arabian Horse News is the only publication in the interest of the Arabian
horse in the United States.

"Mattaria, bred at Count Potocki's Behen Stud, and a producing broodmare in Poland.

"Nahrawana, bred at Er Rasul, the stud of Guilherme Echenique, Jr., and adjudged 'best Arabian in the show' at Pelotas, Brazil.

"Niwka, bred at Polish State Stud, Janow-Podlaski, Poland.

"Nora, bred at Polish State Stud, Janow-Podlaski, Poland.

"Przepiorka, bred at Polish State Stud, Janow-Podlaski, Poland.

"Sielanka, bred at Estate of Jana Kleniewski, Zagloba-Opole, Poland, foaled at Travelers' Rest.

"Ugra, bred at Prince Roman Sanguszko's Gumniska Stud in Poland."

The following is a list of Arabian horses purchased in the U. S. for Travelers' Rest Stud:

"Aire, bred by Hernan Ayerza, Cabana El Aduar in Argentina; foaled at Haras Er Rasul in Brazil. Champion of the Arabian breed at Porto Alegre, Brazil. Imp. U. S. for exhibition in National Arabian Show for Guilherme Echenique, Jr.

"Alya, bred by Chickrallah Abdallah, Jebel, Syria, Imp. by M. K. Bistany.

"Aziza, bred at Prince Mohamed Aly's Manial stud in Egypt. Imp. by W. R. Brown.

"Exochorda, bred by Royal Agricultural Society, raced successfully as Leila II. Imp. by Dr. Heberman.

"H. H. Mohamed Ali's Hamama, bred at Prince Mohamed Aly's Manial stud in Egypt. Imp. by W. R. Brown. Nat'l. Ch. Arabian mare, and prizewinner under saddle.

"H. H. Mohamed Ali's Hamida, bred at Prince Mohamed Aly's Manial Stud, Egypt. Imp. by W. R. Brown.

"Hazna, bred at Crabbet Park, England. Imp. by W. R. Brown.

"Kasztelanka, bred at Polish State Stud, Janow-Podlaski, a successful racer and a producer in Poland. Imp. by H. B. Babson. Prizewinner at Illinois State Fair.

"Kola, bred by Mlle. Cushing, Pau, France. Imp. by W. R. Brown. Produced winners on track, the trail and in the show, in England, France, and U. S. A.

"Kostrzewa, bred at Polish State Stud, Janow-Podlaski. One of the most celebrated mares on track and a producing broodmare in Poland. Imp. by H. B. Babson.

"Nasr, bred at Prince Mohamed Aly's Manial stud, for which he raced with great success and at which he served as chief stallion knowr. as 'Manial'. Imp. by W. R. Brown. Internationally famous.

Mason's Farrier and Stud-Book—New Edition.

THE GENTLEMAN'S
NEW POCKET FARRIER:

COMPRISING

A GENERAL DESCRIPTION OF THE NOBLE AND USEFUL ANIMAL,

THE HORSE;

WITH MODES OF MANAGEMENT IN ALL CASES, AND
TREATMENT IN DISEASE.

BY RICHARD MASON, M.D.

FORMERLY OF SURRY COUNTY, VIRGINIA.

TO WHICH IS ADDED,

A PRIZE ESSAY ON MULES;
AN APPENDIX,

CONTAINING RECIPES FOR DISEASES OF HORSES, OXEN, COWS,
CALVES, SHEEP, DOGS, SWINE, ETC. ETC.

WITH

ANNALS OF THE TURF, AMERICAN STUD-BOOK, RULES FOR
TRAINING, RACING, ETC.

WITH A SUPPLEMENT:

COMPRISING

AN ESSAY ON DOMESTIC ANIMALS, ESPECIALLY THE HORSE,

WITH REMARKS ON TREATMENT AND BREEDING;

TOGETHER WITH

TROTTING AND RACING TABLES,

SHOWING

THE BEST TIME ON RECORD, AT ONE, TWO, THREE, AND FOUR MILE HEATS;

PEDIGREES OF WINNING HORSES, SINCE 1839; AND OF THE
MOST CELEBRATED STALLIONS AND MARES;

WITH

USEFUL CALVING AND LAMBING TABLES, &c. &c.

BY J. S. SKINNER,

Editor now of the Farmers' Library, New York; Founder of the American Farmer, in 1819;
and of the Turf Register and Sporting Magazine, in 1829: being the first Agricultural and the first Sporting Periodicals established in the United States.

PHILADELPHIA:

J. B. LIPPINCOTT & CO.

1857.

The third edition of *Mason's Farrier* of 1828 contained the
first attempt at a stud book published in the United States.

"Rimini, bred at Crabbet Park, a producing broodmare in England. Imp. by Roger Selby.

"Roda, bred at Prince Mohamed Aly's Manial stud, Egypt. Imp. by W. R. Brown. A national prizewinner.

"Rose of France, bred at Crabbet Park. Imp. by Roger A. Selby. A prizewinner.

"S. S. Byron, desert bred. Foaled at sea. Imp. by M. K. Bistany.

"Warsaw, bred at Polish State Stud, Janow-Podlaski. Imp. in utero by H. B. Babson.

"Zarife, bred at Prince Mohamed Aly's Manial stud in Egypt. Imp. by W. R. Brown."

In addition to the index of horses bred and owned by Travelers' Rest which appeared in previous catalogues, the 1947 catalogue listed a pedigree index of ancestors of Travelers' Rest Arabian horses. This index was published in the same order as the index of horses owned and bred and occupies the last forty-nine pages.

I visited Travelers' Rest Farm briefly during the period of its greatest activity, at which time the stud owned approximately fifty brood mares. The greatest number of Arabian horses owned by Travelers' Rest at any one time was probably about eight-five head, and the aim of the stud was to have sufficient mares to produce approximately fifty foals each year.

In 1937 Roger A. Selby, owner of the Selby Stud, then of Portsmouth, Ohio, published a very elaborate illustrated book of his Arabian stud. This catalogue contains 104 pages, and more than one hundred illustrations, several by those famous animal painters, Lynn Bogue Hunt and George Ford Morris.

Of particular interest in this catalogue are articles entitled, "An Appreciation of the Arab Horse," by Lynn Bogue Hunt, the famous painter of wild life, and "The Appeal of the Arabian Horse," by the most famous painter of horses in the United States, George Ford Morris. "Facts About the Arabian Horse" are given in a short article by Albert W. Harris, then Vice-President of the Arabian Horse Society, and Roger A. Selby reproduced a short article called "Why an Arab?"

A detailed description is given of the principal stallions and brood mares of the Selby Stud. Many of these have produced the foundation stock of the leading Arabian breeding studs throughout the United States as well as in several foreign countries. Some of the most famous stallions described and pictured in this book include Champion Mirage and his son, Image, and Raffles, probably the greatest of them all. Among the noted mares described and shown are Champion Rifala, the dam of

Raffles, and Image and a daughter of the famous Skowronek; and Kareyma, one of the greatest brood mares of all times.

Other features are quotations taken from the works of many famous authors on the Arabian horse, including "The Horse of the Desert," by William R. Brown, "The History of the Horse," by John Lawrence, and "The Diaries of Sir Wilfrid Scawen Blunt."

I do not hesitate to state that in my opinion this catalogue is one of the most valuable, comprehensive and authoritative pieces of literature on the Arabian horse ever published in this country.

In 1919 the Maynesboro Arabian Stud owned by William R. Brown and situated at Berlin, N. H., issued its first breeding catalogue consisting of twenty-two pages. In this catalogue a total of eighty-eight pure-bred registered Arabs are listed, several of which were at the original stud farm at Berlin, N. H., others at Decorch, Iowa, and a few at Cody, Wyoming.

This catalogue is unique inasmuch as it lists the various Arabs owned by Maynesboro Arabian Stud according to their families. The breeding and a short description of each animal is included, and many horses are described as to height and weight.

Among the famous stallions shown are Abu Zeyd, Rodan, Sargon, Sinbad, Berk and many others. Certainly this collection of pure-bred Arabian stallions is one of the greatest ever owned by any single individual in the United States, if not in the world, up to that time.

Among the famous mares listed in this catalog are: Rijma, Ramla, Ramim, Onrust, Bathsheba, Ghazala, Guemura, Gulnare, and many more. Some of the greatest mares the breed has ever known appear, and their names will be found in the pedigrees of many of the finest Arabian horses owned in this country. The 1919 catalogue was not illustrated.

In 1922 Maynesboro Arabian Stud published another breeding catalogue that was well-illustrated with pictures of its principal stallions and mares and containing quite a lot of general information on the Arabian horse. In the back of this catalogue appears a very good illustration of the Anglo-Arab mare Halcyon, quite a famous endurance winner, bred by Interlachen Stud of Fall River, Massachusetts. Some mention is also made of endurance tests, one of which was sponsored by the Morgan Horse Club. An illustration showing Rustem Bey and Crabbet finishing the endurance test of 1920 is also included.

In 1925 another stud catalogue was published containing some additional illustrations but following generally the form of the 1922 catalogue. Prominent illustrations in this 1925 catalogue are of imported Rodan, Khaled and Astraled, also a very good illustration of Ghazala at twenty years.

The 1929 stud catalogue follows the same general line as the 1925 catalogue, but very noticeable is the young stallion, Ribal, who at that time was one of the leading sires along with Rehal, both bred by Maynesboro Arabian Stud. Another young stud also bred by Maynesboro was Gulastra, who at that time was but a five-year-old. These stallions all became very good sires of pure-bred Arabs and many of the pedigrees of the most prominent Arabs in the United States contain crosses to them. Another stallion illustrated in this catalogue and bred by Maynesboro Stud was Ghazi, prominent for many years at William R. Hearst's San Simeon Farm until his death in 1948. Among the mare illustrations is Gulnare, one of the famous "G" mares bred by Col. Spencer Borden, and the dam of Gulastra and several other very fine Arabs. Another mare is Bazrah, the daughter of Rodan out of Bathsheba, which foaled and raised her twentieth colt at twenty-eight years of age. This mare is the dam of several very fine Arabs, among her foals the "Peerless Show Horse" Bazleyd.

Chapter 20

The Arabian Horse In The Show Ring

THE number of breeders of Arabian horses in the United States increased so rapidly during the thirties and forties that a need arose for an organization to promote the best interests of the Arabian horse. Greater numbers of Arabian horses were being produced in California than in any other state and it was only natural that such a movement would originate in California.

The first such group to organize on a committee basis was the Arabian Horse Breeders' Society of California. The first meeting was originated and called by Mrs. Joanna Phillips, of Glendale on December 12, 1944, and from this meeting twenty dues-paying members were secured. Elected officers were: R. Warren Phillips, President; Raymond W. Cosly, Vice-President; and Mrs. Joanna Phillips, Secretary and Treasurer. This organization sponsored the first All-Arabian show ever held in the United States on October 14, 1945, at Flintridge, California, with sixty-three horses entered in 105 classes. Two of the Club members, Bill Low and Ted Steere, were largely responsible for show arrangements. Since then, there has been an annual All-Arabian horse show each year and each has had a greater number of entries than the previous one. Interest has become almost nation-wide from an exhibitors' standpoint in this greatest show of its kind in the world.

The Society, in 1950, reported a membership of nearly 200 members. From this organization have sprung several other smaller groups, of which the Midwest Arabian Horse Owners and the West Central Arabian Horse Association are probably the largest and best-known at this time.

The second All-Arabian show was held on October 13, 1946. This show was fully as successful as the previous one and had classes for breeding, saddle and harness Arabs.

The third show was held at Devonshire Downs, San Fernando Valley, on September 28, 1947. It was the largest Arabian horse show ever held in the United States, and there were in excess of 300 entries and an attendance of about 3,500 people.

In this show was one class for senior stallions in which thirty-four horses were entered. All working classes were well filled and the performances were excellent. The grand champion stallion of this show was Ramah, and the show was judged by Dr. Amin Zaher from Egypt.

The fourth show was held on October 23 and 24, 1948, at the Los Angeles Fair Grounds. There were more horses entered than in any

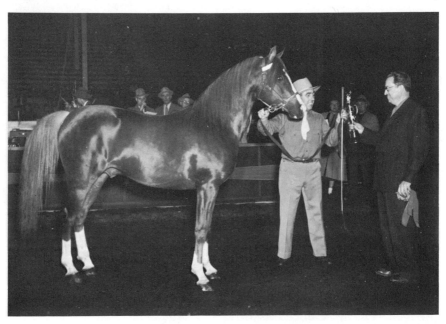

SKORAGE A.H.C. No. 4030. Stallion.

Left: ARABI KABIR. A.H.C. No. 2379. Chestnut Arabian stallion.
Right: ALLABU. A.H.C. No. 4329. Chestnut Arabian stallion.

previous one and there was a considerably greater attendance. There was a total of thirty-one classes in this two-day show and there was an average per class of slightly more than fifteen entries.

The show was judged by Col. F. W. Koester. The class for mares at this show had twenty-one top entries and was probably the most impressive class of its kind ever held in this country. The grand champion in the mare division was the eleven-year-old gray mare, Moneyna, owned by Mr. Harvey Ellis. The reserve championship was won by a two-year-old filly named Jedrazel bred and owned by Dr. Claude Steen, of Fullerton.

Hearst's San Simeon Stables exhibited its recent Arab importation, together with a considerable number of native-bred Arabs.

This show was managed by Guy Williams, of Artesia, while Dr. Harold Capper officiated as ring steward, and Cecil L. Edwards, the president of the Arabian Horse Society of California, served as announcer.

RAFFCON No. 7495, at 3½ years of age.

Comments and reports on the fifth show held at Pomona, California, on October 15 and 16, 1949, indicate that this was by all odds the greatest Arabian horse show ever held in America if not in the world. With more than 300 entries it was truly great. Wayne Dinsmore, for thirty years the able secretary of the Horse Association of America, was the judge of the breeding classes, and Del Kear the performance classes other than dressage classes, which were judged by Maj. George de Roaldes.

During the second day twenty-six pure-bred Arabian classes were judged. The champion Arabian stallion four years old and over, was a bay, Gayr, by Ronek. He later became grand champion stallion of the show. In the Arabian mare class four years old and over, the chestnut Joanna, by Rabyias, owned by Charles and Donald McKenna, was the champion, and later became the champion mare of the show. The following quotation about the show, by Wayne Dinsmore, is taken from the December 1949 issue of *The Bit and Spur*:

HASSAN IBN THABIT. A.H.C. No. 3613. Bay Arabian stallion.

"Arabian horses — a few over 200 in the breeding classes and about 160 in performance classes — some of which were duplicated, competed at the Los Angeies County Fair Grounds, Pomona, California, October 15th and 16th, in what breeders say was the strongest show of Arabian horses ever made in the United States. In addition, 61 half-Arabians were shown in classes for grade Arabians. Del Kear, formerly of Wyoming, now a Californian, judged the performance classes and the writer judged the breeding classes.

"Half Arabian horses only were judged on Saturday, the 15th, which left a very heavy schedule for Sunday, the 16th. The classes were so large — 19 in the under yearling colts, 28 in the yearling fillies, 20 in the one year under two colts, 19 in the same age fillies, 16 in the two year and under three colts, 11 in fillies of the same age, 12 in the three and under four colts, 10 in fillies of the same age, with no less than 32 Arabian stallions shown in the four year old and over class and 26 in the class for mares of that age — that it was a matter of sheer necessity to sort out a short leet without moving all horses that were competing.

"I accordingly gave every animal a critical examination as they stood, sorted out the 10 or 12 that appeared to be the best, and excused the remainder from further showing, without moving them. I regretted this, as I would have preferred to move them all; but time did not permit.

"The animals selected for the short leet were those that appeared to be most satisfactory in underpinning, conformation, quality, symmetry and Arab breed type. These were then moved at walk and trot, critically re-examined and placed as their merits seemed to justify. Decisions were very close in many instances, and many that did not get in the prize money would be worthy of the blue in an average state or regional show.

"Arabian horses are primarily riding horses. They are in demand for pleasure riding by those who can afford to ride pure Arabs; but their principal market must be to cattlemen who can use Arabian stallions to improve the riding qualities and endurance of stock horses they use regularly after cattle.

"Arabian breeders realize this, hence featured many performance classes calculated to show what Arabians can do under saddle — their speed, agility, alertness and quick response to the wishes of the rider. These performance classes, together with the merit of the half Arabians shown, will go far to convince many stockmen that they will do well to use an excellent Arabian sire on mares of good riding type, to enhance the endurance, quality and finish of the young stock horses they are producing for use under saddle on their own ranches.

"It is conceded by all horsemen of experience that the Arabian horse is the most prepotent, stamping his own characteristics more definitely on the progeny than any other breed does; hence there is a place for the Arabian as a sire of good using, durable, attractive riding horses that will furnish good service on ranches, yet sell for pleasure riding purposes at 7 or 8 years of age, to persons who want good riding horses."

Interest and entries continue to increase each year and Arabian breeders with little or no experience in showing are rapidly learning some of the fundamentals of showing their Arabian horses properly and to the best advantage. There is little doubt that these All-Arabian shows will continue to be of great value in popularizing the breed both from the standpoint of the breeder and the individual who will eventually own an Arabian horse.

Several state fairs now have classes for Arabian horses, particularly in those states where there are influential breeders of Arabian horses. These state fairs help greatly in popularizing the breed since attendance is usually very large and covers not only one state but frequently portions of surrounding states.

The American Horse Shows Association, Inc., of New York which licenses the principal saddle horse, hunter and jumper, and similar horse shows, in 1950 recognized the Arabian breed in its show classifications. An Arabian committee was appointed consisting of Donald L. Jones, of California, Ward W. Wells, of Oregon, and C. H. Asmis, of Maryland. Rules and regulations governing the showing of Arabian horses are listed under Rule twenty-one entitled "Arabian Horse Division" as follows:

"Part I. General — Section 1. Entries must be serviceably sound and in good condition. To wear long, natural unbraided mane and natural unset tail, heavy shoes and long toes discouraged. Horses shall be shown without artificial appliances, stimulants and sedatives.

"Section 2. Horses shall be worked at all gaits both ways of the ring

BACARAM No. 3029. Mature Arabian stallion. Winner of many show prizes.

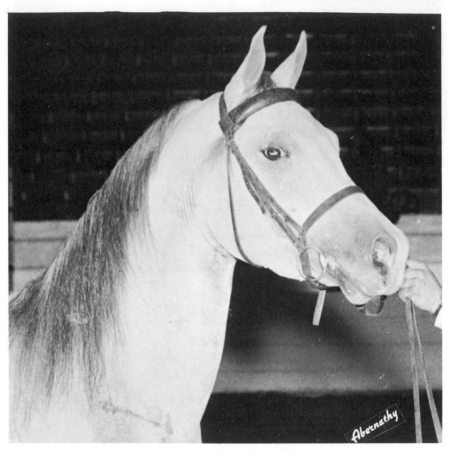

RAFFCON No. 7495, head view at 3½ years of age.

and otherwise at the judge's discretion. May be asked to back individually. Stripping of horses is optional in other classes, but mandatory in stake classes. Horses not to stretch on the line.

"Part II. Breeding Classes — (a) Head straight or (preferred) concave; small muzzle, large nostrils, extended when in action; large, round, expressive, dark eyes, comparatively short distance between eye and muzzle, wide between eyes; large, prominent forehead, small ears (smaller in stallions than mares), thin and well shaped, tips curved slightly inward; long, arched neck, set on high and running well back into withers; long, deep chest; ribs well sprung; short back; loins broad; croup comparatively horizontal; natural high tail carriage. Viewed from the rear, tail should be carried straight, hips strong and rounded; well muscled thigh and gaskin; straight, sound flat bone; large points; prominent, well defined hocks, sloping pasterns of good length; feet of proportionate size. Height from 14.1 to 15.1 hands, with an occasional individual over or under.

"(b) Dark skin; solid color, except legs and face (an occasional small white spot on the body permissible but not desired); fine coat.

"(c) Stallions especially should have an abundance of natural vitality, animation, spirit, suppleness and balance.

"(d) Horses to be shown at walk and trot. Should stand square on all four feet, not stretched. Handled and shown by one person only; unruly horses to be excused from the ring.

"Part III. English Classes — Section 1. Qualifying gaits are:

"(a) The walk: true, flat-footed, rapid and elastic.

"(b) The trot: brisk, smart, cadenced, gliding trot, without loss of form. Smoothness more essential than extreme speed.

"(c) The canter: smooth, slow, collected and straight on both leads.

"Section 2. Appointments.

"(a) The bridle should suit the horse. No breast-plate or martingale.

"(b) Flat, English-type, leather-lined (preferred) saddle. Girth either leather or web.

"(c) Informal dress is suggested for day time classes. Gaudy colors should be avoided. A coat is essential.

"(d) Formal dress is preferred for evening classes.

"Part IV. Pleasure Classes, Western — Section 1. The qualifying gaits are:

"(a) The walk: true, flat-footed.

"(b) The trot: square, slow and easy. (A ground-covering gait.)

"(c) The canter or lope: smooth, slow and easy.

"(d) The gallop: hand gallop; extreme speed to be penalized.

"(e) Special emphasis should be placed on a reasonably loose rein with the horse under control at all gaits.

"Section 2. Appointments.

"(a) Western attire and equipment. No martingale or tie-down.

"Part V. Driving Classes — Section 1. Gaits. Horses are to enter the ring at a park trot, also to be shown at a walk and road gait at the judge's discretion. Extreme speed to be penalized. Entries should stand alone quietly and back readily.

"Section 2. Appointments. Formal: to be shown in light harness to a four-wheeled vehicle suitable to the horse. Fine harness or combination bridle optional. Informal: to be shown to a two or four-wheeled vehicle suitable to the horse. Equipment to be in sound condition.

"Part VI. Mounted Native Costume Class — Section 1. Qualifying gaits. Horses shall enter the ring at a gallop, then be shown at a walk, canter and extended hand gallop both ways of the ring. Extreme speed shall be penalized. Horses may be asked to stand and back.

"Section 2. Appointments.

" (a) Horses shall be shown with added fringe, tapestry or tassels, depicting the colorful desert regalia. They shall be shown with bridle, hackamore or suitable head stall which will enable the rider to have full control of his horse.

" (b) Riders shall be attired in native type costume, including flowing cape or cloak, pantaloons, head dress, scarf or sash.

"Part VII. Arabian Horse Class Specifications — Entries in the Arabian Horse Division are judged on some of the following qualifications:

"Appointments, Performance, Substance (strength), Conformation, Presence, Suitability, Manners, Quality (fineness), Uniformity (of group).

"The particular qualifications for each class are hereinafter set forth and in each class the order of precedence indicates how the emphasis is to be placed in adjudication.

"Any class may be confined to a desired area by prefixing 'Local' to the class title and clearly describing the area included.

"Entry fees, trophies and cash awards should always be indicated in class specifications.

"If classes other than described herein are offered, extreme care should be exercised in the proper wording of the specifications.

"THREE-YEAR-OLD ARABIAN HORSES. To be shown at a walk, trot and canter. To be judged on quality, performance and manners.

"NOVICE ARABIAN HORSES. Open to horses which have not won three blue ribbons in this division at Recognized Shows. To be shown at a walk, trot and canter. To be judged on quality, performance and manners.

"LIMIT ARABIAN HORSES. Open to horses which have not won six blue ribbons in this division at Recognized Shows. To be shown at a walk, trot and canter. To be judged on performance, quality and manners.

"ARABIAN *MARES OR GELDINGS, STALLIONS, OPEN.* To be shown at a walk, trot and canter. To be judged on performance, quality and manners (also conformation if stallions only).

"ARABIAN COMBINATION HORSES. To be judged on quality, suitability for saddle and harness work.

"ARABIAN HORSE PAIRS. To be judged on uniformity as a pair; quality and manners. *Combined ownership permitted. Post entries.*

"ARABIAN HORSE *CHAMPIONSHIP* STAKE. To be eligible, horses must have been entered and shown in one previous class in this

Left: SKOLMA A.H.C. No. 3445. 4-year-old gray mare.
Right: JOANNA A.H.C. No. 2592. 5-year-old chestnut mare. Both are champion show mares.

division. To be shown at a walk, trot and canter. To be judged on performance, presence, quality, conformation and manners.

"ARABIAN PLEASURE HORSES. English type. To be shown at a flat-footed walk on a reasonably loose rein, a collected and an extended trot, a good easy canter and a hard gallop with ability to push on if required. At the judge's discretion horses shall change from any gait to a flat-footed walk on a loose rein. To be judged on performance, manners, quality and conformation. No martingale or tie-down.

"ARABIAN PLEASURE HORSES, WESTERN TYPE. To be shown at a flat-footed walk on a reasonably loose rein, slow and easy trot, a smooth, easy canter or lope and a hand gallop, extreme speed to be penalized. To be judged on performance, manners, substance and conformation. Special emphasis will be placed on a loose rein at all gaits. No martingale or tie-down.

" (Other Western type classes, such as Jaquima, stock horse and parade horse to be held under rules in AHSA Stock Horse Division.)

"ARABIAN DRIVING HORSES, *OPEN*. To be shown to a suitable four-wheeled vehicle at a park trot, road gait and walk. To stand quietly and back readily. To be judged on performance, manners, quality and conformation.

"ARABIAN DRIVING HORSES, PLEASURE TYPE. To be shown to a suitable two or four-wheeled vehicle at a park trot, road gait and walk. To stand quietly and back readily. To be judged on manners, quality and performance.

"ARABIAN HORSE MOUNTED NATIVE COSTUME CLASS. To be shown in bridle, hackamore or suitable head stall. To be shown at a walk, canter and hand gallop and to back readily. To be judged 50% performance; 30% appointments and 20% conformation."

In 1948, Illinois Arab owners formed an organization called the Illinois Arabian Owners, similar to the aforementioned California group. Evidently the founders very early conceived the idea that their organization would have greater value to the breed if it included members from surrounding states, and for this reason the name was changed to Midwest Arabian Horse Owners.

The Midwest Arabian Horse Owners rapidly became known in a considerable area around Chicago, through its shows and classes. There is no doubt but that Mrs. Bazy Tankersley should be given most of the credit for promoting these shows which have steadily increased since their inception in early 1948.

At the December 1949 meeting, the organization decided to accept members in Michigan, Indiana, Wisconsin and Iowa, for a total membership of thirty.

In 1950 it was decided to accept members in the states of Minnesota and Missouri.

In 1948, at Cheyenne, Wyoming, the organization known as the West Central Arabian Horse Association was formed and Dr. Glen H. Joder, of Cheyenne, was elected President, M. W. Osborn, of Sydney, Nebraska, Vice-President, and Mrs. Lloyd Moss, Fort Collins, Colorado, Secretary and Treasurer. This organization included the territory of thirteen Rocky Mountain states, Montana, Wyoming, Colorado, Idaho, Utah, Arizona, New Mexico, North Dakota, South Dakota, Nebraska, Kansas, Oklahoma and Texas. It was decided that there would be three members from each of the states who would serve as a board of directors and that the annual meeting would be held in January at Denver, Colorado, during the National Western Stock Show.

During the first year of its existence this association started a publication for the purpose of promoting the Arabian horse, and it also promoted its first All-Arabian show at Cheyenne, Wyoming, on July 10, 1949, with 137 entries from twelve states. *The Arabian Horse News* was the first journal or magazine in the United States devoted entirely to the Arabian horse. It grew from a two-page first issue into a forty-page magazine during the first year. Edited and published by Mrs. Anna B. Joder, it is the official publication of the West Central Arabian Horse Association.

Several other smaller groups of Arabian horse breeders have been organized for much the same purpose as the three principal ones listed here.

During 1950 an organization was formed for the grouping together of Arabian horse breeders and owners throughout the world, in other words, an international association of Arabian horse owners and breeders. A short description of this association as prepared by the executive secretary, Mrs. Vivienne H. Rulien, is quoted as follows:

"As the Arab horse population grew by leaps and bounds so did the Arab clubs. It was soon evident to far-sighted Arab breeders that a parent organization was needed to integrate all the organized Arab groups so that we might pursue our course with greater effectiveness. Accordingly Mr. E. E. Hurlbutt, then president of the Arabian Horse Breeders' Society of California, after contacting several organized groups — all that there were at that time — called for the first meeting at Salt Lake City, Utah, March 1950. Namely, delegates attending this initial meeting and their respective regional groups were: Arabian Horse Breeder's Society of California, Mr. Glen Purvine, Mr. E. E. Hurlbutt. Arabian Horse Club of San Diego Co., Mr. Harry Harness, Mr. Minal Young. Arabian Horse Association, San Francisco, Calif., Mr. Edmund T. Smith, Mr. Larry Duff. Intermountain Arabian Horse Association, Mr. A. L. Holland, Mr. Earl Bell. Arabian Horse Breeder's Society of Oregon, Mr. Ken Hall. Montana Arabian Horse Association, Dr. James Thompson, Mr. H. O. Bell, Mrs. Faye Saylor. West Central Arabian Horse Association, Dr. Glenn Joder by proxy Mr. G. E. Austin, Mrs. Ward Rulien.

"These seven groups were a fair representation of the entire country except the eastern areas which at that time were not organized and the middle western area which did not send delegates until later.

"After some general discussion and getting acquainted with new breeders the group wished to formally organize and Mr. Hurlbutt was elected president by acclamation. This was proper recognition for a man who has so unselfishly devoted much time and effort toward making the International a success. Other officers elected were: Dr. James R. Thompson, Vice-President, Mr. Harry Harness, Secretary, and Mr. Ken Hall, Treasurer.

"The naming of the organization was given no small attention since it was desired to adopt a name which depicted a true over-all picture of our intent, and still it must not conflict with the title of the Arabian Horse Club Registry of America. It should also be clearly established that this International group in no way conflicts with the Registry; rather it complements it.

"To avoid any misunderstanding the ultimate goals of the two groups are distinct although congruous. The Registry prefers to remain as a distinct registry for pure-bred Arabian horses and to limit itself to that duty while the International is devoted to the promotion of the breeding, exhibiting and perpetuation of the breed. The two groups naturally are dependent one on the other to a degree, but the International definitely does not offer any substitute for the Registry and values its counsel. With all these pertinent facts in mind and still wishing to encompass a wide territory the name Arabian Horse Association (International) was adopted. It was hoped that we would have member associations outside the limits of the United States and to date one has materialized in neighborly Canada and plans are being negotiated for an additional member in Cuba.

"The rules for membership as established in the by-laws are that any non-profit organized Arab group of not less than ten members may make application to the board of directors for membership. Each member association may be represented by directors according to the number of its members: those from 10 to 50 members are entitled to one director, over 50 are entitled to two directors. No member association, regardless of its membership may have more than two directors. Thus the smaller groups will have a fair representation and no one group may dominate by authority of the larger clubs, some of which number more than two hundred. In other words, the future of the Arab in America now is partially under the control of the 'grass-roots' breeder.

"In July at the third meeting, three additional Arab groups joined the ranks of the Arabian Horse Association (International) when the Mid-West Arabian Horse Owners, The Iowa Arabian Horse Association and the New York Arabian Horse Association were represented. They have all three since become officially affiliated. Thus all twelve of the now organized Arab groups in America are member associations of International.

"Since its inception the International has concentrated on two primary goals — that of staging an International Championship Show and providing an executive secretary. Neither is a reality today, January 1951, but definite progress has been made and as educational programs are improved and disseminated to the various member associations, and as news releases are improved, and national advertising programs are launched, so the prestige of the International group will increase.

"Arab breeders feel that with the authentic Registry behind them and now the International to complement the Registry, they can look forward to an Arab breeding era patterned by a definite program and purpose and guided by experienced minds."

A group of Arabian horses at the Indianapolis Horse Show at the September 1938 state fair of Indiana.

Chapter 21

The Arabian Horse As A Parade, Trail And Pleasure Horse

M R. Cecil Edwards, President, Arabian Horse Breeders Society of California, has outlined in a clear and concise manner the adaptability of the Arabian stallion for use as a sire of good type riding horses in an article in the August 1948 issue of the *Western Livestock Journal,* quoted as follows:

"Horseback riding of the 'strictly for pleasure' classification has become a major recreational activity of the nation's outdoor enthusiasts during recent years. The riding associations boasted by every section of the land — metropolitan centers, suburban areas, country communities — are convincing evidence that the riding horse is here to stay.

"This increasingly evident demand for better breeding and quality, plus the fact that the pleasure horse fan has demonstrated willingness to pay commensurately for a good horse, tends to focus the attention of the country horse breeder on the phenomenal capacity of Arabian blood to improve the produce of riding type mares.

"By and large, the greater number of mounts seen in pleasure horse circles today are, if their breeding is known, of mixed light horse bloodlines. A number of reasons account for this — the most influential factor being availability. Historically the 'using' light horse of our great cattle country, the main source of pleasure horses, is a mixed bred horse — most of the better ones having a dash of 'hot blood' tracing to the Arabian, either directly or indirectly thru other light breed infusions.

"Not to be discounted in evaluating the popularity of mixed bred horses are reasons involving the extreme development of certain pure breeds along specialty lines, which while representing the normal and fashionable goal of the breed concerned could not be described as wholly meeting the desideratum for a top pleasure riding horse.

"It is evident from reviewing light horse breed objectives today, that there is a genuine dearth of quality horses about which it could be said 'These were produced primarily for use of the pleasure and trail rider'.

KAMAN A.H.C. No. 2738. Mare.

"Prior to the 'carbon monoxide' era in America when the light horse served the transportation needs of duty or pleasure, several of the fusion breeds we now know pointed to a corresponding role. This was during their zenith for useful purposes and prior to the extreme development of their recognized specialties. What then constitutes a pleasure riding horse?

"At the risk of being facetious, it could be said that the modern pleasure riding horse must be first facile: he must fit fancy, fashion, physique and finances.

"Pleasure riders the world over take pride in the appearance of their mounts. The factors of appearance cover conformation, color, character and quality. Many of the essential points that contribute to the overall beauty of a riding horse, grace of curve and other seemingly aesthetic matters actually connote much more than mere beauty. The various factors that make for durability, intelligence, ease of riding, flexibility, lightness, manners and handiness are intimately connected with and a part of the points of beauty.

"The chiselled 'breedy' head with its small muzzle, large sensitive nostrils, kind open eye, is not only a mark of blood quality but regularly indicates intelligence, willingness and courage. A beautifully set on neck, with muscular emphasis near the shoulder, extending long lean and finely to the head which it enters between widely spaced jaw bones gives not only an appearance of grace but aids in balance, flexibility and ease of breathing. Withers, well defined, aid in securing the saddle as well as locomotion. Shoulders long and sloping minimize possibilities of the horse being heavy on the forehand. A good shoulder is the major part of the concussion absorbing and spring engineering mechanism of a riding horse. In fact the length and slope of the shoulder is the basic factor governing much of the horse's entire conformation, and often the factor that determines his suitability for riding or draft work, the short upright shoulder being less objectionable in a horse destined to pull heavy loads.

"Good sloping shoulders imply agility and freedom of movement. The slope shortens the back — insures that the girth will ride well behind the elbows to avoid galling. Also the length relates to the heart room — which if matched in the remaining anatomy generally provides ample room or middle for the internal organs and 'groceries'. This is a part of durability. The croup, being a part of the propelling mechanism, should be muscular and of good length. The loin, too, should be full, long and strong. It like all muscles contracts through its entire length. The arm should be long, because when extended it effects ease and flexibility of stride — the elbows, similarly the stifles should be

KHOORSHEAD No. 714. Arabian stallion being ridden by Philip K. Wrigley.

sufficiently wide apart to permit easy movement without body inter-ference. Knees and hocks should be free from meatiness, well defined and wide from front or side; this relates to leverage and strength. The bones below them should be short with strong tendons set far back giving a 'flat bone' appearance. The pasterns should be clean and smooth with sufficient length and slope to absorb concussion. They should enter the center of the feet . . . pointing straight to the front. The foot should

TEL-EL KABIR No. 1554, a 3-year-old gelding.

FAD ZARKA A.H.C. No. 1892.

be of sufficient size to carry the horse, free from contraction, show strong concave soles — and have good tough texture in the hoof horn.

"These physical factors plus nerve and substance qualities combine for temperament, ability, symmetry, ruggedness and all around equine beauty and satisfaction in a pleasure riding horse.

"Coloring for a fashionable pleasure horse need not be flashy. There is something to be said about a whole color with dark points being associated with rugged constitutions. As to size . . . a pleasure horse should 'fit' the physique of the rider . . . women riders usually prefer a horse built on slimmer lines . . . whereas a heavy person should choose a weight carrying animal. It should be remembered that a well made small horse can do a better job than an ill-conformed large one.

"Generally speaking a pleasure horse seldom need be more than 15.2 and well conformed smaller horses are more convenient and handier for mounting, trail and pleasure horse riding.

"As to finances — it costs a ranchman breeder much more money to produce one marketable quality pleasure horse 4 years old, than it does to produce two prime 2-year-old beef animals, and everyone knows what a prime beef animal is worth today. Mortality in foals is much higher than in cattle; and whoever heard of a beef animal becoming valueless because of unsoundness or wire cut? Nor is the beef breeder required to train his beef animal for the slaughter pen. Also on the average, good blood stock in the horse field and stud fees are far more expensive than those encountered by the beef producer.

"Therefore, the prospective purchaser of a top quality pleasure horse should bear in mind the cost of producing such an animal.

"Progressive breeders of pleasure riding horses are interested more and more in the dominance of the Arabian stallion as the best side to use in profitably developing quality and desirable characteristics in horses for this market.

"Actually there is nothing new about this trend — it is simply a return to practices proved 'tried and true' in centuries past. The Arabian horse was the initial stimulant and quality ingredient in the formation of the 'Blood Horse' and his related breeds centuries ago.

"In recognition of the value Arabian blood brings to American riding stock, the American Remount Assn., Washington, D. C., maintains an accurate registry for part Arabians got by pure-bred sires. This well patronized registry assures purchasers of grade Arabians on the authenticity of Arabian lineage, removing the 'heresay' and 'guess work' . . .

"Now in this new era of the horse, marked by redeveloped roadside bridle paths, rediscovered historical trails through fields and forests — a new country side — all agreeably adapted to the increased interest in riding for pleasure, health, recreation and fashion we present to you a solution for the production of superior pleasure riding horses — the use of Arabian stallions on grade type mares."

An excellent article that appeared in the October-November 1948 issue of *The Horse Lover*, by Phil O'Connor, entitled "The Arabian — Horse of the Future!" is quoted as follows:

"The Arabian is one of the 'greats' in the world of Parade Horses. The relative rarity of the ones entered compared to the horses of other breeds entered — shows him winning Parade Classes in spite of the percentage in numbers against him.

"The Arabian is one of the great endurance breeds of the world — look at the records; there again, not many Arabians are entered in endurance rides, but percentage-wise his winnings are ahead of all other breeds combined.

"It has often been said that no man is a true authority on one breed of horse unless he can appreciate all breeds. The men who appreciate all breeds will readily agree that the greatest individuals in all breeds have been and are, the horses with the most substance. The great Thoroughbred horses have all had it — a good example of which is Man-O-War. He has not only blinding speed but he also had the power to stay or substance.

"Our great American Saddle-bred horses which have gone to the top

278

NIBL No. 1179 as a 6-year-old gelding.

in the stake division have all had a great deal of substance. This holds true of all great individuals in the breeds of light horses. AND WHEN ONE SPEAKS OF SUBSTANCE, THE BREED SYNONYMOUS TO THAT WORD IS THE MODERN ARABIAN HORSE! The Arabian horse has all the qualities that most horsemen are very eager to find in a horse.

"In the following paragraphs, we will point out a few examples where the Arab horse is being used successfully as a stock horse — and as Dick Holliday pointed out in the Feb.-March, 1941 issue of *The Horse Lover,* 'To date not a single rancher who owns Arabs has a word to say against them. And that goes from Texas to Nebraska, from Florida to Montana!' This is best demonstrated by Mr. Van Vleet on his Lazy V. V. Ranch in Nederland, Colorado — but this is a great and inspiring story of the Arabian horse in itself — and cannot be told here.

"The Arabian Horse breeders regret that many people are uninformed for the Arab is really a 'working' horse.

"They are proving that the Arab can work by bringing their horses into open competition and competing against the best horses in the field. The outstanding achievement of the Arabian stallion, Shereyn, was certainly a step in the right direction.

"Shereyn was being used purely for a pleasure horse and for breeding purposes. He was entered in the Redlands Trail Ride, the Merced-Mariposa Trail Ride and the extremely arduous Concord-Mt. Diablo Trail Ride in 1946 and, under adverse conditions; that is, he was not properly conditioned for such a campaign. An important point, too, is that Shereyn carried over 200 pounds, including rider and saddle, on his 850 pounds. His consistent, easy way of going and endurance over the rough trails astonished the other contestants, combined with his 14 years of age and his placid disposition around mares and geldings. He never placed lower than fourth on any ride and was the only horse among 64 contestants, on the Concord-Mt. Diablo Ride, who received NO points off for fatigue.

"His fame, however, was yet to astound the horse world. Immediately after his return from his strenuous trip he was seen by Jim McCann, eminent stockhorse trainer, who was amazed to note that, although Shereyn was along in years, his legs were clean and he did not gaunt up. Mr. McCann observed his good conformation and recognized an excellent stockhorse prospect.

"He began to train Shereyn for stockhorse work on September 5, 1946, and on October 13, 1946 — 37 days later — he showed and placed third in the Horse Show at Flintridge. The following week he placed second to Champagne, then California State Champion, at La Habra. Three

AADRAFFA A.H.C. No. 2075. Gray Arabian mare.

weeks later he went into competition at the Cow Palace in San Francisco in a class of twenty-three 'top' stockhorses and won the Blue Ribbon in the Lightweight Class.

"Shereyn was a distinct credit, not only to his breed but to stockhorses in general. He performed exactly as the rules specify with speed and smoothness, carrying a spade-bit he had worn only a MONTH.

"Mr. Donald Jones, an Arabian breeder in Porterville, Cal., has 'working Arabians'. His stallion Faronek has gained an excellent reputation as a stockhorse in open classes and has enviable agility in cutting

KALUBLU A.H.C. No. 2530. Gray Arabian mare.

through stakes at top speed. Mr. Jones is enthusiastic about his horses; they have wonderful pedigrees but he is not 'pedigree mad,' he wants to see his horses accomplish something as well as look beautiful.

"On El Rancho Escondido, Catalina Island, the Arabian is used exclusively and found to be an excellent roping horse out of a chute and at the same time a reliable pleasure horse. Mr. Millard Johnson, trainer, is high in his praise of the Arab as a cow horse.

Purebred Arabian stallion ZARIFE, A.H.C. No. 885 at an altitude of 12,500 feet. (Continental Divide in background.)

"Down in San Antonio, Texas, Bill Manning who owns a brahma ranch has an eight-year-old Arabian stallion which his foreman works daily. This stallion, Zariff, is by the California Champion stockhorse, Farana.

"Atop Mt. Diablo, in Contra Costa County, on a treacherous 3,000 acre cow ranch, there is another remarkable stallion; this stallion is as quick and alert, yet easy going, as any cowboy could want — he is the gray horse, Farah, owned by Mr. Charles M. Fryer, prominent San Francisco attorney. Farah can work all day cutting cattle out of the brush with such speed and efficiency, that it is a constant thrill to ride him. He never tires and is ready and willing to work the following day for cutting or roping in the corrals. He is now fifteen years old and has spent his life on this ranch and sired many fine colts and has performed unerringly for eleven years and there isn't a blemish on him.

"This horse would certainly contradict the uninformed opinion that Arabians are not suitable for such work.

"There are countless more working Arabians, a great many of them, like Farah, who are too busy working on cattle ranches to be exploited in the show ring.

"In answer to the question, 'Are Arabians difficult to train?' Jimmy McCann averred. 'Any competent horseman can train an Arabian and will find pleasure in doing so, if he will take an interest in them and TEACH them. They are apt pupils and anxious to learn and are honest and eager to work and CAN and WILL do anything or go anywhere the rider has NERVE enough to go'.

"Many people refer to the Arabian horse as the horse of the future because they say: Where can you find a more beautiful horse? Where can you find a better Parade Horse? The competitive trail rides are proving the horses with Arab blood to be among the finest.

"Arab horses — (to the breeder who wants to breed uniform type) breed true to form. Arabs are gentle, sweet natured and intelligent for the entire family.

"Their comparative rarity throughout the world will always make them a sought after horse."

The following quotation from the December, 1947, and January, 1948, issue of *The Horse Lover* proves the endurance of horses with Arabian blood as trail horses.

"On this, the seventh Concord-Mt. Diablo Trail ride, horses with Arab blood swept all first places and one second place. 'After judging six of these rides', said Mr. Kent Weaver, 'and observing the horses as carefully as I must, I have no hesitation in coming to the conclusion that Arab blood, either in part or in whole, makes for the kind of endurance necessary in a contest of this kind'.

"The Ride, held on August 30-31, 1947, and sponsored by the Concord-Mt. Diablo Trail Ride Association, is nationally famous for the efficient and up-to-date management, and for general toughness requiring great stamina for both horse and rider. The distance covered is approximately 90 miles, being divided evenly into two days of 45 miles each. The start is from Concord and winds out through the Clayton valley, across Marsh creek and up the slopes of Mt. Diablo to Barbecue Terrace which lies about two-thirds of the way to the top. Here the riders and horses spend the night. The following day the same route

AMIDORE No. 925. Arabian stallion, sire of part-bred Arabs bred at Michigan State College and foaled in 1943.

is followed back to Concord. Horses not able to finish the ride are brought back by truck. Starting time each day is 7 a.m. and all horses must finish between 4:30 and 5:00 p.m. Horses are examined before, during, and after the ride by competent judges and a veterinarian, and are graded by the score card for stiffness, soreness, sore or heated tendons, puffy hocks, sore backs, wind galls, saddle or cinch sores, fatigue, etc.; 150 points being a perfect score.

"In the heavyweight class (horses carrying 190 lbs. or over), Real Silk was the winner. He is a registered half-Arab being sired by Baraki No. 997 (Baraki is owned by Mrs. Worth Albert of Lafayette, Calif.), and was ridden by his owner, Joe Hallett, of Lafayette, Calif. Real Silk carried 268 pounds. He stands 14.3 hands and weighs 950 pounds. The Sweepstakes prize, most coveted of all of the honors, also went to Real Silk and for the second straight year. He was the highest scoring of all horses in both the light and heavyweight divisions.

"Second place in the heavyweight class went to a three-quarter Arab

SHARIK A.H.C. No. 1784. Stallion.

sired by Akil No. 552 and owned and ridden by Fred Bennett, of Orinda, Calif. This horse carried 218 pounds. He stands 14.2 and weighs 900 pounds.

"In the lightweight division, Kumait, a registered U. S. Remount half-Arab owned and ridden by Mrs. Betty Taylor, El Sobrante, Calif., was first. He is sired by El Kumait No. 1124.

"In the junior class, Edna Lee Draper and Jubilo carried home not only the Junior Trophy, but also the Junior horsemanship trophy, the trophy for the highest scoring pure-bred horse in the 1947 ride, and the trophy for the highest scoring Contra Costa County-bred horse in the junior class. Jubilo is a pure-bred Arabian stallion (by Caravan, out of La Planta), five years old and carried 165 pounds. He weighs 830 pounds and was in competition for the first time on the Concord-Mt. Diablo Trail ride. His score was 139 out of a possible 150.

"Sixty-four horses competed for honors this year (1947) and approximately the same number competed in the 1946 ride. Almost all breeds of horses were represented. Worthy of mention is the fact that Real Silk

KADIR No. 1999. Arabian stallion used in calf roping.

carrying 268 pounds in each of these rides won the Heavyweight and
Sweepstakes honors both years . . . winning over approximately 128
horses during his 2-year reign as king of them all.

"Kumait, ridden by Betty Taylor of El Sobrante, was the 1946 lightweight winner, as well as winning his division this year.

"The performance of these two horses is a great tribute to the con-
sistency as well as the endurance of horses having Arabian blood."

The Arabian has long been recognized as a natural parade horse and
one of the most popular of them all is Barad (No. 1220), the grey stallion who made such a notable record in 1947, in California shows. The
following account in the December, 1947, and January, 1948, issue of
The Horse Lover, under the title, "The Parade Horse of the Year,"
gives the winnings of this stallion:

"Tumultuous applause greeted this great horse wherever he appeared
. . . 'In a class by himself', says Charles Eblen, his trainer and rider.

"The Grand National Livestock Exposition and Horse Show saw the

ARABI KABIR. A.H.C. No. 2379. Chestnut Arabian stallion.

final performance for the 1947 horse show season, of that outstanding Arabian Stallion, Barad. Barad won the open parade horse class at this show, competing against 32 of the finest parade horses in the State. Barad, who is owned by the Dollie Farms of San Luis Obispo, California,

RAFFERA. A.H.C. No. 3533. 3-year-old gray Arabian stallion. (English equipment.)

has acquired the popular reputation of being the outstanding parade horse on the West Coast. To review Barad's winnings most certainly substantiates this claim. The Dollie Farms was convinced that the Arabian had all of the requirements of a good parade horse, and throughout

289

WARDAMAR ALLA No. 2539. Arabian stallion with western equipment.

the 1947 horse show season Barad proved to his owner, as well as many Arabian breeders, that this was a certainty. The Arabian's brilliance and animation are unexcelled, and Charles Eblen master horseman was able to bring out the best the horse had to offer.

"In April, Barad made his first public appearance at the gala, well attended Desert Circus parade in Palm Springs. It was here that this Arabian Stallion, number 1220, began to attract the attention of the

Purebred Arabian stallion KABAR, A.H.C. No. 748.

most outstanding California horsemen. Barad's brilliance, alertness and bold way of going brought him numerous newspaper comments.

"The Bar-O-National Horse Show in San Diego was the first horse show ring in which Barad had ever performed. He was winner of the blue in the class for Open Parade horses. His performance at this show, and the comments from the spectators, left no doubt in the mind of his owner that Barad was destined for an outstanding and brilliant career in the 1947 horse show season.

"Barad made his third appearance of the year at the Bit and Bridle National Horse Show in Los Angeles. This show was said to have drawn more outstanding parade horses from various parts of the State than at any previous time. Working under extreme pressure, Barad emerged winner of the coveted award, and was the recipient of a tremendous ovation from the spectators. After his winning at this show, his stall was the scene of innumerable visitors who came to observe this gray stallion who stands 14.3 hands. By the comments made it was evident that Barad had won approval of all. Charlie Eblen's riding was superb.

"The Santa Barbara National Horse Show was the scene of great accomplishments for Barad. It was at this show that Barad emerged the winner of The Arabian Model Stallion Class. His competitors were stallions from stables of national repute. Arabian breeders commented that they were amazed by the animation and brilliance that this stallion showed during the judging of this class. At a later date in this show, Barad again entered the ring to win the Open Parade Horse class against a field of outstanding parade horses of varied breeds and types.

SARAJIH A.H.C. No. 1409.

"In August, the Dollie Farms took Barad to the County Fair in Stockton where he again was master of the field. His performance at this show was outstanding, and he gained much popularity in the northern part of the State at this show, his first Northern appearance.

"The State Fair at Sacramento has long been noted as being the one horse show in the State that attracts one of the largest groups of exhibitors in each section of the show. Barad was shown in the open parade horse class against a field of 36 horses. As soon as this Arabian stallion entered the ring he immediately became the cynosure of all eyes. His winning this class appeared to be the highlight of his 1947 show season.

The Arabian had emerged victorious over other pure breds that were also in the ring at that time. Barad's white coat and gray mane and tail make him stand out in any company. This together with his intelligence and all-around beauty, stamp him as one of the most conspicuous members of his breed in this section of the nation. Witnessing this particular performance and hearing the tremendous ovation that this Arabian stallion received from the crowd, was proof enough that this horse, Barad, was the master of parade horses.

"Barad continued his winning career under the capable hands of Chas. Eblen by annexing the blue ribbon in the parade horse class at the annual All Arabian Horse Show that was just recently held at Devonshire Downs in Los Angeles. At this show, Barad paraded among no other horses than those of his own breed."

WARDAMAR ALLA No. 2539. Arabian stallion used in calf roping.

Chapter 22

The Lazy V. V. Ranch

Abuot fifty miles northwest of Denver, Colorado, is a ranch formerly known as Tom Tucker's Bar Rump Ranch, now the Lazy V.V. Ranch. For many years it has been the home of one of the largest studs of pure-bred Arabian horses in this country. The Ranch is now owned by Lynn Van Vleet, of the Trinidad Bean and Elevator Company of Trinidad, Colorado. Some folks call him "King of Beans."

In 1938, Mr. Van Vleet started to stock up this ranch, which runs a large herd of white-faced cattle, with pure-bred Arabian horses. He did not follow the usual practice which is to buy a small number of acceptable mares and one or more stallions and then build up a herd. Evidently Van Vleet was sold on Arabian horses from the start and within a space of two or three years he owned one of the country's largest breeding studs of Arabian horses an accomplishment brought about by his buying a large number of small lots of Arabian horses from many sections of the United States.

It is of considerable interest to review his ideas about the value of Arabian horses, and the advisability of having a using stud on his ranch at an 8,600 foot altitude, an environment far different from the hot, dry climate of their desert home.

Purebred Arabian stallion RIFAGE, A.H.C. No. 1286. (L. W. Van Vleet up.)

Statements made by Mr. Van Vleet as published in *The Western Horseman,* March-April 1944 issue, in an article by Bob O'Shaughnessy, are quoted:

" 'Primarily, the Arab is valuable because of his blood', says Van Vleet, 'The reason this blood is so desirable is because it is hardy, rugged, courageous blood. It was prized in Arabia above gold and diamonds. A man's true wealth was calculated on the basis of the number and quality of horses he owned.

" 'Bedouins fought for them — emperors and queens connived for them — and the world's horsemen now are attempting to perpetuate them. All this is not only because the Arabian is a beautiful horse. Primarily, it is because the Arabian blood is the fountain from which the world's greatest horses have come.'

Three white and one bay purebred Arabian stallions at far right, during the round-up for branding calves on The Lazy V V Ranch.

"So Van Vleet decided there would be no glass-barred stalls, no tasseled trainers, no formal riding rings, no jewel boxes on his ranch.

" 'Instead,' he said, 'I wanted to bring out all the hardy, battle-born characteristics for which the Arab horse has been noted since the time of Christ. I wanted to transplant this horse into totally different surroundings and revive, even intensify, the traits of courage, intelligence, resourcefulness, and endurance which necessity and the experience of thousands of years of adversity in desert hardships bred into him.

" 'I wanted to bring the Arab into this mountain setting, which is as much the opposite of the desert as daylight is to dark, and substitute the rich diet of plentiful mountain meadows for the scarcity of desert lands; to substitute cooling, soothing mountain breezes for the hot winds of the desert'."

The Lazy V.V. Ranch grew until the stud consisted of around seventy-five head of pure-bred Arabian horses of all ages and sizes. At all times there were from three to five mature stallions present and each and every one was used regularly in cattle work just the same as quarter horses, cow ponies and other western-type horses. The ranch foreman and the riders at this ranch do not hesitate to claim that these Arabian stallions make a highly satisfactory horse, and since they work at a range of from 8,600 to an altitude of 12,500 feet it is evident that they must have a great deal of endurance and stamina in order to adapt to these extreme changes.

Among the magazines that published material on this stud was *Liberty,* which carried an article by Henry W. Hough entitled, "Champs of the Bit," in the November 17, 1945, issue.

In the March-April 1944 issue of *The Horse,* published in Washington, D. C., there is a detailed article by Sibyl L. Davis entitled, "Our Aristocratic Friends," which deals at considerable length with the friendliness of the Arabs and the enjoyment visitors get from associating with them. Mention is made of the principal sires and many of their offspring and considerable details are given about the work that these Arabian stallions do on the ranch.

In the April 1946 issue of *The Westerner,* published at Denver, Colorado, by the Record Stockman Publications, there is a well-illustrated and interesting article on the Stud.

In the April 1947 issue of *The Westerner* appears another article on the Lazy V.V. Ranch entitled, "Arabian Horses Older Than History," by Ruth Tallman, which discusses in a general way the background and early history of the Arabian horse.

One of the largest and most elaborate articles on Arabian breeding was published in the *Boulder Daily Camera,* of Boulder, Colorado, on August

A group of Van Vleet purebred Arabian brood mares and their colts.

297

16, 1941, under the authorship of Robert C. Looney. It is well-illustrated with eleven photographs and gives a very lengthy and detailed general description of the Arabian horse in America and the history and purposes of the Van Vleet Arabian Stud in particular.

In the spring of 1941 the Associated Press assembled a full newspaper page of pictures of the various horses and activities at the Lazy V.V. Ranch. This was probably the most extensive piece of publicity that any Arabian horse breeding farm ever had.

For several years past the Lazy V.V. Ranch has put on a free show every Sunday afternoon patterned after the show put on for several years by the Pomona Ranch, in California. Because Denver is on one of the principal routes from east to west in the United States, the attendance figures have been extremely large and tens of thousands of persons unfamiliar with the Arabian horse have had an opportunity to observe the breed.

The V.V. Arabian Stud has shipped surplus colts to many foreign countries and to every section of the United States in recent years. Its colt crop has run as high as twenty-five head or more in favorable years.

In addition to the many articles published in general magazines, horse papers and other publications on the Lazy V.V. Ranch two movie shorts were made at this ranch, which have evidently been of great value in popularizing and calling the attention of the general public to the Arabian horse.

Chapter 23

Arabian-Bred Riding Ponies

Pony breeders throughout the world have long recognized the value of using an Arabian stallion on pony mares for the production of high-grade riding ponies. England has for many years produced through this method many high-grade saddle ponies, and the practice has become quite common in certain parts of the United States.

Usually pony classes have only two grades or divisions, one not to exceed eleven point two hands and the other from eleven point two to not more than fourteen point two hands. This method of dividing ponies has been rather unsatisfactory in many areas because the smaller type ponies of the larger division were often handicapped because of their size. It seems more desirable to have the three divisions of ponies used for showing purposes which are now being used by the Maryland Horse Breeders Association.

The use of an Arabian stallion on Shetland, Welsh, Hackney or other pony mares results in unusually fine, stylish riding ponies with excellent dispositions, especially well suited for young children.

Arabian breeders who are producing the classic or beauty-type Arabs can well afford to give a lot of attention to the use of these stallions for the production of riding ponies. The practice is being quite com-

NAHR. A pony brood mare sired by an Arabian stallion. A prize winner.

monly followed in eastern states like New York, Maryland, Virginia and elsewhere.

Mr. Humphrey S. Finney, of the Maryland Horse Breeders' Association was invited to discuss riding ponies and their showing and how they were bred, at a meeting of the Horse and Mule Association of America. His remarks were published by one of the Association's circulars:

"Two things are closely correlated: the development of good riding children and the production of riding ponies. When the Maryland Horse Breeders' Association was incorporated some twenty years ago, one of our prime objectives was to develop something many of our children are born with, that being the instinct to ride. It is natural that in a country which has been famous for fox-hunting, cross-country racing and horse sports since Colonial times, there should be a great number of enthusiastic young riders. It is from these young enthusiasts that we eventually obtain the buyers for the produce of our stud farms and our surplus racing stock, many of which go into the hunting field.

"As Field Secretary of the Maryland Horse Breeders' Association, it has been my duty to have had considerable connection with the development of many of the horse and pony shows in Maryland. It was early found that the custom, prevailing still in most states, of either lumping all ponies together in one class, or dividing them into two size groups from 12.2 down and up to 14.2, shut out many would-be exhibitors. We found that children, showing 11-hand or under ponies had little chance, in the small division, the same being true of those standing 12.3 or so in the larger group. There was no way, however, of getting uniformity in the matter then, as there were no rules to go by.

"The Association of Maryland Horse Shows, which has operated some eighteen years and which embraces about forty shows held annually in the Old Line States, has shows which operate under uniform rules. They have regular dates allotted and must put on classes which are approved by the Association. The Association has established three divisions of ponies, to-wit: 11.2 and under; over 11.2, not exceeding 13.0; and over 13.0, not exceeding 14.2, at all of our shows where there are pony classes. As soon as this change was made, pony entries picked up at the shows, and more children were in the market, because of the enlarged opportunity to win some sort of ribbon.

"All ponies have to be registered with the Association of Maryland Horse Shows to be eligible to compete for the high-score trophies that the Show Association presents to the owner of the pony piling up most points in its division. These awards are hotly contested for. I believe 96 ponies were registered and competed in the three divisions in the 1947 shows.

"Top winner among the large ponies is one that is half-Arabian, the other two quarters being Thoroughbred and polo-pony. His name is Easter Hal, and he was bred at McDonogh School, where they have kept an Arabian, a Dartmoor and a Thoroughbred stallion, and have crossed these back and forth with Thoroughbred and other mares, including ponies of all breeds. The result is that the boys, who range from six to eighteen years, are all well mounted on ponies or horses of appropriate size. The disposition of the animal, rather than breed or type, has been the deciding factor in selecting those used for reproduction purposes.

"Easter Hal went up to Madison Square Garden recently and took a pair of blue ribbons and two reds as well. He'd have done better, but the boy riding him just went to sleep in one class and let his pony stop for a rest in the in-and-out. The champion of our middle-sized division

SOUTHLANDS KATHA. Gray pony mare sired by KARNAK No. 1396, an Arabian stallion. (Picture taken at 2 years of age.)

also is shown, this being the grey Surprise, a very fine pony for which offers of many hundreds of dollars have been refused. Surprise is the only foal of a great little Welsh pony, Jiminy Cricket, by imported Stormy Weather, a top Virginia pony stallion for years. Surprise's dam was part Welsh and part Thoroughbred. Surprise has been top point winner in Maryland for three years. The small division champion, Napoleon, a veteran of the rings, is said to be by a Shetland sire from a dam of unknown breeding. He's a fine going pony anywhere.

"In England the Arab sire has exerted great influence on the various pony breeds in their formative years, and the same is true in the case of many of the ponies we find in America today. The majority of the larger ponies you see in the various photographs shown have more or less Thoroughbred or Arab blood in them. In the East we see, at least in Maryland and Virginia, few of the fine saddle-bred ponies so often found in Midwestern shows. We are in a hunting country, and therefore we find that a pony of the type of a miniature Thoroughbred is the most valued, and best for our requirements. We find that by breeding top-class pure-bred sires to selected mares we naturally get a more intelligent pony, therefore one that wins more and is more useful and saleable.

"In our shows, small ponies are asked to jump two feet, the medium division to jump up to 2½ feet and the larger ones about three feet. If you ask the children to jump higher in the show ring the parents are horrified, but most of our show ponies go out with hounds when their owners get a chance to take them, and many hunt pretty regularly. While out hunting they are apt to run into all sorts of jumps, lots of them almost as big as the ponies, but they get over them somehow, and think nothing of it. The result is that we have to have a pony with good sloping shoulders, clean, well-defined withers, well set on head and neck, and particularly having good feet, legs and way of going. Some of these ponies hack five or six miles to a meet, hunt all day, then hack home in the evening. It takes a horse or pony with a good 'bread basket' to do that. In short I am trying to describe a tiny Man o' War, or Holystone, or any other good Thoroughbred type. . . .

"In the main our small ponies are Shetlands, or Shetland crosses. We have many pure-breds. Some are crossed with Welsh ponies direct, and many small ponies are by Shetland sires, out of daughters of Welsh stallions. The Chincoteague shows up often, particularly when crossed with the Shetland stallion. Some pure-bred Welsh are occasionally found with us, but not very many. There are numerous middle-division ponies that are half Welsh, with the other half very often from small mares of Hackney, Arabian or Thoroughbred extraction. The Welsh stallion, imported Stormy Weather, has had a lot to do with our best ponies. As in every other breed, there occasionally develops some sire of prepotent character who is able to stamp his individuality on a large group through his offspring, just as Steeldust did for the Quarter Horse of old, and Old Sorrel for the King Ranch. . . ."

Appendix

The Author Establishes an Arabian Breeding Stud

THE author established an Arabian breeding stud in 1943 consisting of five broodmares and including one three-year-old mare from The Travelers Rest Stud of Dickinson of Tennessee, her number 2009 and registered as CARIOCA. She was bred to CHAMPION INDRAFF 1575 and this mare foaled a colt for us every year for the next 10 years. This mare cost a total of $850, which was at least $350 above what mares of this age and class were selling for three years earlier. Most Arabian mares at this time we speak of—which would be about 1940—could be bought for $500. Two mares, namely KHIFFAH 1333 and PERA 1107, were purchased for a total of $1100 and the total cost of these five mares in 1943 was considerably less than $4000. Five mares of the same type of breeding and the same quality today in 1971 would probably cost $25,000.

In 1943 Arabian horse colts at weaning time sold anywhere from $200 to $300 each, but for the next ten years after 1943 prices for horse colts at weaning time often went as high as $750 to $800 each.

It is difficult to reconcile the fact that Arabian horse colts often sell at such unusually low prices compared to the females of the breed, while the stallions or horse colts of other breeds generally outsell the females of the breed.

At the present time there are probably 19,000 owners of purebred Arabian horses in the U.S.A. and there are probably the same number of owners of part-bred Arabs in the U.S.A.

In the early 1940s there was only a handful of breeders of Arabian horses in the U.S.A. who had as many as 50 registered Arabian horses. At the present time there is quite a sizeable number of breeders who have 75 to 100 registered Arabian horses while there is a considerable number who have above 100.

The growth of the Arabian horse in America has been extremely heavy during the last ten years, or since 1960, and much of this growth has been the result of the pressure of some breeders and owners who sold these new owners on the basis that they could produce and sell high-priced offspring as fast as they could be produced. In actual practice thousands of these breeders have been disappointed and are dissatisfied with their ownership of the Arabian horse.

The Formation of an Arabian Breeding Stud as Developed by the Author of *The Arabian Horse in America*

The background for the formation of the breeding stud of the horses of Dr. and Mrs. George H. Conn started in 1935 and consisted of trips to some well-known breeding studs in the central part of the U.S.A. and an occasional visit to other studs during the period from 1935 to 1941. In 1941 the Conns purchased their first purebred Arabian namely, NIBL 1179, a son of ASIL 785 and the dam was NEJMAT 501. This bay gelding was six years old and was bred by Brig. Gen. J. Arthur Ball, Muncie, Indiana.

In 1943 NABIKA 653, whose sire was RIBAL 397 and whose dam was NEK 461, who at that time was suckling her foal, CASSIM 2556, was purchased as the beginning of a small breeding stud. NABIKA was bred by William R. Brown, who was the largest breeder and importer of Arabian horses in the early 1900s and who was also the author of *The Horse of the Desert*.

PERA 1107, daughter of *MIRAGE 780 and whose dam was SLIPPER 442 and who was bred by the Selby Arabian Stud of Ohio.

GASARA 1039, daughter of BAZELEYD 648 and a daughter of GUEMURA 277 was bred by The Travelers Rest Arabian Stud of Tennessee. GASARA was also registered as a Thoroughbred in the Thoroughbred Stud Book.

KHIFFAH 1333, whose sire was ASIL 785 and whose dam was SANTA FE 882. This mare was one of the largest Arabian mares in the United States, being fully 15.3 hands tall, and was bred by Brig. Gen. J. Arthur Ball of Indiana.

At the time this stud was founded the demand had greatly increased for Arabian breeding mares and it required quite a diligent search to find mares that could be purchased. Since the price of Arabian mares had made a sizeable increase going from $500 each to a common price of $750, it required quite a lot of work to get mares even at the higher price because it was evident that there were several buyers for every mare that was available.

These five mares were foaled and owned in Ohio, Indiana, Tennessee and Georgia. This includes CARIOCA 2009 from Travelers Rest Arabian Stud of Tennessee. The author has given some details of the formation of this Arabian stud for the reason that Arabian horses were starting to increase in price at this time and most owners and breeders who had an animal they could dispose of were very slow in making up their minds to price this animal at the increased price, thinking that by holding the animals for a period of time an increased price could be secured. Many present owners and breeders have, during the last several years, been able to organize a breeding stud of a considerable number of horses of the Arabian breed without the necessity of a long-drawn-out extensive search for Arabian animals such as the author secured for founding his breeding stud in 1943.

The following information with reference to the registration of Arabian horses in the U.S.A. should be of considerable interest due to the one fact that registrations as of June 1, 1971, total 70,000 head. The first attempt àt registering purebred Arabian horses was made in 1908 and registered about 78 horses. While copies of this bulletin or small booklet have been in existence, it was not recognized as an official stud book. The first official Arabian Stud Book was published in 1913, and from 1913 to 1937 three more volumes were published and have been listed as Volumes 2, 3 and 4 of the Arabian Stud Book. Volume 4 of this series registered all purebred Arabians not found in Volume 3 until the close of 1944. This Volume 4 registered Arabians in the U.S.A. from No. 1 to 2924.

In 1945 the Arabian Association decided to adopt a new type and the first volume was The Arabian Stud Book Vol. 5, and this Vol. 5 includes all the registrations of Vols. 1, 2, 3 and 4 known as the old series of The Arabian Stud Book.

When the current volume, 20, was published in 1971 it covered only Arabian horses that were registered in 1969. The difference between this date and June 30, 1971, indicates that more than 11,000 purebred Arabians were registered in the U.S.A. between these two dates given here. It is now evident that Volume 21 of The Arabian Stud Book will soon be due for publication.

Considerable details are given with reference to the registration of Arabian horses in the U.S.A. In the early 1940s there were fewer than

3000 registered Arabians in the U.S.A. Quite a number of other Arabian breeders developed breeding studs during the same time and the difference in registration figures will definitely prove the great growth of this breed in the U.S.A.

Since Volumes 19 and 20 of *The Arabian Stud Book* had each been published after 6000 additional Arabians had been registered, and since Volume 20 had registered 58,686 horses as of 1969, and since there have been registered as of June 30, 1971, a total of 70,000, it is therefore evident that Volumes 21 and 22 of *The Arabian Stud Book* should be in the process of publication.

The present address of The Arabian Horse Registry of America, Inc. is 1 Executive Park, 7801 E. Belleview Ave., Englewood, Colorado 80101. The registry had moved from Chicago some time ago.

The new and present address of The Arabian Horse World is 2650 E. Bayshore, Palo Alto, Calif. 94303.

There are now two new magazines being published in the interest of the Arabian horse, *The Arabian Horse Times,* 819 E. Alm Ave., Waseca, Minnesota 56903, a magazine sent free to Arabian breeders and owners in the U.S.A. and elsewhere without any subscription rate and therefore no informational and educational material about the Arabian horse. As of September 1, 1971 this magazine has reached Volume 2.

The other magazine is *Arabian Adviser,* the national newspaper of the Arabian horse, published at 66 So. Riverside Drive, Batavia, Ohio. 45103. Subscription rates to this monthly magazine is $4.00. This magazine, as of August, 1971, has produced eight issues of Volume 2.

The International Arabian Horse Association, 224 E. Olive Ave., Burbank, Calif. 91503 is a long-standing organization that registers part-bred Arabians and Anglo-Arabs and promotes the purebred Arabians for showing, breeding and owning.

Another Sleeping Sickness Disease Appears in the United States

Another sleeping sickness disease known as Venezuelan Equine Encephalomyelitis has now appeared in the U.S. and is commonly known to the horse owners as well as to the veterinary profession as VEE. This condition has been spreading steadily for the past several years from Venezuela, where it was originally found. From there it started to spread slowly northward, and it reached Mexico in mid-1971. In late June this condition was first discovered in Texas, and about three weeks later, on July 19, it was formally announced from headquarters in Houston that this condition was at present in Texas. It was stated at that time that 825 horses were reported dead in Texas and that more than 1000 were reported sick. As early as July 23 there were a total of 1150 suspected cases. As of July 28, 1971, no cases in the United States have been found outside of Texas, and all cases have been south of a line between Houston and Laredo.

The veterinary profession have extracted the offending virus from 58 horses in Texas where at this date they reported deaths of 1350 horses, not all of which could be confirmed as being caused by VEE infection. At this time 21 human cases, all in the lower Rio Grande Valley, were reported. The U.S.D.A. also reported that the virus causing VEE has been found in 11 different species of mosquitoes. They also report that a spraying campaign covering more than two million acres was set up to destroy or control the mosquito population.

On July 28 the Animal Health Division of the U.S. Department of Agriculture stated that officially the five states of Texas, Oklahoma, New Mexico, Louisiana and Arkansas were under federal quarantine.

Unofficially Arizona, California, Mississippi, Florida and Georgia are expected to be placed under quarantine and the vaccination program extended to these states.

The U.S. Department of Agriculture set up headquarters in Houston for the purpose of attempting to control VEE and to confine it in a total of 10 of the southern and southwestern states. As of August 20, 1971, this base reported that a total of 1,638,000 horses had been vaccinated against VEE.

It was reported at this time that not all the final figures were in from some of the states. Although in Oklahoma over 226,575 vaccinations were performed, which was almost 100 percent of the total horse population. It was reported in Louisiana 95 percent were vaccinated, in Arkansas 93 percent, Mississippi 92 percent and New Mexico 85 percent.

In the state of Texas, where the disease has made considerable inroads, it was reported that 570,142 of the horses in the state of Texas, which represents about 86 percent, have been vaccinated.

Sleeping sickness of the western variety has been appearing in the U.S.A. at intervals during the last several years. The writer of these notes recalls that he vaccinated a number of farm horses and others during that outbreak, and following that first outbreak of this sleeping sickness the condition got pretty well under control very soon.

In current information in the June 1971 Newsletter of the Department of Agriculture of the State of Illinois, we find their quotations from the U.S. Department of Agriculture as very pertinent to this condition. We herewith quote four paragraphs about the Department statement about this disease:

"Venezuelan equine encephalomyelitis (VEE) is a highly fatal virus disease of horses and other equidae. The disease may also affect other mammals and some non-mammals. The infection is transmissible to human beings in whom it usually produces a disease of variable symptomology, but is not generally fatal. Children are usually affected more severely than adults. The disease is insect transmitted, primarily by mosquitoes. The possibility of contact transmission between horses has been reported. Rodents are susceptible to VEE and it has been suggested that they may be important as reservoirs of the virus and in the natural perpetuation of the disease.

"VEE was first diagnosed in Venezuela in 1936 and has been reported in several South American countries since that time. During the last few years, epidemics have occurred in Central America. In 1970, Mexico experienced a severe outbreak in which the death of approximately 6000 horses was attributed to VEE. Mexico reports clinical evidence of the disease in the States of Veracruz, Oaxaca, Chiapas, and Michoacan.

"VEE has not been found in horses in the United States. A strain of VEE virus of apparent low pathogenicity for horses has been isolated from mosquitoes and cotton rats in Florida. In 1968, the disease was diagnosed clinically and serologically in three humans in Florida. Virus was not isolated from these individuals."

The American Veterinary Medical Association has recently issued a news release on the Sleeping Sickness disease that appeared in southern Texas in early July and against which a very vigorous vaccination program has already been carried out. We quote the following paragraphs from this memorandum:

"This mosquito-borne virus disease that began killing large numbers of horses in Texas in early July was a topic for lengthy discussion by veterinarians working in public health and regulatory programs throughout the nation who met at the recent (July 18–22) joint annual meeting of the AVMA and the Canadian Veterinary Medical Association in Detroit, Mich.

"The disease known simply as VEE, is so new in this country that few U.S. Vets have had experience with it or know a great deal about it. But most who are familiar with VEE believe that with sound control and eradication procedures it can be contained.

"If we can keep infected animals quarantined to prevent their movement into uninfected areas, we should be able to keep the disease from spreading outside the infected areas, Dr. Saulmon explains. And if we can break the mosquito reproduction cycle within the infected area and vaccinate susceptible horses, we should be able to reduce the spread of VEE in the infected area. This is what we're trying to do.

"On June 28 the state of Texas quarantined its southernmost 13 counties and the USDA and Texas Animal Health Commission began a massive horse immunization program. Two weeks later, on July 10, a widespread insect control program was started along the Rio Grande River northward from the Gulf of Mexico. This week [July 20 and 21] the spray program was extended along the Texas-Louisiana border and immunizations expanded into Louisiana, Oklahoma, Arkansas and New Mexico.

"With these measures, Department of Agriculture and public health officials hope to bring VEE under control within the next few weeks."

We again quote from the memorandum of The American Veterinary Association:

"Exactly what the facts are about VEE is somewhat difficult to determine because the disease has never before appeared in the United States and veterinarians* here have had limited experience with it.

"Experience in other countries indicates that the disease is readily spread by mosquitoes and often but not always deadly to horses. Human beings also are susceptible, but the disease in man is reported to be generally mild, somewhat resembling influenza, and very rarely fatal.

"Horses are affected in a variety of ways. Some animals contract VEE and recover without ever showing signs of disease, while others die from it.

"VEE strikes swiftly. Animals may show signs within two days after being bitten by infected mosquitoes and death can occur from two to six days after the disease becomes apparent. As many as 50 to 80 percent of the horses that show signs of infection may die.

"Infected horses may show one or many of a variety of signs. In the early stages of VEE infection, a horse may run a fever, go off feed, or become depressed. Abdominal distress and diarrhea may also be seen in the early stages of infection. In the advanced encephalitic or 'sleeping sickness' stage, a horse usually shows marked depression. The 'twitching' reflex commonly exhibited by horses when their skin is touched usually disappears. The lips almost always droop loosely and the pupils may contract. Blindness or nervous convulsions may also develop, and an infected animal will sometimes hang its head or press it against a wall, post or some other immoveable object. Many victims develop a stumbling, circling gait, and some wander off in a straight line as though sleepwalking, oblivious to fences and other objects that may be in the way. Eventually the horse sinks to the ground, unable to get up, and dies."

VEE is known to have existed in South America since 1938 and remained there until 1969. Since this disease also inhabits the human, cases

---

* The author has been a veterinarian for 58 years and has been involved in the sleeping sickness outbreak that appeared in the U.S.A. several years ago.

of human infection followed very rapidly during the last few days of July 1971. All reports on this disease as affecting the human, state that it is usually very mild and rarely fatal. In the late 1940s an experimental vaccine was developed for treating humans affected with this disease and it has been reported to be of considerable value in preventing it. This same vaccine has also been used in horses.

A vigorous spraying campaign was undertaken in the areas of the U.S.A. where this disease has been prevalent. Another factor in the control of this disease is that of quarantine. It is generally believed by many officials and others that by vaccinating the entire horse population in certain areas, using a spray treatment against the offending mosquitoes, and quarantining the horse population this disease will be brought under control. With the great movement of horses throughout the U.S. and in and out of areas adjacent to the U.S. it is quite evident that a program such as this is going to be very difficult to effect as planned.

Arabian Racing Association Promoting Pari-Mutuel Racing for the Arabian Breed in the U.S.A.

About three or four years ago a small group of breeders got together for the purpose of having Arabian horses trained for racing. Most of the races so far have been made at Turf Paradise in Phoenix.

Up to the present time these races have been conducted once each day for a week's racing. Most race meetings have anywhere from seven to ten races daily, and the Arabian race was usually held once each day.

Early races were held for horses four years and older and in some instances horses 15 years or older have been raced.

Most of these Arabian races have been for purses of $1000 each. In several races the number of starters has been six or seven head, and in a recent three-year-old allowance race nine horses went to the post. As of August 1971, there have been about 60 Arabian horses in training. Some racing association has made the statement that in their opinion, if the Arabian owners get 100 horses trained to start that some racing association would be inclined to set up more races for them. The author's own opinion about this is that it will require several times 100 head trained and ready for racing to make this a profitable and satisfactory proposition.

Some ambitious plans are already under way to have very rich stakes available for racing of Arabian horses in the not too distant future. A $50,000 American Arabian Breeders Derby for five-year-old horses is to be raced in February 1973 at a Pari-Mutuel track under Jockey Club rules, and for this race the entry fee will be $5000 per horse. The race is to be limited to ten entries of horses foaled in 1968 and the entries must have been received by Labor Day 1971.

The other important race is known as the President's Classic. The purse is $20,000 and is for foals of 1970. It is to be raced in July 1973. The entry fee for this race is $100. The details of this and the previous race can be secured from The Arabian Horse Registry of America.

The author has compiled a short summary of several Arabian horses either imported or bred in the U.S.A. at an early date and which had a record, while foreign owned, of some racing ability. You will note from this short summary that none of these horses produced any offspring that showed any great amount of racing speed.

Some Information on Racing Arabians in the U.S. of an Early Date

ANTEZ 448—Ch. S. Sire HARARA 122; Dam MOLIAH 109. Foaled in 1921 and bred by F. E. Lewis II, Spadra, Calif. Later owned by Gen. Dickenson of Travelers Rest. He was tried for speed and the tests were good enough so that he was sold and exported to Poland where he raced for 5 years, after which he was returned to the U.S. where he was again put to breeding at around 20 years of age.

ANTEZ sired 33 offspring registered in Vol. 5 and 20 offspring in Vol. 6 of the Arabian Stud Book.

Only one of his offspring was given enough training to determine if he was fast enough for racing. His training was by the late Carl Raswan and he made several records at different distances.

This horse was registered as SARTEZ 2500 Ch. S. Sire ANTEZ 448 foaled 5–18–43. Only one offspring was registered as sired by him in Vol. 6.

CZUBUTHAN 1499—gr. stallion. Foaled in Poland 6–17–33. Imported by Gen. Dickenson where he sired 49 offspring registered in Vol. 5 and 47 in Vol. 6 of Arabian Stud Book. This stallion was a famous racer in Poland yet none of his offspring in the U.S. were ever tried for speed.

NASR 889—Gr. S. Poland—August 23, 1918. Imported by Gen. Dickenson and was rated as one of the great Arabian racers in his native country. He sired 59 registered in Vol. 5 and 15 in Vol. 6 of the Arabian Stud Book. We saw this horse at Travelers Rest in Tennessee and he looked more like a Thoroughbred than an Arabian. None of his offspring were tried for speed as far as we know.

While Travelers Rest of Tennessee imported several foreign mares at the time they had CZUBUTHAN 1499 and NASR 889 there was no offspring from the mating of these mares with these two stallions that showed any evidence of unusual speed. We do know, however, that these imported mares were soon disposed of.

In 1938 Henry B. Babson imported some Arabian bred racing horses from Poland such as KASZTELANKA B—M—foaled 1929 No. Arabian Stud Book 1542. Other Polish horses imported by him are registered in Vol. 5 of The Arabian Stud Book U.S.A., Nos. 1541, 1543, 1544, and 1545. The gray stallion SULEMAN was a famous Polish racer but he was a failure in the breeding stud and was finally given outright to an Arabian breeder at no cost to him and later on only one of his offspring showed any speed worthy of note.

KASZTELANKA B—M—foaled 1929
Imported 1938
Sire—KOHEILAN 1 P.A.S.B.
Dam—BEALOGRADKA P.A.S.B.
Bred by the Polish State Stud—Janow—Podlaske
Imp. by Henry B. Babson 1938
This mare was imported in Dec. 1938 and had a foal WARSAW 1682—S on Feb. 1, 1939. This mare did not breed for the next 27 months and I started to treat her in May 1941 and treated her for several months making about 15 calls, each 90 miles, for which I received no fee. The foal resulting from my treatment was FADHEILAN S—B—2603 foaled on December 24, 1942.

Babson disposed of these Polish mares after a few years and we have no record that they produced any offspring with unusual speed.

Arabian Horse Shows Are Increasing Greatly in Numbers Each Year in the U.S.A. and They Are Having a Great Effect on the Development of This Breed

At the time the author finished his book entitled *The Arabian Horse in America* in 1954, there were only a very small number of Arabian shows, because the breed was principally centered in the central and western states. Probably not more than a dozen or so shows of any importance were held annually in the early 1950s. In 1971, according to an Arabian calendar published in *The Arabian Horse News,* 183 shows are to be held in the United States and Canada, and some of them are quite large. There is some chance now that some of these shows will not be conducted because of the outbreak of VEE.

The Arabian horse shows are conducted under the rules of The American Horse Shows Association and there has been considerable agitation about some of the rules at some of the leading shows.

The Arabian breed has been known for a long time as the foundation of all horse breeds. Due to this factor most breeders were supposed and expected to produce typical high-grade offspring from the horses they obtained. The speed at which many of these people got into the showing of their Arabian horses proves very definitely that all they were interested in was showing these horses and winning with them. This speed with which many Arabian horse owners got into the showing of their horses evidently did not work out too well for them due to their lack of experience and knowledge required to do a correct job of showing their animals in competition.

For many of us who have had many years experience with the Arabian horse it is now evident that it is going to take a long time to get the owners and breeders back where they were many years ago in their relation to the Arabian horse.

In the September 1971 issue of *The Arabian Horse World* a total of 24 Arabian shows is reported. These shows have already been held in 1971 in all sections of the U.S.A.

There has been considerable criticism of the necessary expense for showing Arabian horses at most of these shows, for the very extreme prices charged for the privilege of showing horses in competition. It is quite likely that with this dissatisfaction there will soon be a slowing down of the number of new breeders of Arabians interested in showing them. Some of this financial trouble is probably due to the fact that the time payment when buying many Arabians has left owners without enough ready cash to show them as they would wish. It seems quite evident that there is a problem of too many Arabian breeders. It will probably require some little time to work anything out for the advantage of the breeder who now faces this problem.

Recent Importations of Arabian Horses Have Definitely Changed the Situation with Reference to This Breed in America

In the last few years importations have been made largely from horses bred and owned in Poland and Egypt. Publicity of these imports has been unusually large. Since these importations encourage a lot of breeders in the U.S.A. to expand their breeding operations it became necessary for some of these large importers to conduct auction sales to dispose of their horses that they then had for sale. In brief, here is how the situation developed:

At the Ann McCormick dispersal sale at Scottsdale, Arizona, in 1969, an Arabian stallion which McCormick had imported in 1963 and then registered as NABORR, 25472, was sold at auction for $150,000. This sale set up quite a lot of excitement and it is rumored that the International Revenue Service has made some investigations about this and other sales because of the very high price reported.

One of the leading auction sales from a prominent breeder in the Scottsdale area was put on as a stock reduction auction by the Lasma Arabian Stud of that area. This sale was held on February 11, 1971, and in the sale 27 purebred registered Arabians were sold for a total of $535,200.

In this sale three Arabian mares sold for totals of $56,000, $51,000, and $50,000 respectively. One old mare of 18 years in foal sold for $25,000. In this sale 20 mature mares sold for an average of $22,775 each.

Some other Arabian auction sales have done quite well for the breed in the way of getting high prices for many of their animals. It is quite evident that this great increase in prices for breeding Arabians will probably hinder their future development in America.

At the present time at least two Arabian breeders with a large number of horses for sale are conducting auctions during September 1971 that will have a marked influence on the future of the breed in this country.

As mentioned elsewhere, it does not seem that the author should pursue this factor any further because it will be many weeks before the final results of some of these auctions will be available in detail, and naturally they will be featured in great detail by the Arabian magazines.

Index

Index